The French Tradition in America

DOCUMENTARY HISTORY OF THE UNITED STATES

Edited by Richard B. Morris

Chronological Volumes:

Topical Volumes:

The French Tradition in America

Edited by

YVES F. ZOLTVANY

Harper & Row, Publishers
New York, Evanston, and London

THE FRENCH TRADITION IN AMERICA

Introduction, editorial notes, compilation, and translations by the editor copyright © 1969 by Yves F. Zoltvany.

Printed in the United States of America.

First edition: HARPER PAPERBACKS, 1969, Harper & Row, Publishers, Incorporated, 49 East 33rd Street, New York, N.Y. 10016.

The clothbound edition of this title is published by the University of South Carolina Press.

Library of Congress Catalog Card Number: 72–625502.

Contents

Acknowledgments

The Editor would like to thank the following institutions and persons for their assistance in the preparation of this book: the French Canada Studies Center of McGill University; the New York State Library at Albany; M. Roland-J. Auger, Acting-Archivist, Quebec Provincial Archives; Mr. Donald J. Horton, a doctoral student at McGill University.

Y.F.Z.

The French Tradition in America

Introduction

THE FRENCH presence in America dates from the sixteenth century, from the first great period of European overseas expansion. France was drawn to the northern part of the new continent in search of the passage that would lead to the spice-producing regions of the Far East and to the gold and silver that would enable her to match the wealth of Spain. These two goals, and the second one particularly, formed the basis of French colonial strategy during much of the sixteenth century. They explain the attempt of 1541 to found a settlement near Quebec on the St. Lawrence River, which the Breton mariner, Jacques Cartier, had discovered and explored seven years before. It was expected that this outpost would enable the French to control the kingdom of the Saguenay, an ill-defined territory on the north shore of the river, which was believed to hold rich deposits of precious metals. The failure of the expedition to turn up anything except worthless quartz crystals and iron pyrite, combined with the harshness of the climate, resulted in the liquidation of the enterprise the following year.

For the next fifty years, no further attempt was made to settle these cold and barren northern lands. The codfisheries, however, which from the start had proved profitable to the French, continued to attract large numbers of their fishermen to the Grand Banks of Newfoundland and to the lower St. Lawrence. Fur trading began as a secondary activity when these men put ashore and met with the Indians, but it soon grew into a major enterprise when an important market for this commodity developed in France. Beaver pelts, as the hatmakers soon realized, made a superior grade of felt, and other types of skins, such as mink and marten, were required by furriers to trim the robes of Churchmen and civil officials. Soon, several ships were traveling to the St. Lawrence Valley each year solely for the purpose of engaging in the fur trade. The discovery of this valuable staple gave fresh life to the idea, discredited by the misadventure of the 1540's, of establishing a colony in the northern part of America.

The first successful attempt to carry out this project was made in the opening years of the seventeenth century by a company of merchants organized and led by a Huguenot, Pierre du Gua, sieur de Monts. In 1605, this group founded Port Royal on the Bay of Fundy, which became France's first permanent establishment in the New World and the capital of the colony of Acadia, which ultimately included Nova Scotia, New Brunswick, Prince Edward Island, and part of the state of Maine. Economically this territory had much to recommend it, for it could serve as a base for the fur trade and the fisheries and also held good agricultural possibilities; but the area, as subsequent events revealed, was weak and vulnerable, for it constituted essentially a geographical extension of New England, cut off by the Appalachian highlands from the main body of settlements in Canada. In Canada, furthermore, the St. Lawrence River would act as a pole of attraction for settlement, agriculture, and commerce; but Acadia's long shore line, broken by many coves and inlets, and the lack of physical unity resulted in disconnected settlements and divided jurisdiction. In such a setting, effective systems of government and defense, both sorely needed because of the constant threat of attack from New England, were nearly impossible to establish.

These developments still lay in the future in 1607 when the French government deprived de Monts of his monopoly of the Acadian fur trade, on which he depended to maintain his small colony. But instead of withdrawing from colonial ventures after suffering this blow he followed the advice of one of his assistants, Samuel de Champlain, and turned his attention to the St. Lawrence Valley. A secondary figure in Acadia, Champlain played a role of far-reaching importance in determining the pattern of Canadian colonization. It was he who, in 1608, chose the site of the present city of Quebec as the principal seat of the new colony. It was he also who initiated the first systematic exploration program and who laid the foundations of that network of Indian alliances that reached continental proportions less than a century later. Champlain hoped that these measures might lead to the discovery of a passage to the Pacific Ocean and promote the growth of the infant colony's commerce. Already it was evident that the fur trade would make an expansionist policy necessary.

Champlain, however, wanted Canada to become something more than a mere outpost for exploration and the Indian trade. He hoped to use the profits from this trade—the sole source of capital at this time, since the government had not yet begun to subsidize colonization—to bring out settlers who would develop the full economic potential of the new land and build a strong colony in the St. Lawrence Valley. This plan, which establishes him as the first of the great French North American colonizers, involved him in a series of conflicts with the private companies which had been granted the monopoly of the fur trade. In return for this lucrative privilege, these corporations had contracted with the Crown to bring out settlers, but they consistently eluded their obligation. Solely concerned with the fur trade, they felt no compulsion to encourage the development of a large settlement. The Indians trapped the animals and, in the case of beaver, even did the processing by wearing the pelts, thus loosening the coarse guard hair and rendering the fur soft and supple. Indeed, not only were settlers not necessary, but they might even harm company interests by privately trading with the Indians. Neither Champlain's threats and arguments, nor those of the government, made the merchants change their attitude. In 1627, the population of Canada still consisted of less than one hundred persons—clerks, interpreters, and missionaries. Except for the apothecary Louis Hébert and his family, not one of them could be called a genuine settler.

In that year, important reforms in French colonial policy were carried out by Cardinal Richelieu, Louis XIII's first minister and grand master of navigation. In order to increase the power and prestige of the monarchy, a goal which he pursued with ruthless determination until his death in 1642, the cardinal realized that it was not enough to humble the House of Hapsburg, deprive the Huguenots of their political privileges, and subdue the turbulent French nobility; it was also necessary to increase the nation's wealth. Dazzled by the achievements of Holland, which had replaced Spain as Europe's most successful colonial power, Richelieu decided that such power might most surely be achieved by winning for France a major share of the maritime and colonial trade. With this end in view, he dedicated himself to the task of building a large navy and of chartering powerful companies to develop the colonies.

The cardinal's chosen instrument for the colonization of New

France was the Company of One Hundred Associates, whose charter received royal approval in May, 1627. All earlier concessions were revoked and the new company was granted full title to the land from Florida to the Arctic Circle and from the Atlantic Ocean to the Great Lakes. In return, it was obliged to bring out 200 to 300 settlers in 1628 and 4,000 more during the next fifteen years. Several precautions were taken to ensure that it would not neglect these obligations by placing a higher priority upon the fur trade, as its predecessors had done. Its capital investment of 300,000 livres[1] was much larger than that of earlier companies. An attempt was also made to reduce merchant influence by introducing a majority of noble shareholders, no doubt in the expectation that they would be more interested in taking out landed estates than in engaging in the fur trade.

The One Hundred Associates might have done great things for Canada had not their efforts been plagued by misfortune. The convoy which they sent to Quebec in May, 1628, numbering four ships and bearing four hundred settlers, had cost them 164,000 livres and was France's finest colonization effort to date. Unfortunately, war had just broken out between France and England and the entire fleet was captured in the Gulf of St. Lawrence by the Kirke brothers, privateers who held letters of marque from Charles I. Left without supplies and reinforcements, Quebec barely managed to survive the winter and finally had to capitulate the following summer when the enemy ships appeared before it. Subsequent efforts by the One Hundred Associates to reconquer the colony were unsuccessful and only served to drain the last livres from its depleted treasury. By 1630, with Quebec in English hands and Richelieu's great company on the verge of bankruptcy, French rule in America had apparently come to an early end.

The cardinal wanted the return of Quebec, and he obtained it in 1632 at the Treaty of Saint-Germain-en-Laye. However, in view of the prostrate condition of the One Hundred Associates and of France's growing involvement in the Thirty Years' War, the colony would probably have sunk into neglect had it not been for the emergence of a new agency of colonization: the Roman Catholic Church. During the first part of the seventeenth century France was experiencing a strong religious revival. Religious orders as well

1 The livre was the basic monetary unit in France during the Ancien Régime. It would be worth about $2.00 in 1969.

as pious laymen turned to America to bring the word of God to the Indian tribes. But the Church in Canada did not confine itself to the religious sphere during those years. Partly because of its wealth, organization, and driving enthusiasm, partly because of the weakness of secular institutions, it rose rapidly to a position of political leadership. It lost this temporal authority after 1663, when Louis XIV made colonization an affair of state; but from the Treaty of Saint-Germain-en-Laye to the beginning of the royal régime thirty-one years later, a period which some historians have aptly called the colony's mystical age, the Church was the practical master of Canada.

The strategy of colonization during this period was elaborated by the Jesuits, the strongest and most influential of the religious orders established in Canada. Their goal was the conversion of the Indians to Christianity and the basic function of the colony was to assist the missionaries in the performance of this difficult task. The Jesuits felt that nomadic tribes like the Algonquins and Montagnais who roamed the north shore of the St. Lawrence would have to be converted to a sedentary way of life and Frenchified, that is, assimilated into European cultural patterns, before they could be induced to accept the tenets of Christianity. Effecting these preliminary but vital changes in the habits and outlook of the natives now became the responsibility of the colony. The problem was different with the Hurons, the third of New France's great allies in the first half of the seventeenth century, for these Indians already led a stable community life in the Georgian Bay area. It was therefore relatively easy for the missionaries to take up residence among them; but it was quite another matter to have their teachings accepted. Indeed, they were frequently insulted and reviled by those whom they sought to convert. The Jesuits considered that a strong French colony would help to make the savages more respectful and receptive, for they would then associate the missionaries and their teachings with the idea of strength and power. Such, in brief, was the blueprint of colonization during the mystical age. Church and state, missionary and layman would join together to build a spiritual New France.

To this ideal the colony which emerged by 1632 did not conform in any way. It had been built by fur traders who were primarily interested in making economic contact with the Indians. What it now required was groups and institutions that would serve as social and cultural bridges between the white and native populations: a farming community to instruct the nomads in the ways of agriculture, schools and convents to teach their children, hospitals to nurse their sick. The Jesuits explained their program and issued appeals for assistance in their famous publication, the *Relations*, which was widely read in France. They met with an enthusiastic response. Several devout persons, among them a number of wealthy widows, donated substantial sums of money and even volunteered their services for the Canadian missions. Unfortunately these persons, whose personality and outlook had been shaped by the religious fervor and mysticism of the Catholic Reformation, frequently lacked the practical realism that would have enabled them to channel their energies in truly constructive directions. They were idealists, eager to build schools and hospitals for the Indians but frequently oblivious to the colony's material needs. As a result New France did not develop along basically sound lines from 1632 to 1660. A roof had been built while the foundations were still lacking.

In those years when the colony was primarily the nerve center of a vast field of missionary endeavor, a secular society was also being born. When the Company of One Hundred Associates found itself without the funds to satisfy the terms of its charter, it resorted to a technique of colonization which marked the beginnings of the seigneurial system in Canada. It made outright grants of large tracts of land to persons of some substance who agreed to clear these properties and settle them with colonists whose numbers would be credited to the company's account. These first Canadian landowners came mainly from the provinces of Normandy and Perche and were a closely knit, enterprising group. In 1645 they formed a company called the Community of Habitants, which sublet the fur trade from the One Hundred Associates. In 1647 they obtained representation on the Council of Quebec—a body made up of the governor-general, the governor of Montreal, and the superior of the Jesuits, which had extensive attributions in matters of administration, commerce, and finance. The birth of this small Canadian society possessing both economic and political power is one of the more significant developments of the 1640's.

With an approximate population of only 300 persons in 1642, and of 2,000 in 1653, Canada remained nonetheless a weak and vulnerable colony. In 1641 its very existence was suddenly threatened by the outbreak of war with the Iroquois Indians. With the exception of a brief respite from 1667 to 1682, this conflict would last until 1701 and disastrously affect economic expansion and demographic growth. It is therefore important to understand its basic nature.

Since the publication in 1940 of G. T. Hunt's *The Wars of the Iroquois*,[2] most historians have accepted the thesis that the war waged by the Iroquois against New France and her native allies was economically motivated. The French in the St. Lawrence Valley depended largely on the Huron Nation to bring them their supply of pelts. The Hurons, in turn, did not obtain these by hunting but by trading with tribes located in their commercial empire, a vast territory fanning out from Georgian Bay and bordered roughly by the Saguenay River to the north and Lake Michigan to the south. Meantime, in present-day New York State, another trading alignment had emerged. The Dutch West India Company, which had founded a post at Albany in 1624, had been obliged to establish commercial relations with the Iroquois Five Nations in order to obtain their fur, for the settlements of these Indians, extending from the Mohawk River westward to Niagara, cut off the company from all contacts with the tribes farther west. Initially, the Iroquois were able to supply the Dutch with beaver trapped on their own hunting grounds, but the disappearance of this animal from their area toward 1639 made it necessary for them to gain a share of the Huron trade. When they failed to accomplish this by means of negotiations, they decided to make war.

At first the Iroquois were satisfied to lurk along the Ottawa River, New France's great commercial highway, and to intercept the fur convoys moving toward the colony. Perhaps they felt that they lacked the strength to adopt a more aggressive policy, for the Hurons, despite the great losses they had suffered when a plague swept through their country in the late 1630's, were still their superior in numbers and at least their equal in intelligence and cunning. But Huron attempts to encircle and divide their enemy by means of alliances with the Susquehannas and the Onondagas, one of the Five Nations, made the rest of the Iroquois realize that they would have to strike a great blow in order to smash the ring closing around them. In March, 1649, a force of approximately

2 G. T. Hunt, *The Wars of the Iroquois: A Study in Intertribal Trade Relations* (2nd ed., Madison, Wis., 1960).

1,000 Mohawks and Senecas, which had advanced silently through late winter snows, struck at the very center of Huronia. They stormed and fired the towns of St. Ignace and St. Louis, routed the populations, and martyred the Jesuit fathers Brébeuf and Lalemant. Terrified by the suddenness and force of the attack, the rest of the Hurons fled in order to save themselves from the Iroquois fury. In a matter of weeks the nation which had been the heart of the Canadian missionary Church and the principal of New France's commercial allies had ceased to exist.

Following this great victory, the Iroquois no doubt expected to fall heirs to the Huron commercial empire. Their hopes were soon deceived, however, for the French were able to establish a fresh relationship with the Ottawa Indians and to maintain a grip on the western fur trade. This obliged the Iroquois to remain at war. They resumed their blockade of the Ottawa River and also intensified their attacks against the colony itself. Over one hundred settlers were killed in 1661 alone and many others were probably frightened into returning to France. At this dark moment, the colony's very survival appeared to be in jeopardy.

The sorry condition to which New France had been reduced, while indicative of Iroquois military strength, also forcefully underlined the failure of the One Hundred Associates, the Canadian seigneurs, and the Church to build a strong colony in the St. Lawrence Valley. The deficient record of these agencies of colonization did not escape the attention of the new king, Louis XIV, and his ministers. In 1663, in order to clear the way for an extensive program of colonial defense and reform, the new government revoked the charter of the One Hundred Associates and brought the colony under direct state control. This measure marks the beginning of the royal régime and constitutes a turning point in the history of French colonization in America. Henceforth, unlike the British colonies which always remained primarily the responsibility of private enterprise, New France would look to the state for its most vital needs.

American historians, viewing New France from a vantage point of laissez-faire liberalism, have deplored this development. Francis Parkman, the famous New Englander whose epic series *France and England in North America* appeared between 1851 and 1892, claimed that the preponderant role of the state in New France after 1663 resulted in "perpetual intervention of government, regulations, restrictions . . . a constant uncertainty what the authorities would do next . . . volition enfeebled, self-reliance paralyzed . . ."[3] Almost seventy-five years later L. H. Gipson also upheld the view that the people of New France were drained of individual incentive and initiative by governmental overregulation.[4] From statements such as these emerged an image of New France, still widely accepted today, as a static, unprogressive community ruled by the heavy hand of authority in civil and religious matters.

The validity of this traditional view has been challenged by historians who in recent years have restudied the evolution of New France. W. J. Eccles has pointed out that the form of statism practiced by the Crown, far from being reprehensible, was necessary to compensate for the deficiencies of French private enterprise. Wealthy persons in France tended to invest their money in land or bonds, which guaranteed a secure income, or to purchase titles of nobility, positions in government, and commissions in the army, which conferred social prestige; manufacturing, trade, and commerce were shunned because of the risks and because they did not enable one to rise in the social hierarchy. As a result of this pattern of investment, considerable sums were either frozen or channeled into the hands of government, which thus became the most powerful agency of socioeconomic growth.[5] For this reason, it considered itself duty-bound to subsidize the economy, plan its development, and to give money for schools and hospitals and to support the poor. These practices, which appeared so reprehensible to the Social Darwinists of the late nineteenth century, have become perfectly acceptable to persons who have grown accustomed to the policies of the modern welfare state.

One of the first concerns of Louis XIV after assuming control of the colony was to provide it with new political institutions. The system of government that was inaugurated between 1663 and 1666 was derived from that of provincial France but made more simple and effective by the absence of the feudal vestiges and institutions that cluttered the French political scene and occasionally

3 F. Parkman, *The Old Regime in Canada* (Boston, 1887), pp. 394–395.
4 L. H. Gipson, *The British Empire Before the American Revolution:* Vol. 5, *Zones of International Friction: The Great Lakes Frontier, Canada, the West Indies, India, 1748–1754* (New York, 1942), pp. 342–343.
5 W. J. Eccles, *Canada Under Louis XIV, 1663–1701* (Toronto, 1964), pp. 57–8.

jammed the administrative machinery. All power rested with the king, who ruled by divine right, and was delegated to a series of royally appointed officials through a clear-cut chain of command. The most senior of these was the minister of the marine, who resided at the court. With the assistance of deputies known as commis, he exercised a general supervision over the colony's affairs and also formulated the policy that served as the basic framework for its development. Once a year his orders and instructions were transmitted to the governor and the intendant, New France's two leading officials. The former, who was recruited from the ranks of the military nobility, was commander-in-chief of the armed forces and also looked after the colony's relations with the Indian tribes and the British colonies to the south. The latter, who was either a bourgeois or a member of the nobility of the robe, was responsible for the administration of justice and finance and for the internal peace and general well-being of the colony. Within their respective spheres, the two officials were naturally responsible for carrying out the minister's orders, but they also enjoyed numerous opportunities to participate in and sometimes to dominate the policy-making process. They could achieve this either indirectly, by the information which they sent to the minister and the recommendations they made to help him reach decisions, or directly, when, as was so often the case because of the distance separating colony and mother country, they found themselves obliged to act without the benefit of ministerial instructions.

The most important institution after the offices of governor and intendant was the Sovereign Council, established by a royal decree of 1663. Its membership consisted of the governor, the intendant, the bishop, an attorney-general, and five councilors who were later increased to seven and finally to twelve to cope with a volume of business that grew with the population. Its functions, like those of the parlements of France on which it was modeled, were threefold: to register and promulgate the laws of the kingdom, to act as a court of appeal and first instance in civil and criminal cases, and to legislate for the needs and well-being of the people by means of police ordonnances. Initially, the councilors were appointed by the governor, who also had the right to dismiss them from office; but in 1675, following attempts by Governor Frontenac to use this power to intimidate the council, the Crown decided to grant its members royal commissions. This made them virtually independent of the governor and greatly increased their authority and prestige.

The intendant for his part always exercised important functions within the council. As its president, he was responsible for "collecting the voices" of the councilors, after which he drafted legislation or delivered judgment. The procedure of "collecting the voices" did not merely consist of counting votes. It meant that after all the councilors in turn, beginning with the most junior, had given their verdict, the intendant took action in accordance with what he considered to be the consensus of opinion. This technique had much to recommend it, for it combined the intendant's legal training with the councilors' knowledge of the condition and needs of the colony, but it was gradually abandoned in the eighteenth century. The intendant tended more and more to issue police ordonnances on his own authority while the council limited itself to its judicial functions. Thus, during a period when the power of the *parlements* of France grew, that of the Sovereign Council, renamed Superior Council in 1703, declined.

Below the central government the colony was divided for administrative and judicial purposes into the districts of Montreal, Trois Rivières, and Quebec. Each had a local governor—except Quebec, where the governor-general performed his functions—a civil and military establishment, and a court of law. Representatives of the people were excluded from all executive, legislative, and judicial functions but it is important to note that they met frequently in consultative and deliberative assemblies. The governor and the intendant often summoned assemblies of Canadian notables to consult with them on matters affecting the general welfare of the colony. The opinions expressed by the notables on these occasions frequently influenced the decisions of the officials. Merchants also met regularly to consider the state of their affairs and to draw up petitions for presentation to the authorities in Canada or France. In the villages and the seigneuries, assemblies of *habitants* exercised a great deal of control over such local matters as the building of churches, roads, and bridges. Thus, it would be totally inaccurate to state that the people of New France had no voice in the administration of their affairs. On the contrary, they enjoyed numerous opportunities to express their views and an effort was made to legislate in accordance with them.

Such in bare outline was New France's machinery of government from 1663 to 1760. It was highly centralized and, having been conceived to further Louis XIV's grand design of securing total obedience from all his subjects, authoritarian. Obedience, however, was not to be secured callously by the use of force but humanely by giving the people good and fair government in order to win their loyalty and devotion. This master idea was frequently embodied in the king's instructions to the governor and the intendant, urging them to be kind and just toward the Canadians, mindful of their needs, and to protect the poor and the weak against the rich and the strong. Supreme authority, in other words, sought to maintain itself by using confidence, not force, as its bond with the people.

This strong civil government, run by officials who were determined to assert the royal authority, soon came into conflict with the Church, the colony's most powerful institution for many years. In the 1660's, under its able and strong-willed leader, Bishop François de Montmorency Laval, the Church of New France was expanding its activities to meet the needs of a growing population. The ecclesiastical system which Bishop Laval established had originated at the Council of Trent but had ceased to function in Europe. Instead of founding permanent parishes, he created a seminary at Quebec which received the tithe—set at one-thirteenth of the fruits of the soil in 1663 but subsequently reduced to one-twenty-sixth because of popular opposition—and where all the secular priests of the colony resided. From there they were sent out to serve the parishes or to perform other duties and were transferred or recalled as the bishop saw fit. This system had much to recommend it, for it facilitated the enforcement of ecclesiastical discipline and the extension of religious services to areas that would have been too poor to maintain a priest. The civil government, however, considered that its centralized character gave the bishop too much power and it repeatedly but unsuccessfully tried to force him to establish permanent parishes.

While these important changes were being made in the internal structure of the Church, the Jesuits were adopting a new strategy to convert the Indians. By the 1660's it had become obvious that the policy of Frenchification in which they had formerly placed such great hopes had been a failure. Most of the Indians who had been subjected to the experiment had returned to their old way of life at the first opportunity, while those who had cohabited with the French had gained nothing from the contacts unless it was new vices. The worst of these was an immoderate taste for alcoholic drink. According to all reports the Indians drank solely to get drunk and then became like wild beasts. In an effort to solve these problems, the Jesuits replaced their policy of integration by one of segregation, which consisted of grouping the Indians on isolated missions under close religious supervision. At the same time, they joined with Bishop Laval in a vigorous campaign to force the civil government to prohibit the sale of intoxicants to the natives.

In the Church-state controversy that flared in the latter part of the seventeenth century, the issues of the brandy trade and to a lesser degree of parish organization proved to be the most exacerbating. The bitterness of the conflict was largely due to the fact that these two questions were related to the more basic one of who should dominate in New France, the civil or the religious estate. While it might be an exaggeration to describe Laval's purpose as theocratic, he did require the co-operation of the civil government on a number of issues in order to be able to enforce his code of religious and moral precepts. But he met instead with the opposition of the minister of the marine, Jean-Baptiste Colbert, who had determined to subordinate the Church to the state and instructed the colonial administrators to resist clerical pretensions. Of the two designs it was the minister's that ultimately prevailed. As the flames of the Catholic Reformation flickered out, the Church in New France lost its militancy and the bishops who succeeded Laval accepted without qualms the doctrine of royal Gallicanism which subordinated the Church to the Crown and gave the king extensive powers in ecclesiastical matters. In this new context the questions of the brandy trade and parish organization lost their explosive potential and produced nothing more than occasional minor discord in the eighteenth century.

Another institution which underwent important modifications under the royal régime was the seigneurial system. Now that the state had assumed the responsibility for sending settlers out to the colony the seigneurs no longer had to act as immigration agents, which had been one of their principal functions before 1663. Their role after that date consisted essentially of making land grants and of adopting concrete measures to develop their estates. The government concluded that the principal reason why these ends had not been attained in the past was that the seigneurs had been granted more territory than they could possibly clear. It therefore reunited to the royal domain the huge tracts conceded by the One Hundred Associates, which covered hundreds of square miles in some cases, and granted them out again in blocks averaging one or two leagues of frontage on the St. Lawrence River and two or three leagues in depth. So that anyone in the colony might obtain concessions on these estates, the dues payable to the seigneurs were kept low; to discourage speculation a tax known as the *quint*, amounting to one-fifth of the sale price, was payable to the state whenever a seigneury was sold; to oblige seigneurs and tenants to develop their concessions, laws were enacted obliging tenants to reside on their farms and providing for the forfeiture of uncleared territory at the end of fixed periods. These various measures enable the historian to reconstruct with accuracy the purpose of the seigneurial system in New France. It was an instrument of colonization derived from French feudalism by virtue of which an agent, the seigneur, distributed to settlers the land which he held in trust from the Crown. Because of the prestige connected with the ownership of land the seigneurs enjoyed a high social status but they wielded little political power. It was not the seigneur but a selected *habitant*, known as the captain of militia, who acted as the representative of royal authority in the countryside. As for the seigneuries themselves, they were too restricted in size to serve as a base of personal power. Thus it was difficult for the seigneur to oppress his tenants and impossible for him to threaten royal authority.

What did the seigneurial system achieve in New France? It did not make the colony into a thriving agricultural community but no system of land tenure could have done so, for the obstacles were too great. The quantity of arable land was limited to a narrow belt along the St. Lawrence and the farming season was reduced to a few months annually by the long winters. The labor force was inadequate because of the small population and further diluted by the fur trade's superior economic appeal. Agricultural expansion was limited throughout the seventeenth century by the Iroquois wars and until 1715, when a new colony was established on Cape Breton Island, by a complete lack of external markets. In spite of these unfavorable conditions, historians have traditionally viewed the seigneurial system as one of the basic institutions of the French régime. One school depicts the seigneury as a well-organized social unit where the rights and obligations of everyone were carefully defined by the government and where the seigneur or his representative was present to provide leadership, service, and protection. Another, more critical, school accepts the seigneurial system as one of the centers around which the colony grew but claims that it was made defective by the impoverished condition of the seigneurs and their lack of interest in agriculture. In 1966, both views were challenged by a geographer, R. C. Harris, who argued that the seigneurial system was irrelevant to the way of life which developed in New France.[6] In a colony where land was a source of expense rather than revenue, few seigneurs bothered to develop their concessions. Seigneuries, Harris claimed, remained vague markings on the landscape and the pattern of settlement would not have been much different had all land been held directly from the Crown. Ultimately, historical opinion will probably come to rest somewhere between this radical negation of the system's importance in the colony's history and the idealized image of the seigneurial community painted by the older school. Some seigneuries did lie neglected, but others were developed and became very valuable, particularly after 1715; some seigneurs did regard their estates simply as status symbols, but others attempted to make the most of their economic potential.

These institutional reforms were accompanied by a number of measures prepared by Jean-Baptiste Colbert, Louis XIV's great minister of the marine, that were designed to expand the colony's economy. Intensely patriotic, this son of a Reims draper wanted to make France a great power, but his views of how this might be achieved differed from those of the monarch. While Louis XIV thought that his glory might best be served by military conquests, Colbert, true to his bourgeois origins, strove to make his king rich. He not only encouraged or compelled his countrymen to participate in his program of economic aggrandizement but even tried to uproot the military and aristocratic values that were so deeply ingrained in the French mentality, in order to replace them by the middle-class virtues that prevailed in Holland and England. Factories were begun, the poor were put to work, the rich were urged to invest their money in commerce and industry instead of in land and bonds. For a time Colbert even considered launching a frontal

6 R. C. Harris, *The Seigneurial System in Early Canada: A Geographical Study* (Madison, Wis., 1966).

assault on what he regarded as the principal obstacles to economic progress by suppressing the monasteries and that "den of chicanery" the legal profession, equalizing the tax load, and prohibiting the sale of government offices. Financial considerations and the resistance of powerful vested interests prevented him from carrying out these revolutionary reforms, but he did make sure that the practices which he would have liked to eliminate in Old France were not introduced in the new.

A great maritime and colonial empire that would produce the goods France lacked and perhaps eliminate the need for costly imports was very important to Colbert, who strove for economic self-sufficiency. To increase the French share of world trade, he chartered several large, semipublic corporations to act as instruments of state policy. Their role was twofold: to provide ships to compete with those of other nations on the oceans of the world and to take charge of colonial development. Canada, however, was not significantly affected by this policy. The Company of the West. Indies, to which it had been granted, soon became completely involved in a struggle to drive Dutch shipping from the West Indies and this obliged the government to exercise its rights in North America.

Colbert's aim was to transform Canada from a weak fur trading settlement into a strong self-sufficient extension of the French kingdom. The first step was to establish the colony on firm foundations by making it self-supporting in the necessities of life, such as food, shelter, and clothing. The second was to build an economy that could produce goods for the export trade. Up to that time, the colony had produced nothing except furs, but the market for this luxury product was an uncertain one. In the 1660's prices for beaver had begun to fall, in part because of the introduction of new techniques in the manufacturing of men's hats. Thus, Colbert was understandably eager to place the economy on a sounder basis by developing the fisheries, lumbering, mining, and manufacturing. Eventually, these resources might enable Canada to provide France with naval stores and the West Indies with agricultural products and dried fish to feed the plantation slaves, as well as staves to build barrels for the shipment of sugar. But before this ambitious plan could become a reality a prodigious effort was necessary, for the colony was destitute in almost everything. Colbert did not hesitate to make such an effort. Population grew from 3,215 in

1665 to 7,200 in 1672 as a result of a state-sponsored immigration and of measures to encourage early marriages and the raising of large families. State subsidies were made available to support new enterprises. Jean Talon, an intendant of great ability, was sent to Canada to direct the program of economic development.

In Acadia, the royal régime did not mark the beginning of a new era of colonization. In the 1630's, the colony had been divided into three vast and ill-defined domains which had been granted to Nicolas Denys, Charles de Menou d'Aulnay, and Charles de La Tour. Denys devoted himself to the development of his estate but La Tour and d'Aulnay, as rival lords and fur traders, engaged in a private war that raged on land and sea until 1658, when the colony was conquered by the English. France regained title to it in 1667, by the Treaty of Breda, but perhaps because of its preoccupation with Canada did very little to promote its development. The population in 1686 was only 885 persons and the entire economy was controlled by the New Englanders, who treated Acadia merely as an extension of their own settlements. In 1682, Louis XIV and Colbert had attempted to correct the situation. They had granted extensive fishing and trading rights in Acadia to a private company and issued an edict stipulating that any foreign vessel found within the limits of its concession would be confiscated. Enforcing these orders, however, proved to be impossible because of the naval superiority of New England. The French seaboard colony continued to vegetate until the 1690's when the outbreak of war with England obliged the mother country to send out some reinforcements.

In Canada, meantime, the 1670's had witnessed the collapse of Colbert's plans for a diversified economy and the parallel triumph of the fur trade. Such a development was perhaps inevitable, for the minister's system was a costly one to put into operation and no profits could be expected from it for many years to come. When state subsidies were discontinued in 1672 because the outbreak of war with the Dutch Republic made a diversion of funds necessary, the new industries were deprived of their chief sources of financial support. The fur trade, on the other hand, was a natural economy. Furs were always in demand in Europe and all that was required to obtain them from the Indians was a canoe, a few men to take it up country, and a supply of trade goods. Colbert had understood that because of this superior appeal the fur trade could well cripple the rest of the economy by drawing off into the wilderness the colony's most able-bodied men. To prevent this from happening he had issued a series of edicts ordering the Canadians to remain within the confines of the main settlements under pain of severe penalties. Unfortunately all his efforts were in vain, for the geographical and economical factors arrayed against him were too great. Canada, unlike the British colonies, which were cut off from the interior by the Appalachians, was connected to the heart of the continent by a magnificent system of lakes and rivers. The French had been unable to take advantage of their geographical situation as long as the war with the Iroquois had lasted; but this obstacle was lifted in 1667, when the regiment of Carignan-Salières sent to Canada by Louis XIV forced these Indians to sue for peace. Finally, marketing arrangements concluded in 1675 gave the fur trade an irresistible appeal. In that year a syndicate of French financiers known as the Company of the Farm was granted a monopoly on the purchase and sale of Canadian beaver, on condition that it buy at a fixed price the pelts brought to its stores. This assured the Canadians of an outlet that would not vary according to market conditions and it encouraged them to overtrade recklessly with the Indians.

Ironically, it was Colbert himself who set in motion the events that led to the undoing of his "compact colony" policy. The minister was interested in the discovery of a water route from Quebec to the south sea that would give New France access to an ice-free port and open up new commercial possibilities for the colony. So greatly, however, did he fear the dispersion of population that might result from scattered settlements that in 1674 he refused to grant a seigneury in the Illinois country to Louis Jolliet, the discoverer of the Mississippi. But only four years later the famous Cavelier de La Salle, by a clever use of influence and by concealing his real motives, obtained what Jolliet had been denied. He was commissioned by the government to explore the Mississippi River to discover if it flowed into the Gulf of Mexico. Since the court would not finance the venture, he was also authorized to establish posts and to trade with the Indians in the new land as a means to an end. Once in the Mississippi Valley, however, La Salle, with the support of his protector Governor Frontenac, promptly reversed these priorities. The discovery of the mouth of the river became not the end but the means to monopolize the trade of half a continent. This development obliged other merchants, who had previously been satisfied to wait for the Indians to bring their pelts to the colony, to modify their tactics. To avoid being driven into bankruptcy by La Salle and other Frontenac allies who had begun to trade in regions farther north, they had to send their own agents to the interior. The upshot of all this was an enormous increase in the number of men deserting the colony for the west.

The consequences of this expansionism proved momentous for Canada. As late as 1670 the colony still consisted of a small settled area in the St. Lawrence Valley. Fifteen years later, in spite of the opposition of the ministry of the marine, a huge hinterland which embraced the entire Great Lakes and Mississippi Valley regions had been annexed to the inhabited portion. To hold this vast area, which they had neither the means nor the desire to settle, the French relied on the ability of their agents to control the Indian tribes: the *coureurs de bois*, who took trade goods to the natives and frequently ended up by adopting their way of life; the missionaries, now as much political figures as religious ones; the soldiers, who were garrisoned at military posts located at strategic points across the west. Thanks to the influence and prestige these men enjoyed among the Indians, unruly and undisciplined tribes became instruments that enabled the French to maintain and extend their sway in the interior of the continent. It was the relentless demographical pressure of the Thirteen Colonies upon this wilderness empire which, in the 1750's, ignited the war that led to the fall of New France.

The first to challenge French control of the west, however, were not the English but the Iroquois. The territory invaded by La Salle and his men was also the one from which the Five Nations drew a large percentage of their furs for the trade which they carried on with Albany. It was primarily to protect these vital economic interests that they decided to break the peace of 1667. In 1680, some six hundred of their warriors invaded the Illinois country as the first step in a campaign designed to conquer the principal western tribes and to drive the French from the interior.

Thus, after only thirteen years of peace, Canada once again found itself involved in a cruel and costly war with the Iroquois. Against their 2,800 warriors, the colony deployed a force made up of militiamen and newly arrived regulars on the one hand and the western tribes on the other. In this alliance with the Indians of the west lay the colony's strength and at almost any cost it had to be preserved. The Iroquois could always flee when large French expeditions advanced against them, but they were practically defenseless against the raiding parties of Ottawa and Miami Indians that mercilessly ravaged their western flank. Although the clumsy policy pursued by Frontenac came close to causing the breakdown of this alliance on a number of occasions, the war fortunately ended before such a disastrous development could materialize. In 1701 the Iroquois, their fighting force cut in half by twenty years of war, came to terms with the French and all their native allies, thus ending the second and last of the colony's great Indian wars.

It was also during the 1680's and 1690's that the French and the English first became aware of their clashing interests in North America. In the north, the English were striving to make themselves the masters of Hudson Bay and in the south were supporting with arms and ammunition the Iroquois effort to win control of the western fur trade. The French realized that this pincerlike movement had to be broken in order to relieve the economic and military pressure that bore on the colony. To check the English in the north, the Canadian merchants formed a company—La Compagnie du Nord—which attacked the installations of the Hudson Bay Company. To curb English hostility in the south, a series of savage raids was launched against the border settlements of New England and New York. Governor Frontenac, who was the instigator of these attacks, expected that they would demoralize the English and deter them from assisting the Iroquois, but in the case of New England they produced exactly the contrary effect. The cruelties perpetrated by the French and Indian raiders so outraged the Puritan colony that it decided to attempt the conquest of New France. In October, 1690, a fleet commanded by William Phips laid siege to Quebec but was repelled by the defenders commanded by Frontenac.

The outbreak of the War of the Spanish Succession in 1701 marked the beginning of a new phase in Anglo-French colonial rivalry. Shortly before the outbreak of this war, the French government, in a dramatic reversal of Colbert's compact colony rule, decided to consolidate its control of the west from the Great Lakes to the Gulf of Mexico by founding new settlements at Detroit and in Louisiana. This decision was not economically motivated, nor was it merely a grudging recognition of the developments which had taken place since the late 1670's. It was rather a strategy whose aim was to prevent English westward expansion. French statesmen had begun to fear that the overflow of the population of the Thirteen Colonies into the Mississippi Valley would enable the British to build an empire strong enough to conquer the possessions of both France and Spain in America. Louis XIV, for his part, saw Louisiana as a means of furthering his dynastic ambitions. In 1701 his grandson, Philip of Anjou, had acceded to the throne of Spain left vacant by the death of Charles II, the last of the Spanish Hapsburgs. By establishing a buffer colony on the Lower Mississippi, between Mexico and the southern British plantations, Louis XIV hoped to demonstrate to the Spaniards that now that they were under a Bourbon king they could rely on French protection.

The first attempt to erect a barrier in the rear of the English settlements was short-lived and did not yield appreciable results. Because of her involvement in the War of the Spanish Succession, France could do little for Louisiana and the colony eked out a precarious existence during its early years. Detroit, under the command of the incapable Cadillac, proved to be a liability rather than an asset for the French in the region of the Great Lakes. This settlement shifted the center of New France's hinterland too far to the south and brought the western allies inside Albany's economic orbit. In 1708, after the colonial administrators had repeatedly called his attention to the dangers of the situation, the minister of the marine finally abandoned his plan of controlling the northwest from a power position at Detroit. Thus, the grand design of 1701 was allowed to lapse; but the idea of encircling the British plantations in order to prevent their westward expansion was not forgotten.

The War of the Spanish Succession ended in 1713 with the signing of the Treaty of Utrecht. The French had been defeated in Europe and had suffered a major setback in North America in 1710, when Acadia was conquered by the English. These military reverses forced France to make several concessions at the peace table which seriously weakened her colonial empire. Hudson Bay, Newfoundland, and Acadia, three outposts of vital importance for the fur trade and the fisheries, were ceded to the British. The British also managed to have a clause inserted in the treaty which granted them suzerainty over the Iroquois confederacy and the right to trade with all the western tribes. This article, perhaps even more than the others, dismayed the Canadians, who knew very well that their control of the Great Lakes and Mississippi Valley depended on their alliance with the key tribes of those regions. Might not these natives grow cool toward the French and eventually abandon them completely once British traders began to circulate among them with their cheaply priced, high-quality trade goods?

New France thus came out of the War of the Spanish Succession with her economic foundations undermined and her positions in the west under serious challenge. French statesmen, colonial administrators, and businessmen soon realized that unless an energetic program of reconstruction were adopted the future development of their North American colonies, and perhaps even their very existence, would be placed in jeopardy. They also understood that action on this problem could not long be deferred, since Britain's growing strength lay principally in a rapidly expanding colonial empire. Soon after 1713 the French government and the colonial administration began to carry out a program which aimed to contain British power in North America by anulling the effects of the Treaty of Utrecht. The vagueness of this document on two important points greatly facilitated this strategy. It had not defined the Anglo-French boundary nor had it specified which Indian nations should be deemed subjects of which country. These contentious points were to be settled by a joint commission that was to meet at an unspecified date in the future. The omissions enabled France to claim suzerainty over all her traditional allies and ownership of much of the territory claimed by Britain under the terms of the peace treaty.

Three areas were principally affected by this policy. On Cape Breton Island, renamed Ile Royale, in the North Atlantic, the French built the fortress of Louisbourg. This stronghold was to serve both as a fishing station to replace the ones formerly located in Newfoundland and Acadia and as a naval base to guard the approaches to the St. Lawrence. In the northwest, a chain of posts was built from Lake Superior almost as far as the Rockies to intercept the Indians before they could reach British-owned Hudson Bay. Finally, in the Great Lakes and Mississippi Valley, Canada and Louisiana extended their system of fortified trading posts in order to increase their control of the Indian tribes and if need be to turn them against the English, who might venture into Trans-appalachia under cover of the peace treaty. This strategy enabled New France to rebuild her shattered frontiers and to maintain her positions in the fur trade and the fisheries; but these objectives were only accomplished at the cost of mounting friction with the British settlements, friction that made another armed encounter with them practically inevitable.

Accompanying these measures to defend the frontiers were others designed to strengthen Canada internally. Under Frédéric de Maurepas, minister of the marine from 1723 to 1748, and his able intendant, Gilles Hocquart, a determined effort was made both to increase the colony's population by means of a state-sponsored immigration and also to diversify the economy by subsidizing certain sectors of agriculture and some industrial enterprises. This program was essentially the same as the one pursued by Colbert half a century before, but it met with far greater success, for the population, which passed from 20,531 in 1716 to 55,009 in 1755, was now sufficiently large to support a complex economy. By the 1740's, there were unmistakable signs of prosperity and growth. Exports no longer consisted simply of furs but also of large quantities of wheat for the new colony of Ile Royale. Two important industries employing a few hundred men were in full operation: shipyards at Quebec and ironworks near Trois Rivières. In brief, between the Treaty of Utrecht in 1713 and the outbreak of war with Britain in 1744, Canada outgrew the stage of a primitive fur-trading economy and began to exploit the other resources of the St. Lawrence Valley.

The different ways in which historians have analyzed the society established on these economic foundations constitute an historiographical study in themselves. The traditional school of French Canadian historiography, which was at the peak of its influence in the early years of this century, considered that Roman Catholicism and the peaceful work of the countryside had been the most formative social influences of the French régime. Their attempt to explain the colony's development by means of spiritual and agrarian factors was acceptable as long as the church and the farm were the dominant institutions of French Canada. After 1920, however, the influence of this interpretation began to wane. The face of the Province of Quebec was being rapidly transformed by the advent of large-scale industrialization and urbanization, and French Canadians felt a growing need to redefine their past. In the 1950's the rising generation eagerly accepted the interpretation of the history of New France put forward by Guy Frégault of the Université de Montréal. Frégault contended that the driving force in the colony's history had been neither the Church nor the farm-dwelling *habitant* but an economic class—the French Canadian *bourgeoisie*—which had built, controlled, and defended the colony before being destroyed by the British conquest of 1760.[7]

A working hypothesis rather than a conclusive study based on exhaustive research, this interpretation soon ran into strong criticism. Jean Hamelin of Quebec's Université Laval flatly denied that a class of powerful French Canadian *bourgeois* had existed before 1760.[8] W. J. Eccles, for his part, conceded the existence of moneyed elements but, unlike Frégault, maintained that wealth did not have the same significance in New France, where the ethos was military and aristocratic, as in the English colonies, where it was *bourgeois* and commercial. For the British, the accumulation of wealth was an end in itself; for the French, it was but a means to an end, this end being entry into the ranks of the nobility.[9] This interpretation has a special utility in that it underscores basic similarities in the mentality and outlook shared by the French upper classes of colony and mother country. Both societies were very status conscious and both placed the accent, not on the basic *bourgeois* values of thrift, industry, and prudence, but on the gentlemanly ones of honor, courtesy, and breeding.

Although the same outlook prevailed in France and New France, the structure of the two societies was differentiated by environmental factors. In France, the great dividing line in society was drawn between the privileged first and second estates and the non-privileged third. During the reign of Louis XIV it had been relatively easy for a wealthy and ambitious member of the *tiers-état* to enter the ranks of the nobility, but this became progressively more difficult during the eighteenth century when French society began to harden into a caste system. In New France, on the other hand, classes tended to shade off one into the other. This was due in part to the opportunity enjoyed by everyone to own land and to

---

7 G. Frégault, *Canadian Society in the French Regime* (Ottawa: Canadian Historical Association Booklets, 1962).

8 J. Hamelin, *Economie et société en Nouvelle France* (Quebec, 1960).

9 W. J. Eccles, *Canadian Society During the French Regime* (Montreal: E. R. Adair Memorial Lectures, 1968), pp. 20–26.

participate in the fur trade; in part to the existence of numerous means of social promotion, of which the principal was an edict of 1684 which allowed the Canadian nobility to engage in trade and commerce, an occupation that was closed to them in France. This edict was primarily meant to stimulate the economy but, although this may have been unintended, it also lowered the barriers between the nobles and the merchants and enabled many of the latter to join the ranks of the nobility. As a result, these two social elements were fused into one group at the summit of the social hierarchy. It constituted an open oligarchy—Frégault's *bourgeoisie* —which, in the words of this historian, "shared the trading posts, occupied most of the public offices, and distinguished itself in military expeditions."[10] At the bottom of the scale were the *habitants*, who had nothing about them of the French peasantry's air of sadness and resignation which the Le Nain brothers have captured in their paintings. According to all reports they were well-built, proud, independent, and notoriously insubordinate.

In 1744 the long period of peace which had prevailed since the Treaty of Utrecht and so greatly favored the development of New France came to an end. Great Britain entered the War of the Austrian Succession in which France was already engaged and the world's two great imperial powers fought a global conflict which, except for a brief respite from 1748 to 1754, only ended in 1763 with the cession of New France and the collapse of the first French empire. In previous wars, North America had been a very secondary theater. French strategists had regarded it as remote and unimportant and had concentrated their efforts in Europe. England, while more concerned, had only pursued limited objectives, such as those it had managed to achieve in 1713. In the late 1740's the policy of both nations began to change and control of the North American continent became one of the crucial issues of the Seven Years' War.

The man primarily responsible for the French change of attitude was Roland-Michel Barrin, comte de La Galissonière, scholar, naval officer, and colonial administrator. During the years he spent in New France as acting governor-general, from 1747 to 1749, he developed the ideas that formed the basis of his great "Memoir on the Colonies of France in America," which he submitted to the government in December, 1750. In it he argued with compelling

10 G. Frégault, *Canadian Society in the French Regime*, p. 14.

clarity that the balance of power in Europe was linked directly to
the balance of power in America. The conquest of the French
colonies by the English would so greatly increase the power of
Britain that France would lose her hegemony in Europe. To
prevent this from happening, La Galissonière advocated a general
strengthening of Canada and Louisiana and the occupation of the
Ohio Valley, which he regarded as the key to America. If the English should succeed in winning control of this area they would be in
a position to wreak havoc on New France's system of Indian alliances, attack the posts on the Mississippi, and sever communications between Canada and Louisiana. France acted on his suggestion in 1753, when it sent a force of 2,300 men to build a chain of
posts south of Lake Erie toward the Ohio River. This was a fateful
move, for it sparked the war which led to the fall of New France in
1760.

In the English world, public opinion was slowly rallying to the
idea that the security of the Thirteen Colonies and the expansion
of British trade could only be assured by a total victory over the
French in America. The idea of a conquest of Canada had originated in Massachusetts in the closing years of the seventeenth
century. It had gradually been taken up by the fur traders of New
York and the land speculators of Virginia after 1713 when the
French built an empire that directly threatened their interests. It
became one of the key points of the aggressive program of the great
London commercial interests who believed that their country's
greatness depended upon its capture of world trade. Held in check
by Sir Robert Walpole, who considered that England existed for
substantial country squires and not for commercial adventurers,
these aspirations gained partial recognition at the start of the Seven
Years' War, when British regulars landed in Virginia to resist
French pretensions in the Ohio Valley and finally triumphed under
William Pitt, who committed his nation to the task of driving the
French from America.

The strategy of Britain was simple and effective. It consisted of
subsidizing an ally, Prussia, which drew France's financial and military resources into the vortex of a continental campaign. Britain,
for her part, was free to devote her undivided energies to the
maritime and colonial conflict. In 1755, her war fleet numbered
131 ships mounting 8,722 guns as compared to 71 ships and 4,790
guns for the French. This naval superiority was chiefly responsible

for Anglo-American successes, for it enabled them to control the seas and to mount a decisive assault against New France. The campaign plans themselves followed the pattern established during the War of the Spanish Succession. A naval attack against Quebec was to be accompanied by a thrust against Montreal by way of the Richelieu.

In spite of the great superiority of the forces massing against them, the Canadians, reinforced by a few thousand regulars newly arrived from France, were remarkably successful in the early stages of the war. They drove back the English along the Richelieu and took the offensive in the Great Lakes country, where they captured Oswego in 1756. The strain of war, however, soon had a disastrous effect on society and on the still fragile economy. Frequent mobilization of the militia slowed down agricultural production and caused a food shortage, while heavy wartime expenditures resulted in the proliferation of paper money and spiraling costs. These miseries were aggravated by administrative corruption practiced on a giant scale by the intendant François Bigot, who used the great powers of his office to embezzle public funds and to gain a monopolistic control of the colony's internal and external trade.

By 1758, Canada still held onto the Richelieu but her eastern and western flanks were being driven in. While Anglo-American forces were capturing key posts in the Ohio Valley and Great Lakes regions, the British were making themselves the masters of the Gulf of St. Lawrence. In 1755 the Acadians, whose doubtful loyalty made them a security risk in an area of high strategical importance, had been deported. On July 27, 1758, Louisbourg capitulated after enduring a siege of one and a half months. The road to Quebec now lay open and the following year the British fleet appeared before the capital of New France. Had the French general Montcalm been able to defeat the army under James Wolfe which scaled the city heights on the morning of September 13, he might still have saved the colony; but his errors of judgment led to his defeat and to the surrender of the city a few days later. In September, 1760, with three armies advancing against it from different directions, Montreal capitulated and all resistance ceased. The French régime in America had come to an end.

What did the conquest mean for French Canada? A very large book could be written on the answers that have been given to this question. Francis Parkman and many historians of the English-speaking world regarded it as a happy calamity, a form of liberation from Bourbon absolutism. The traditional school of French Canadian historians, on the other hand, argued that the fall of New France created a situation that was full of perils for the language, laws, and religion of the settlers. Led by their clergy, however, the people victoriously defended these vital elements of their nationality against the policy of Anglification which the British either openly or secretly pursued. This interpretation, which dwelt almost exclusively on the cultural aspects of nationality, did not satisfy Guy Frégault and his followers, who advanced instead the theory of social decapitation. They claimed that the conquest caused the disintegration of the influential *bourgeoisie* of the French régime. Some members of this group realized that their social and economic role was jeopardized outside the framework of the French empire and returned to France; others, who remained in Canada, were soon eliminated from commerce and industry by the newly arrived British settlers who enjoyed the support of London's great banking and financial firms. Thus, French Canadians fell back upon the soil and became an agrarian people. This thesis, which seemed to prove that French Canada's traditional absence from commerce, finance, and industry had not been a matter of choice but necessity, was enthusiastically received by a generation which had become anxious to acquire and exercise economic power. Some historians, however, only gave it qualified support and others rejected it altogether. Jean Hamelin, for instance, argued that the absence of a strong French Canadian *bourgeoisie* after 1760 was not a result of the conquest but of the French régime itself. The economy of New France, he pointed out, had not been built and controlled by the Canadians but by the Crown or by merchants whose base of operation was located in France.

Was the conquest, then, a catastrophe which completely changed the course of French Canadian history or merely an incident that did not cause profound changes in the fabric of society? Much more research will have to be done before a definitive answer can be given to this question, but evidence presently available favors the second hypothesis. During the first thirty years of British rule the major institutions of the French régime were not disturbed. The seigneurs not only kept their estates but even took advantage of the new government's unfamiliarity with the nature and purpose of Canadian feudalism to increase the dues payable by their tenants and to gain fresh political powers. The Roman Catholic Church, enjoying official recognition and freed from the restraints of royal Gallicanism, also increased its influence. The fur trade remained the basis of economic life and French Canadians continued to participate in it successfully until the 1780's, when they began to lose ground to the British merchants. Their eclipse appears to have been caused by their insistence upon conducting their affairs individually or in small partnerships when rising costs and growing distances made large capital concentrations necessary.

Originally it had not been Britain's intention to allow a French society to perpetuate itself on the shores of the St. Lawrence. Her initial policy for the new colony, outlined in the Royal Proclamation of October, 1763, and in the instructions to Governor James Murray, was one of radical reconstruction. The new colony of Quebec was to be made British in fact as well as in name by the introduction of British laws, freehold tenure, an assembly to be called when conditions warranted, and the shutting out of Rome's ecclesiastical jurisdiction. This program, however, was soon opposed by Murray and his successor Guy Carleton particularly. By character and background, these men were military, aristocratic, and authoritarian. On the one hand, they felt a strong attraction for Canadian society with its landed nobility, its authoritarian government, and its legal system which, in the words of Carleton, assured "subordination, from the first to the lowest"; on the other, they were repelled by the low-born British merchants who took up residence in the colony after 1763 and clamored for the implementation of the royal proclamation. In an age when lines of loyalty were frequently drawn horizontally between classes rather than vertically between nations, it is not surprising that the governor and the Canadian upper classes should have joined together in defense of an aristocratic-type society against democratic attack.

Carleton enjoyed the advantage in his struggle with the British element, for conditions in the colony increasingly favored a pro-French constitutional settlement. The influx of British Protestant settlers into Quebec, which would have given the royal proclamation a broad base of popular support, did not materialize; except for a few hundred merchants who trickled in, the population remained entirely French. To enforce the proclamation under such circumstances was impolitic, for it might weaken British control over a strategic territory at a time when war with France was threatening and the rumblings of discontent in the Thirteen Colonies were growing louder. Faced with this dangerous situation, the British government decided to accept Carleton's recommendation, which had not carried much weight before 1769, to give Quebec a constitution that would confirm its French character. In 1774 the proclamation was abandoned and replaced by the Quebec Act, which reconstituted the Canada of the French régime. Once again, the frontiers of the colony extended to the Ohio and the Mississippi. French civil law, the seigneurial system, and the right of the Church to collect the tithe from all Roman Catholics were officially recognized. Plans for an assembly were put aside in favor of an authoritarian form of government composed of the governor and an appointive council to which Roman Catholics were admitted without having to take the Test Oath.

Carleton expected that the Quebec Act would not only keep democracy in check, but would also align firmly on the British side the entire Canadian population which, he anticipated, would follow the directives of its social superiors unquestioningly. That the governor was mistaken was strikingly demonstrated during the American Revolution when the *habitants* refused en masse to mobilize against the invading Americans when urged to do so by the seigneurs and the priests. While all historians agree that Carleton's policy did not produce the desired effect, there is considerable disagreement among them over where it went wrong. A. L. Burt, an authority on Quebec during the first thirty years of British rule, believes that Carleton's aristocratic designs were wrecked by the resistance of a frontier-bred democracy which permeated the lower levels of Canadian society.[11] Michel Brunet, a follower of Guy Frégault, claims that the seigneurs and the clergy had discredited themselves in the eyes of the people by their collaboration with the traditional enemies of New France.[12] These two interpretations are interesting but they seem to miss the point. Carleton's strategy was not defeated by the people's democratic instincts nor by their outraged nationalism but by his own unfamiliarity with the nature of government before 1760. During the

11 A. L. Burt, *Guy Carleton, Lord Dorchester, 1724–1808* (Ottawa: Canadian Historical Association Booklets, 1964), pp. 5–6.
12 M. Brunet, *Les Canadiens et les débuts de la domination britannique, 1760–1791* (Ottawa: Canadian Historical Association Booklets, 1962), p. 12.

French régime the administration had carefully restricted the powers of both the Church and the seigneurs; Carleton had increased them. The massive disobedience of 1775 thus appears as a form of protest against the domination of an upper class that was alien to the French Canadian tradition.

In spite of this deviation from the methods of government of the French régime, the institutions and social structure of New France remained basically unchanged fourteen years after the conquest. Soon afterward, however, disintegration began to set in. Following the ratification of American independence in 1783, a large number of United Empire Loyalists immigrated to Quebec and Nova Scotia, Britain's last two possessions on the North American continent. Because those who came to Quebec could not be denied the British institutions for which they had risked their lives and sacrificed their property, changes in the constitution became necessary. These were carried out in 1791 under the Constitutional Act. The part of Quebec lying west of the Ottawa River and north of the line of the Great Lakes, where approximately 6,000 Loyalists had settled, became the Province of Upper Canada. This new colony and Quebec, now called Lower Canada, were granted a government composed of an elective assembly and, as a safeguard against the democratic excesses for which many British statesmen blamed the American Revolution, two appointive councils. The grant of this democratic lower house fatally undermined the aristocratic settlement of 1774. Given the opportunity to choose their political representatives, the *habitants* turned to shopkeepers, doctors, lawyers, and notaries, men who were of the common people and in whom they had confidence. The rise to prominence of this professional middle class was the most important social change in French Canada up to that time.

This change was accompanied by others that were no less decisive for the future of French Canada. The torrent of nationalism which the French Revolution and the Napoleonic Wars loosened upon the western world made the new French Canadian élites conscious of themselves as the national leaders of a people. On the side of the British, the Francophile administrators of the post-conquest period passed forever from the scene. They were replaced by men like Governor James Craig (1807–1811) who actively distrusted the French and were determined to Anglicize the province. The decline in the fur trade in the first decade of the nineteenth century and the emergence of timber as a new staple added to these tensions. The fur trade in the late eighteenth century had been a great co-operative venture between two groups of men, the Scottish merchants and the French Canadian *voyageurs*, who had been united by bonds of mutual sympathy and respect. The timber magnate was a new type of entrepreneur who could not accommodate himself to existing institutions. He insisted on internal improvements and on the chartering of banks to make Lower Canada into an effective commercial state, and he became increasingly angry and impatient with the French Canadian agrarian majority in the assembly for its failure to carry out such a program. The province was now dividing along national rather than class lines.

In the first decade of the nineteenth century, as a result of these multiple changes in society, in the economy, and in governmental policy, the Ancien Régime may be said to have died in French Canada and a new age to have been born.

I

The Origins of New France, 1534–1663

1. Jacques Cartier
Visits the Island of Montreal,
1535

OF THE three voyages Jacques Cartier made to Canada from 1534 to 1541, the second (1535–36) was unquestionably the most important, for it resulted in the discovery and exploration of the St. Lawrence River, which became Canada's principal economic axis in the following century. The visit to the island of Montreal constitutes one of the high points of this voyage. From the information given to him by the Indians who inhabited the island, Cartier concluded that there was gold to be found in the regions to the north. This in turn led to France's abortive attempt of 1541 to found a colony in the St. Lawrence Valley.

The following passage, taken from the journal of Cartier's second voyage, describes this visit to Montreal.

Further Reading: G. Lanctot, A History of Canada, Vol. I, From its Origins to the Royal Régime, 1663 (Cambridge, Mass., 1963) provides the history of the period covered in this chapter. See also, C. A. Julien, Les Voyages de découverte et les premiers établissements (Paris, 1948); M. Trudel, Histoire de la Nouvelle France, Vol. I, Les Vaines tentatives, 1524–1603 (Montreal, 1963).

SOURCE: H. P. Biggar (ed. and trans.), The Voyages of Jacques Cartier (Ottawa, 1924), pp. 162–172.

As we drew near to their village, great numbers of the inhabitants came out to meet us and gave us a hearty welcome, according to the custom of the country. And we were led by our guides and those who were conducting us into the middle of the village, where there was an open square between the houses, about a stone's throw or thereabouts in width each way. They signed to us that we should come to a halt here, which we did. And at once all the girls and women of the village, some of whom had children in their arms, crowded about us, rubbing our faces, arms and other parts of the upper portions of our bodies which they could touch, weeping for joy at the sight of us and giving us the best welcome they could. They made signs to us also to be good enough to put our hands upon their babies. After this the men made the women retire, and themselves sat down upon the ground round about us, as if we had been going to perform a miracle play. And at once several of the women came back, each with a four-cornered mat, woven like tapestry, and these they spread upon the ground in the middle of the square, and made us place ourselves upon them. When this had been done, the ruler and chief of this tribe, whom in their language they call *Agouhanna*, was carried in, seated on a large deer-skin, by nine or ten Indians, who came and set him down upon the mats near the Captain, making signs to us that this was their ruler and chief. This *Agouhanna*, who was some fifty years of age, was in no way better dressed than the other Indians except that he wore about his head for a crown a sort of red band made of hedgehog's skin. This chief was completely paralyzed and deprived of the use of his limbs. When he had saluted the Captain and his men, by making signs which clearly meant that they were very welcome, he showed his arms and his legs to the Captain motioning to him to be good enough to touch them, as if he thereby expected to be cured and healed. On this the Captain set about rubbing his arms and legs with his hands. Thereupon this *Agouhanna* took the band of cloth he was wearing as a crown and presented it to the Captain. And at once many sick persons, some blind, others with but one eye, others lame or impotent and others again so extremely old that their eyelids hung down to their cheeks, were brought in and set down or laid out near the Captain, in order that he might lay his hands upon them, so that one would have thought Christ had come down to earth to heal them.

Seeing the suffering of these people and their faith, the Captain read aloud the Gospel of St. John, namely, "In the beginning", etc. making the sign of the cross over the poor sick people, praying God to give them knowledge of our holy faith and of our Saviour's passion, and grace to obtain baptism and redemption. Then the Captain took a prayer-book and read out, word for word, the Passion of our Lord, that all who were present could hear it, during which all these poor people maintained great silence and were wonderfully attentive, looking up to heaven and going through the same ceremonies they saw us do. After this the Captain had all the men range themselves on one side, the women on another and the children on another, and to the headmen he gave hatchets, to the others knives, and to the women, beads and other small trinkets. He then made the children scramble for little rings and tin *agnus Dei*, which afforded them great amusement. The Captain next ordered the trumpets and other musical instruments to be sounded, whereat the Indians were much delighted. We then took leave of them and proceeded to set out upon our return. Seeing this the squaws placed themselves in our way to prevent us, and brought us some of their provisions, which they had made ready for us, to wit: fish, soups, beans, bread and other dishes, in the hope of inducing us to partake of some refreshment and to eat with them. But as these provisions were not to our taste and had no savour of salt, we thanked them, making signs that we were in no need of refreshment.

On issuing forth from the village we were conducted by several of the men and women of the place up the above-mentioned mountain, lying a quarter of a league away, which was named by us "Mount Royal". On reaching the summit we had a view of the land for more than thirty leagues round about. Towards the north there is a range of mountains, running east and west,[1] and another range to the south.[2] Between these ranges lies the finest land it is possible to see, being arable, level and flat. And in the midst of this flat region one saw the river [St. Lawrence] extending beyond the spot where we had left our long-boats. At that point there is the most violent rapid it is possible to see, which we were unable to pass.[3] And as far as the eye can reach, one sees that river, large, wide and broad, which came from the south-west and flowed near three fine conical mountains, which we estimated to be some fifteen leagues away. And it was told us and made clear by signs by our three local Indian guides, that there were three more such rapids in that river, like the one where lay our long-boats; but through lack of an interpreter we could not make out what the

1 The Laurentian Mountains.
2 The northern slope of the Adirondacks and of the Green Mountains of Vermont.
3 The Lachine Rapids.

distance was from one to the other. They then explained to us by signs that after passing these rapids, one could navigate along that river for more than three moons. And they showed us furthermore that along the mountains to the north, there is a large river,[4] which comes from the west like the said river [St. Lawrence]. We thought this river [Ottawa] must be the one that flows past the kingdom and province of the Saguenay; and without our asking any questions or making any sign, they seized the chain of the Captain's whistle, which was made of silver, and a dagger-handle of yellow copper-gilt like gold, that hung at the side of one of the sailors, and gave us to understand that these came from up that river [Ottawa], where lived *Agojuda*, which means bad people, who were armed to the teeth, showing us the style of their armour, which is made with cords and wood, laced and plaited together. They also seemed to say that these *Agojuda* waged war continually, one tribe against the other, but through not understanding their language, we could not make out what the distance was to that country. The Captain showed them some copper, which they call *caignetdazé*, and pointing towards the said region, asked by signs if it came thence? They shook their heads to say no, showing us that it came from the Saguenay, which lies in the opposite direction. Having seen and learned these things, we returned to our long-boats, accompanied by a large number of these Indians, some of whom, when they saw that our people were tired, took them upon their shoulders, as on horseback and carried them. And on our arrival at the long-boats, we at once set sail to return to the bark, for fear of any misadventure. Such a departure did not fail to cause the Indians great regret; for so long as they could follow us down the river, they did so. And we made such good headway that we reached our bark on Monday, October 4.

2. Samuel de Champlain

FROM THE day he founded Quebec on July 3, 1608, until his death on December 25, 1635, Samuel de Champlain worked unceasingly to establish a powerful French colony in the St. Lawrence Valley. The memoir he submitted to the king of France and his council in 1618 to stimulate their interest in the new country is the best single statement

4 The Ottawa River.

of his program of colonization (Document A below). Unfortunately, until the foundation of the Company of One Hundred Associates by Cardinal Richelieu in 1627, Champlain's aims were frustrated by a policy that left the country's development in the hands of small companies whose sole interest was the exploitation of the fur trade (Document B).

Further Reading: M. Bishop, Champlain, The Life of Fortitude (New York, 1948); M. Trudel, Histoire de la Nouvelle France, Vol. II, Le Comptoir, 1604–1627 (Montreal, 1966).

SOURCES: Document A. H. P. Biggar (ed and trans.), The Works of Samuel de Champlain (6 vols., Toronto: Champlain Society Publications, 1922–36), II, 326–337. Document B. Ibid., IV, 349–352. Both selections reprinted with the permission of Champlain Society Publications.

A. His Program of Colonization, 1618

To the King and the Lords of his Council.

SIRE,

The Sieur de Champlain represents to you most humbly that for sixteen years he has toiled with laborious zeal as well in the discoveries of New France as of divers peoples and nations whom he has brought to our knowledge, who had never been discovered save by him; which peoples have given him such and so faithful report of the north and south seas that one cannot doubt but that this would be the means of reaching easily to the Kingdom of China and the East Indies, whence great riches could be drawn; besides planting there the divine worship, as our Récollet friars can bear witness, in addition to the abundance of merchandise from the said country of New France, which would be drawn thence annually through the diligence of the workmen who would go there. Should this said country be given up and the settlement abandoned, for want of bestowing upon it the needed attention, the English or Flemings, envious of our prosperity, would seize upon it, thereby enjoying the fruits of our labours, and preventing by this means more than a thousand vessels from going to the dry and green fisheries, and for whale-oil, as they have already done in the north and in the Sieur de Poitrincourt's[1] settlements as well as in those of the Jesuits, which they have captured and burned, as the said Champlain has reported to the gentlemen of the Chamber of Commerce, who

1 The correct spelling is Poutrincourt.

have properly and duly informed themselves concerning every point of the articles hereto appended. And considering the advantage and profit to be derived therefrom, as well for the glory of God as for the honour of His Majesty and for the good of his subjects, the Chamber of Commerce has passed a resolution to represent to His Majesty and to the said Lords of his Council on the measures which he should take for such a holy and glorious enterprise.

For these reasons the said Champlain most humbly entreats His said Majesty and the said Lords of his Council to grant him the means of strengthening and extending his design. And forasmuch as the said de Champlain, in this present year, is making a voyage to New France, he humbly entreats His said Majesty to consent that the Baron de Roussillon, one of the commissioners of the said Chamber of Commerce, be entrusted with the care of looking after the things necessary for the said undertaking, and of pursuing the fulfilment of the said resolution of the said Chamber of Commerce with His said Majesty and the said Lords of his Council, during the absence of the said de Champlain; who will continue to pray God unceasingly for the prosperity and increase of Your said Majesty.

(Signed) CHAMPLAIN

Firstly.—His said Majesty will establish the Christian faith among an infinite number of souls, who neither hold nor possess any form of religion whatsoever, and nevertheless wish only for the knowledge of divine and human worship, according to the reports of all those who have made the voyage to the said New France.

Secondly.—The King will make himself master and lord of a country nearly eighteen hundred leagues in length, watered by the fairest rivers in the world and by the greatest and most numerous lakes, the richest and most abundant in all varieties of fish that are to be found, and full also of the greatest meadows, fields, and forests, for the most part of walnut-trees, and very pleasant hills upon which there is found a great abundance of wild vines, which yield grapes as large as or larger than ours, cultivated as these are.

Thirdly.—The Sieur de Champlain undertakes to discover the South Sea passage to China and to the East Indies by way of the river St. Lawrence, which traverses the lands of the said New France, and which river issues from a lake about three hundred leagues in length, from which lake flows a river that empties into the said South Sea, according to the account given to the said Sieur de Champlain by a number of people, his friends in the said country; whom he has visited and become acquainted with, having ascended the said river St. Lawrence for more than four hundred leagues into the said lake of three hundred leagues in length, on which voyage he found numerous fortified towns, encircled and enclosed with wooden palissades after the manner used to-day in Muscovy; which towns can furnish two thousand men armed after their fashion; others less.

That His said Majesty would derive a great and notable profit from the taxes and duties he could levy on the merchandise coming from the said country, according to the memorial submitted, as likewise from the customs' duties on the merchandise that would come from China and from the Indies, which would surpass in value at least ten times all those levied in France, inasmuch as all the merchants of Christendom would pass through the passage sought by the Sieur de Champlain, if it please the King to grant them leave to do so, in order to shorten the said journey by more than a year and a half, without any risk from pirates and from the perils of the sea and of the voyage, on account of the great circuit it is necessary now to make, which brings a thousand inconveniences to merchants and travellers.

Furthermore the said Sieur de Champlain declares and proposes, subject to the good pleasure of His Majesty, should he see fit to undertake and pursue the said enterprise, to build at Quebec, the site of the Sieur Champlain's settlement situated on the river St. Lawrence, at a narrow part of the said river, some nine hundred or a thousand yards in width, a town almost as large as St. Denis, which shall be called, if it please God and the King, LUDOVICA, in the centre of which will be built a fair temple, dedicated to the Redeemer, and called the Church of the Redeemer, as a memorial and commemoration of the good that it shall please God to do to these poor people, who have no knowledge of His holy name, to incline the will of the King to bring them to the knowledge of the holy Christian faith and to the bosom of our holy mother Church.

A fort with five bastions will be built alongside the said town, on a certain spot elevated on two sides, which will command the said town and the narrows of the said river. On the other side of the river and directly opposite will be built a fort of the same dimensions in order to bar completely the passage of the said river, as being the entrance and the gateway of the said country, through which alone anyone may enter therein, since from the mouth of the said river to the sea, from which mouth it may be about thirty leagues to the said Quebec, which is distant from the opening into the sea some six score leagues, the country on the right and on the left is very full of horrible mountains and rocks and desert lands, which there is no means of traversing, there being no port nor harbours for laying up vessels, save one, called Tadoussac, where the great vessels come to anchor. And in this place a fort will be built on a very suitable point of land, in which will be placed a garrison, which garrison will be changed every six months.

The said Tadoussac is some thirty-five leagues below the said Quebec. Between the said Quebec and Tadoussac neither friends nor enemies can secure a footing.

What the said Sieur de Champlain declares to be necessary in order to secure a solid footing in the said country of New France is: firstly, in order that this holy enterprise may be blessed by God, to take there first of all fifteen Récollet friars, who will be lodged in a monastery to be erected near the said Church of the Redeemer;

Secondly, to conduct thither three hundred families, composed each of four persons, namely the husband and wife, son and daughter, or man-servant and maid-servant, below the age of twenty years, that is to say the children and servants.

And inasmuch as all existing states are supported politically on four buttresses, which are force, justice, trade and husbandry, having spoken in the first instance of what pertains to the Church, it is necessary to add thereto force, which will consist of three hundred good men well armed and disciplined, and who nevertheless will have to work by turns at whatever will be necessary, as it is inexpedient in founding colonies to carry thither people, whatever their quality may be, who are incapable of earning their living.

And it will be well to consider that, should the said settlement at Quebec not be kept up and strengthened against attack by settlers on the neighbouring lands establishing themselves in the country in good earnest, the English or the Flemings, who are our neighbours, will drive us out, as they have already done the Jesuits and the Sieur de Poutrincourt, whose settlements they have captured and burned.[2]

---

2 These settlements had been located in Acadia.

The Flemings are settled in a place where they permit no one to go save those of their nation, which place is not very far from us. The English are settled in Virginia, where they permit no Frenchman to enter, as likewise in the north, where the said English have established themselves, permitting no foreigners save of their own nation to engage in the whale fishery; and if they should come to get possession of the river St. Lawrence and of our settlement, they would prevent at least six or seven hundred French vessels from going annually to the cod-fishery; against which it is necessary to make provision and to take early measures.

Should it please His Majesty to grant the moneys raised from the above-mentioned sources, which nevertheless the said petitioner, as he has stated above, does not wish to handle or touch, for the period of fifteen years, this accident will be guarded against; and the said Sieur de Champlain, upon the expiration of the said period, promises on his honour and his life, provided that from the said sources he can obtain sufficient to meet the expenses of the said families and soldiers, to hand over the enterprise to His Majesty so firmly established, that no human force need be feared in the four towns built along the said St. Lawrence, nor in the towns and villages, and also all the peoples of the said country tributary to His Majesty. Provision must be made for as many families and soldiers as stated above, the whole in accordance and conformity with the estimate above set out, and to have transported thither in considerable numbers all sorts of domestic animals that we have in France, which are not found in the said country. And it is necessary to reckon for this article fifteen thousand livres annually, and for three consecutive years only. For the establishment of the other three parts of the state, to wit: justice, trade and husbandry, His Majesty will be most humbly entreated to appoint certain of his Council to establish and ordain the fundamental laws of the state, in accordance with which all litigations and suits in these parts shall be decided and all disputes settled at the third hearing of the cases and without the necessity of attorney or lawyer; and that justice be done free of cost.

B. His Conflict with the Merchants, 1618

In the same year 1618 the partners were afraid of being deprived of the fur-trade for not doing something more than they were obliged by their agreement, such as to transport men to that side to inhabit and cultivate the land, to which I urged them as much as I could, offering in their default to introduce others, granting them the same privileges as they had themselves. For my part, I said, I had to inform His Majesty and my Lord the Prince as to the progress which was made from time to time, as I had done; that the usual disturbed conditions in France had hindered His Majesty from correcting the situation, and that they must do better. Otherwise they might be ousted from all their claims, which aimed only at their private gain, quite unlike mine; for I had no other purpose than to see the country inhabited by industrious people, for the clearing of the land, in order not to be subjected to the importation of provisions yearly from France at great expense, and to have the men fall into great necessity through not possessing the wherewithal to sustain life, as had already happened when the ships had been nearly two months behind their usual date, and there had almost been a tumult and revolt on this account on the part of some against others.

To all this our partners said that affairs in France were so unsettled that, although they had gone to great expense, they held no position of security to themselves, since they had seen what had happened in the case of the Sieur de Monts. I told them that there was a great difference between those times and these, in so far as he was a nobleman who had not enough influence to maintain himself at Court against the ill-will in His Majesty's Council. That now they had a prince for patron and viceroy of the country who was able to protect and defend them in respect to and against all, subject to the good pleasure of the King. But I was well aware that they were afraid of something more serious, that if the country became inhabited their power would wane, since they would not be doing just as they liked in those parts, and that they would be defrauded of the greater part of the furs, which they would only get through the channel of the inhabitants of the country, and a little later would be driven away by those whom they had installed at great cost. For all those who have such plans these are arguments for never doing anything; and thus, under plausible pretexts, they promise marvels but accomplish little, and prevent those who would have greatly liked to take up their abode in that country, who would gladly have brought their belongings and spent their lives there, if they had not been prevented from it.

3. The Company of One Hundred Associates, 1627

CHAMPLAIN's efforts to interest France in America finally bore fruit in 1627 when Richelieu founded the Company of One Hundred Associates. More of the kingdom's wealth and talent than ever in the past were now committed to the task of Canadian colonization. The rights and obligations of the One Hundred Associates were carefully defined in the charter issued to them on April 29, 1627.

Further Reading: C. W. Cole, Colbert and a Century of French Mercantilism, 2 vols. (New York, 1939).

SOURCES: *Edicts, Ordinances, Declarations and Decrees Relative to the Seigniorial Tenure, Required by an Address of the Legislative Assembly, 1851* (Quebec, 1852), pp. 5–10.

Act for the Establishment
of the Company of the Hundred Associates
for the Trade of Canada,
Containing the Articles Granted to the Said Company
by the Cardinal de Richelieu,
the 27th April 1627

THE KING, being desirous now, as the late king Henry the Great, his father, heretofore was, of causing to be sought out and discovered in the lands, regions and countries of New-France, called Canada, some fit and proper place for the establishment of a colony, for the purpose, with divine assistance, of introducing to the people who inhabit the same the knowledge of the Only God, cause them to be civilized and instructed in the Catholic, Apostolic and Roman Religion and Faith; his Eminence the Cardinal of Richelieu, Grand Master, Chief and general Superintendant of the trade and manufactures of France, being obliged by the duties of his office to forward the pious intentions and designs of their Majesties, the kings above named, has deemed that the only means of introducing these people to the knowledge of the only God, is to people these regions with french born catholics, who will by their example dispose the people to embrace the christian religion and to lead a civilized life, and by establishing therein the royal authority, be the means of creating, in his said newly discovered regions, some trade which may become advantageous to His Majesty's subjects.

Nevertheless the persons to whom these objects have been entrusted have been so little zealous in their accomplishment, that, even now, but one settlement has been effected, in which forty or fifty french subjects are maintained, rather for the interest of traders, than for the benefit and furtherance of the king's service in the said country; and so little assistance have these settlements received up to the present moment, that various complaints have been made to the king in council, and the cultivation of the country has been so little advanced, that if the surplus of grain and other commodities, necessary for so small a number of individuals had not been brought annually, these people would have perished from hunger, inasmuch as they had not wherewith to subsist upon for a month after the period at which the vessel usually arrived every year.

Those also who have up to the present period obtained for themselves all the trade of the said country, have had so little desire or have had so little power of settling and cultivating it, that in the course of fifteen years, during which their privilege was to endure, it was not their intention to bring into the country more than eighteen men;—and although they have now had their charter for the last seven years, they have not up to this period performed any of the duties, or complied with any of the charges they had taken upon themselves,—for although they are obliged to carry each of those who are desirous of going to the said country called New-France for thirty-six livres, nevertheless they have become so intractable, and they have so frightened the french who were desirous of living in that country, that although it seems that trading with the indians is permitted them, nevertheless such are the restrictions imposed, that if, by their labor, they have a bushel of wheat above what they require for their own consumption, it is not permitted them to assist french subjects, or others who may require it, with the same, and they are obliged to give it up to those who are privileged to carry on trade there, nor are they allowed to give it to those who could bring from France the necessaries of life and supply them with the same.

These abuses having so increased, his Eminence the Cardinal has deemed it incumbent upon him to apply a remedy, and in correcting such abuses, thereby following up the intentions of His Majesty, and acting in such way as,—assisting in the conversion of these people and establishing a powerful colony in that province;— New-France, with all its dependencies, may once for all become a possession of the crown without danger of its being taken away from the french by the king's enemies, as might be the case if precautionary measures were not taken against such a contingency. Wherefore, after having examined different proposals in relation to this matter, and it being ascertained that there were no other means of colonizing the said country but by a revocation of the privileges heretofore granted to Guillaume de Caen and his associates, by reason of their being contrary to His Majesty's intentions, his said Eminence the Cardinal requested the sieurs de Roquemont, Houel, Lataignant, Dablon, Duchesne and Castillon to enter into an extensive association for that object, and for that purpose to assemble together, and to submit notes for the basis of such an association,—Which having been by them effected, they undertook and bound themselves, unto his said Eminence the Cardinal, to form a company of one hundred associates, and to do their utmost to colonize New-France, commonly called Canada, according to the articles hereinafter stated. . . .

I. That is to say, that the said de Roquemont, Houel, Lataignant, Dablon, Duchesne and Castillon, as well for themselves as for others their associates, making up the number of one hundred, will undertake to carry over to New-France aforesaid, in the course of the ensuing year 1628, two or three hundred men of all trades, and during the next fifteen years to increase that number to four thousand of either sex, which fifteen years shall be completed in the year 1643, to provide board and lodging and all things generally which may be necessary to life, during three years only, after which period the said associates will be discharged, if they so desire it, from the obligation of providing for them, by giving to them a sufficient quantity of cleared land to enable them to support themselves, with the necessary wheat to sow them for the first time, and to live upon the same until the next ensuing crop, or otherwise to provide for them in such way that they may, by their labor and industry, subsist in the said country and support themselves.

II. Without nevertheless, its being lawful for the said associates and others, to carry over any foreigner to the said colony, but to people the same with natural born french subjects, professing the catholic religion. . . .

III. In every settlement made by the said associates, there shall be, for the purpose of converting the savage tribes and of affording the consolations of religion to the french who shall have settled in New-France aforesaid, at least three Ecclesiastics, which the said associates shall be bound to lodge, to provide with the means of subsistence, ornaments and generally with every thing necessary to life and for the exercise of their ministry, during the said fifteen years, unless the said associates shall prefer giving to the said Ecclesiastics cleared lands sufficient for their subsistence. . . .

IV. And for the purpose of repaying to the said company the heavy expenses and advances necessary to be made by the said company, for the purposes of the settlement of the said colony and the support and preservation of the same, His Majesty will grant to the said associates, their heirs and assigns forever, in full property, with right of seigniory, the fort and settlement of Quebec, with all the country of New-France called Canada, all along the coast, from Florida, which the predecessors of His Majesty have caused to be settled, ranging the sea shore as far as the Arctic circle for latitude, and in longitude from the Island of Newfoundland, towards the west, as far as the Great Lake called fresh water sea and beyond . . . together also with the lands, mines and minerals, the said mines nevertheless to be used in compliance with the terms of the ordinance, ports and harbors, rivers, ponds, islets and islands, and generally all that extent of the said country, in length and in breadth, and beyond as far as it will be possible to extend and to make known the name of His Majesty,—His Majesty merely reserving the right of Fealty and Homage, which shall be rendered to him and to his royal successors by the said associates or by one of them, with a gold crown weighing eight marks, upon each mutation of the crown, and the appointment of the officers of the royal court, who shall be named and presented by the said associates, when it shall be deemed proper to establish such court: with permission to the said associates to cast cannon, balls, to make weapons offensive and defensive of every description, make gunpowder, erect and fortify fortresses, and generally do in the said country every thing which may be necessary, either for the safety of the said country, or for the preservation of its commerce.

V. It will be lawful for the said associates to improve and

ameliorate the said lands as they may deem it necessary, and distribute the same to those who will inhabit the said country and to others, in such quantities and in such manner as they will think proper; to give and grant them such titles and honors, rights and powers as they may deem proper, essential and necessary according to the quality, condition and merits of the individuals, and generally upon such charges, reserves and conditions as they may think proper. . . .

VI. And to the end that the said associates may enjoy what will be given and granted to them, fully and peaceably, His Majesty will revoke any gift which may have been made of the said lands, or any part or parcel of the same.

VII. Furthermore, His Majesty will grant to the said associates for ever, the trade of all leathers, furs and peltries of New-France aforesaid, [and] for a period of fifteen years only, to commence on the first day of January 1628, and to finish on the last day of December in the year 1643, all other trade either by sea or by land which may be made and carried on in any way or manner whatsoever, throughout the said country, and in so far as the same may be extended, with the exception however of cod and whale fishery only, which His Majesty desires should be open to all his subjects. . . .

VIII. It will nevertheless be lawful for french subjects settled in the said countries with their families, and who will not be supported and maintained by said company, to trade freely with the indians, provided that the beaver obtained by them be afterwards sold to the said company or to their clerks or agents. . . .

IX. His Majesty will further give to the said company two vessels of war, of two or three hundred tons, armed, equipped and ready for sea, without however being victualled. . . .

XIII. And the further to induce the subjects of His Majesty to emigrate to the said country, and to establish therein all sorts of manufactures, His Majesty will permit that all the artisans, which the said company bind themselves to send to the said country, and who shall have exercised their trade and industry in New-France aforesaid, during six years, may be, if they desire to return to this kingdom, reputed masters of their arts respectively, and may be allowed openly to exercise their trades in Paris and other cities, by producing an authentic certificate of their having exercised their trades in the said place. . . .

XIV. And whereas merchandize of any kind whatever, imported

from the said country, and more particularly from New-France aforesaid, will be the product of the industry of french subjects, His Majesty will, for a period of fifteen years, exempt such merchandizes from New-France aforesaid, from the payment of any duties whatever, though they be carried in, brought to and sold in this kingdom.

XV. His Majesty will also declare all munitions of war, provisions, and other things necessary for the victualling of any expedition sent to New-France, free and exempt of any imposts and duties whatever, during the said period of fifteen years.

XVI. Any person or persons of any rank and quality, ecclesiastics, noblemen, officers and others, will be permitted to enter in the said company, without derogating from the privileges of their order; and the said company, if they think fit, may receive among them, associates who may offer themselves hereafter, to the number of one hundred more, if so many there be, and in case that amongst the associates there should be any that are not of noble origin, His Majesty will grant patents of nobility to twelve of the said associates, who will enjoy in future the privileges of nobility, as also their children born or to be born in lawful wedlock. . . .

XVII. His Majesty will order and declare that the children of french subjects who shall settle in the said country, and also the indians who will be brought to a knowledge of the christian faith, and who will profess the same, will be considered and reckoned natural born subjects of France, and as such will be allowed to settle in France whenever they please, acquire property therein, make wills, inherit, accept donations and legacies, in the same manner as those born in France, without being obliged to take letters of naturalization.

4. The Blueprint of Religious Colonization, 1634

FOLLOWING the ruin of the One Hundred Associates, the Roman Catholic Church and more specifically the Jesuit Order became the most powerful institution in Canada. In 1634 Father Paul Le Jeune (1591–1664) formulated a program to convert the Indians, which became the master plan of Jesuit colonization in the years that followed.

Born of Calvinist parents, Le Jeune was converted to Catholicism in 1607 and entered the Jesuit novitiate in Paris in 1613. He came to Canada in 1632 as the superior of the Jesuit missions and kept this position until 1639 when he became a simple missionary. After his return to France in 1649 he was assigned the office of procurator of the Canadian missions. Father Le Jeune was the first editor of the famous Jesuit Relations, in which his views on the means of converting the Indians appeared in 1634.

Further Reading: J. Chaussé, "Le Père Paul Le Jeune, S.J., missionaire-colonisateur," Revue d'Histoire de l'Amérique française, XII (1958–59), 56–79, 217–246; L. Gérin, Aux sources de notre histoire (Montreal, 1946).

SOURCE: R. G. Thwaites (ed. and trans.), *The Jesuit Relations and Allied Documents* (73 vols., Cleveland, Ohio, 1896–1901), VI, 145–155.

THE GREAT show of power made at first by the Portuguese in the East and West Indies inspired profound admiration in the minds of the Indians, so that these people embraced, without any contradiction, the belief of those whom they admired. Now the following is, it seems to me, the way in which to acquire an ascendancy over our Savages.

First, to check the progress of those who overthrow Religion, and to make ourselves feared by the Iroquois, who have killed some of our men, as every one knows, and who recently massacred two hundred Hurons, and took more than a hundred prisoners. This is, in my opinion, the only door through which we can escape the contempt into which the negligence of those who have heretofore held the trade of this country has thrown us, through their avarice.

The second means of commending ourselves to the Savages, to induce them to receive our holy faith, would be to send a number of capable men to clear and cultivate the land, who, joining themselves with others who know the language, would work for the Savages, on condition that they would settle down, and themselves put their hands to the work, living in houses that would be built for their use; by this means becoming located, and seeing this miracle of charity in their behalf, they could be more easily instructed and won. While conversing this Winter with my Savages, I communicated to them this plan, assuring them that when I knew their language perfectly, I would help them cultivate the land if I could have some men, and if they wished to stop roving,—representing to them the wretchedness of their present way of living, and influencing them very perceptibly, for the time being. The Sorcerer, having heard me, turned toward his people and said, "See how boldly this black robe lies in our presence." I asked him why he thought I was lying. "Because," said he, "we never see in this world men so good as thou sayest, who would take the trouble to help us without hope of reward, and to employ so many men to aid us without taking anything from us; if thou shouldst do that," he added, "thou wouldst secure the greater part of the Savages, and they would all believe in thy words."

I may be mistaken; but, if I can draw any conclusion from the things I see, it seems to me that not much ought to be hoped for from the Savages as long as they are wanderers; you will instruct them to-day, to-morrow hunger snatches your hearers away, forcing them to go and seek their food in the rivers and woods. Last year I stammered out the Catechism to a goodly number of children; as soon as the ships departed, my birds flew away, some in one direction and some in another. This year, I hoped to see them again, as I speak a little better; but, as they have settled on the other side of the great river St. Lawrence, my hopes have been frustrated. To try to follow them, as many Religious would be needed as there are cabins, and still we would not attain our object; for they are so occupied in seeking their livelihood in these woods, that they have not time, so to speak, to save themselves. Besides, I do not believe that, out of a hundred Religious, there would be ten who could endure the hardships to be encountered in following them. I tried to live among them last Autumn; I was not there a week before I was attacked by a violent fever, which caused me to return to our little house to recover my health. Being cured, I tried to follow them during the Winter, and I was very ill the greater part of the time. These reasons, and many others that I might give, were I not afraid of being tedious, make me think that we shall work a great deal and advance very little, if we do not make these Barbarians stationary. As for persuading them to till the soil of their own accord, without being helped, I very much doubt whether we shall be able to attain this for a long time, for they know nothing whatever about it. Besides, where will they store their harvests? As their cabins are made of bark, the first frost will spoil all the roots and pumpkins that they will have gathered. If they plant peas and Indian corn, they have no place in their huts to store them. But who will feed them while they are beginning to clear the land? For they live only from one day to another, having ordinarily no provisions to sustain them during the time that they must be clearing. Finally, when they had killed themselves with hard work, they could not get from the land half their living, until it was cleared and they understood how to make the best use of it.

Now, with the assistance of a few good, industrious men, it would be easy to locate a few families, especially as some of them have already spoken to me about it, thus of themselves becoming accustomed, little by little, to extract something from the earth.

I know well there are persons of good judgment who believe that, although the Savages are nomadic, the good seed of the Gospel will not fail to take root and bring forth fruit in their souls, although more slowly, as they can only be instructed at intervals. They imagine also that, if a few families come over here, as they are already beginning to do, the Savages will follow the example of our French and will settle down to cultivate the land. I myself was impressed with these ideas, when we first came over here; but the intercourse which I have had with these people, and the difficulty that men accustomed to a life of idleness have in embracing one of hard work, such as cultivating the soil, cause me to believe now that if they are not helped they will lose heart, especially the Savages at Tadoussac. As to those of the three rivers, where our French People are going to plant a new colony this year, they have promised that they will settle down there and plant Indian corn; this seems to me not altogether assured, but probable, inasmuch as their predecessors once had a good village in that place, which they abandoned on account of the invasions of their enemies, the Hiroquois.

The Captain of that region told me that the land there was quite good, and they liked it very much. If they become sedentary, as they are now minded to do, we foresee there a harvest more abundant in the blessings of Heaven than in the fruits of the earth.

The third means of making ourselves welcome to these people, would be to erect here a seminary for little boys, and in time one for girls, under the direction of some brave mistress, whom zeal for the glory of God, and a desire for the salvation of these people, will bring over here, with a few Companions animated by the same courage. May it please his divine Majesty to inspire some to so noble an enterprise, and to divest them of any fear that the weakness of their sex might induce in them at the thought of crossing so many seas and of living among Barbarians.

In the last voyage there came some women who were pregnant, and they easily surmounted these difficulties, as others had done before them. There is also some pleasure in taming the souls of the Savages, and preparing them to receive the seed of Christianity. And then experience makes us feel certain that God, who shows his goodness and power to all, has, nevertheless, for those who expose themselves freely and suffer willingly in his service, favors seasoned with so much sweetness, and succors them in the midst of their dangers with so prompt and paternal assistance, that often they do not feel their trials, but their pain is turned to pleasure and their perils to a peculiar consolation. But I would like to keep here, where we are, the children of the Hurons. Father Brebœuf leads us to hope that we shall have some, if he goes with our Fathers into those well-peopled countries, and if there is anything with which to found a seminary. The reason why I would not like to take the children of one locality [and teach them] in that locality itself, but rather in some other place, is because these Barbarians cannot bear to have their children punished, nor even scolded, not being able to refuse anything to a crying child. They carry this to such an extent that upon the slightest pretext they would take them away from us, before they were educated. But if the little Hurons, or the children of more distant tribes, are kept here, a great many advantages will result, for we would not be annoyed and distracted by the fathers while instructing the children; it will also compel these people to show good treatment to the French who are in their country, or at least not to do them any injury. And, lastly, we shall obtain, by the grace of God our Lord, the object for which we came into this distant country; namely, the conversion of these nations.

5. The Foundation of Montreal, 1642

THE FOUNDATION of Montreal was one of the outstanding achievements of the mystical period. Founded in 1642 by the Society of Notre Dame, which grouped wealthy laymen and clerics, the settlement conformed to the pattern recommended by Father Le Jeune. It had missionaries, a convent for French and Indian girls, and a hospital to care for the poor and the sick.

In the following document Dollier de Casson (1636–1701) tells the story of the town's origins. After a few years spent in France as a soldier, Dollier entered the Sulpician Order in 1657 and came to Canada in 1666. He worked as a missionary and explorer until 1671, when he became the superior of the Seminary of St. Sulpice in Montreal. His History of Montreal belongs to this latter period. While Dollier did not participate in the town's foundation, he was in close contact with many people connected with the event and considered like them that Montreal owed its origins to divine intervention.

Further Reading: E. R. Adair, "France and the Beginnings of New France," Canadian Historical Review, XXV (1944), 246–278.

SOURCE: R. Flenley (ed. and trans.), A History of Montreal 1640–1672 from the French of Dollier de Casson (London and Toronto, 1928), pp. 59–63. Permission to use this selection was granted by the publisher, J. M. Dent & Sons Ltd.

From the Year of Our Lord 1640
to the Sailing of the Vessels from Canada to France
in the Year 1641

The hand of the Almighty, shown each day in its workings, willed in the fortieth year of this century to manifest itself in a special manner by the foundation of Montreal, planning the enterprise in the minds of a number of people in a way which showed the great good will of God to this country, in desiring to give this post to it as the buckler and wall of its defence. It showed also an unsurpassed wisdom for the success of that which it desired to undertake therein, omitting nothing of what the most politic wisdom could have asked, and also a might tremendous and amazing for the execution of this business, doing marvellous things on its behalf. All the old settlers of New France know how much it has been worth to them to have this advanced post thrust forward against their enemies to occupy and restrain them in their terrible invasions. They are well aware that very often this island has served as a dike against the Iroquois to hold in check their fury and impetuosity, so that they gave up the idea of going farther when they were so vigorously repulsed in the attacks they made there. The course of this history will reveal so plainly how Canada has been saved by Montreal that those who know from their own experiences the truth and sincerity of this story will in reading it bless Heaven a thousand times for having been so benignant as to form and conceive the plan of a work so advantageous. And if the goodness of God has been plainly evidenced in this scheme, His wisdom and omnipotence have shone no less, for it is impossible to bear in mind all the events that happened with relation to Montreal during the year of which we write, without admiring at every point these two divine perfections, which combined one with the other in the subject under consideration. Thus it appeared clearly that this foundation was due not to man but solely to the wisdom of God and to His infinite power, moved by goodness alone to act in this way.

Let us see how these two divine attributes of wisdom and power combined to give birth to this work. The Providence of God desiring to make this island strong enough to be the frontier of the country, and wishing further to see it sufficiently peopled to allow the praises of its Creator, so far unknown, to be heard there, turned its gaze upon several pious and important people in order to secure a company to undertake the affair, the expenses of which were bound to be large. They would have been insurmountable had not certain persons, powerful and of rank, united for the work, and the union would not have endured had not these persons been pious, divorced from material interests, and wholly devoted to the service of Our Lord. Further, this society, of necessity working without any hope of profit, there being even to-day little to hope for in that respect after a number of years, would soon have come to grief had it been looking for gain. For in that case it would have had only the disappointment of being always obliged to give out, with no hope of being able to receive anything for a long time. Beyond that it was requisite that divine Providence should have at its disposal some illustrious commander for this place, who must be a man of courage, strong, experienced, and with no other interests than those of eternity. Again, it was necessary that the selfsame Providence should choose someone likewise free to take care of the poor, the sick and the wounded, until with the growth of population there should be obtained for this island the aid of a hospital to assist or take the place of this person. In this connection it is to be remarked that a girl or woman was required because persons of that sex are more fitted for several occupations not so well cared for as a rule in a place where there are no women. But to be frank, someone full of grace was needed to come into this country so distant, so wild and so rude; and it needed the extreme protection of the Almighty hand always to preserve her purity unscathed from scandal, real or falsely surmised, living thus among military men. Providence miraculously effected all these things, as we shall see in the course of this history, whereby we shall be made to admire both the wisdom and the might of God.

But before speaking of this illustrious commander, and of the person selected for the care of the sick and wounded, let us look back to the formation of our sacred company, for we should not venture as yet to introduce these two persons chosen by Heaven, since the hand of God, working so powerfully in them, preferred to make these two so necessary helpers ready in secret, to the end that our associates should have no knowledge thereof until the next year, when they received them as a bounty direct from above. Therefore let us watch this praiseworthy association begin, originating in the town of Laflèche through a narrative of New France, which spoke forcibly of the Isle of Montreal as being the best place in the country for the establishment of a mission and meeting-place for the savages. This narrative fortunately came into the hands of M. de la Dauversière, a person of outstanding piety, who was in the first place much touched in reading it, and was later even more affected, since God gave him so plain a picture of this place that he described it to everyone in a way that left no doubt that there was something extraordinary in it. For the wars had allowed so little opportunity for acquiring close knowledge of the island that one could scarcely form even the barest idea of it. But he described it from end to end, not merely its shores and outline, but he also depicted it within with the same ease. He described the beauty and richness of its soil, the length and breadth of its different parts. Finally he talked so familiarly about it that, once going to see the reverend Father Chauveau, Rector of the College of La Flèche, his confessor, he told him that God had caused him to know this island, revealing it to him as the scene of the work to which he ought to devote his efforts, and thus aid in the conversion of the savages, by the means of a fine French colony which could give them a taste of a more civilised life. Yet whilst he saw what he ought to do, he wished the Father to say whether he believed it was from God or no. This Father, enlightened from above, and convinced by what he had heard, replied: "Have no doubts on the subject; work at it in earnest."

6. The Destruction of Huronia,
1649

THE HURONS *were the principal allies of New France during the first half of the seventeenth century. They lived in thirty-two villages scattered in the Georgian Bay area and numbered between ten and fifteen thousand persons. In March, 1649, with a suddenness as dramatic as it was unexpected, this nation disintegrated completely under the impact of a lightning Iroquois campaign directed against the mission villages of St. Ignace, St. Louis, and Ste. Marie. Father Paul Ragueneau, a missionary at Ste. Marie, wrote an account of the Iroquois attack and its results, which was published in the* Relations.

Further Reading: G. T. Hunt, The Wars of the Iroquois: A Study in Intertribal Trade Relations (*Madison, Wis., 1960*); A. W. Trelease, "The Iroquois and the Western Fur Trade," Mississippi Valley Historical Review, *XLIX (1962), 32–51;* B. Trigger, "The French Presence in Huronia: The Structure of Franco-Huron Relations in the First Half of the Seventeenth Century," Canadian Historical Review, *XLIX (1968), 107–141.*

SOURCE: R. G. Thwaites (ed. and trans.), *The Jesuit Relations and Allied Documents,* XXXIV, 123–137; XXXV, 79–83.

The 16th day of March in the present year, 1649, marked the beginning of our misfortunes,—if, however, that be a misfortune which no doubt has been the salvation of many of God's elect.

The Iroquois, enemies of the Hurons, to the number of about a thousand men, well furnished with weapons,—and mostly with firearms, which they obtain from the Dutch, their allies,—arrived by night at the frontier of this country, without our having had any knowledge of their approach; although they had started from their country in the Autumn, hunting in the forests throughout the Winter, and had made over the snow nearly two hundred leagues of a very difficult road, in order to come and surprise us. They reconnoitered by night the condition of the first place upon which they had designs,—which was surrounded with a stockade of pine-trees, from fifteen to sixteen feet in height, and with a deep ditch, wherewith nature had strongly fortified this place on three sides,— there remaining only a little space which was weaker than the others.

It was at that point that the enemy made a breach at daybreak, but so secretly and promptly that he was master of the place before people had put themselves on the defensive,—all being then in a deep sleep, and not having leisure to reconnoiter their situation. Thus this village was taken, almost without striking a blow, there having been only ten Iroquois killed. Part of the Hurons—men, women, and children—were massacred then and there; the others were made captives, and reserved for cruelties more terrible than death.

Three men alone escaped, almost naked, across the snows; they bore the alarm and terror to another and neighboring village, about a league distant. This first village was the one which we called Saint Ignace, which had been abandoned by most of its people at the beginning of the Winter,—the most apprehensive and most clear-sighted having withdrawn from it, foreboding the danger; thus the loss of it was not so considerable, and amounted only to about four hundred souls.

The enemy does not stop there; he follows up his victory, and before Sunrise he appears in arms to attack the village of Saint Louys, which was fortified with a fairly good stockade. Most of the women, and the children, had just gone from it, upon hearing the news which had arrived regarding the approach of the Iroquois. The people of most courage, about eighty persons, being resolved to defend themselves well, repulse with courage the first and the second assault, having killed among the enemy some thirty of their most venturesome men, besides many wounded. But, finally, number has the advantage,—the Iroquois having undermined with blows of their hatchets the palisade of stakes, and having made a passage for themselves through considerable breaches.

Toward nine o'clock in the morning, we perceived from our house at Sainte Marie the fire which was consuming the cabins of that village, where the enemy, having entered victoriously, had reduced everything to desolation,—casting into the midst of the flames the old men, the sick, the children who had not been able to escape, and all those who, being too severely wounded, could not have followed them into captivity. At the sight of those flames, and by the color of the smoke which issued from them, we understood sufficiently what was happening,—this village of Saint Louys not being farther distant from us than one league. Two Christians, who escaped from the fire, arrived almost at the same time, and gave us assurance of it.

In this village of Saint Louys were at that time two of our Fathers,—Father Jean de Brebeuf and Father Gabriel Lallement, who had charge of five closely neighboring villages; these formed but one of the eleven Missions of which we have spoken above; we named it the Mission of St. Ignace.

Some Christians had begged the Fathers to preserve their lives for the glory of God,—which would have been as easy for them as for the more than 500 persons who went away at the first alarm, and had abundant leisure to reach a place of security; but their zeal could not permit them, and the salvation of their flock was dearer to them than love for their own lives. They employed all the moments of that time, as the most precious which they had ever had in the world; and, during the heat of the combat, their hearts were only fire for the salvation of souls. One was at the breach, baptizing the Catechumens; the other, giving absolution to the Neophytes,—both animating the Christians to die in the sentiments of piety, with which they consoled them in their miseries. Accordingly, never was their faith, or the love which they had for their good Fathers and Pastors, more lively. . . .

The Iroquois having dealt their blow, and wholly reduced to fire the village of Saint Louys, retraced their steps into that of Saint Ignace, where they had left a good garrison, that it might be for them a sure retreat in case of misfortune, and that the victuals which they had found there might serve them as refreshments and provisions for their return.

[The Iroquois, according to Father Ragueneau, then decided to attack Ste. Marie; but they suffered serious losses in encounters with Huron war parties which had ventured out against them.]

On the nineteenth, the day of the great Saint Joseph, a sudden panic fell upon the hostile camp,—some withdrawing in disorder, and others thinking only of flight. Their Captains were constrained to yield to the terror which had seized them; they precipitated their retreat, driving forth in haste a part of their captives, who were burdened above their strength, like packhorses, with the spoils which the victorious were carrying off,—their captors reserving for some other occasion the matter of their death.

As for the other captives who were left to them, destined to die on the spot, they attached them to stakes fastened in the earth, which they had arranged in various cabins. To these, on leaving the village, they set fire on all sides,—taking pleasure, at their departure, in feasting upon the frightful cries which these poor victims uttered in the midst of those flames, where children were broiling beside their mothers; where a husband saw his wife roasting near him; where cruelty itself would have had compassion at a spectacle which had nothing human about it, except the innocence of those who were in torture, most of whom were Christians.

An old woman, escaped from the midst of that fire, bore the news of it to the village of Saint Michel, where there were about seven hundred men in arms, who charged upon the enemy; but, not having been able to overtake him after two days' march, partly the want of provisions, partly the dread of combatting without advantage an enemy encouraged by his victories, and one who had mostly firearms, of which our Hurons have very few,—all these things obliged them to retrace their steps, without having done aught. They found upon the roads, from time to time, various captives, who—not having strength enough to follow the conqueror, who was precipitating his retreat—had had their heads split by a blow of the hatchet; others remained, half burned, at a post.

In consequence of the bloody victories obtained by the Iroquois over our Hurons at the commencement of the Spring of last year, 1649, and of the more than inhuman acts of barbarity practiced toward their prisoners of war, and the cruel torments pitilessly inflicted on Father Jean de Brebeuf and Father Gabriel Lallemant, Pastors of this truly suffering Church,—terror having fallen upon the neighboring villages, which were dreading a similar misfortune,—all the inhabitants dispersed. These poor, distressed people forsook their lands, houses, and villages, and all that in the world was dearest to them, in order to escape the cruelty of an enemy whom they feared more than a thousand deaths, and more than all that remained before their eyes,—calculated as that was to strike terror into hearts already wretched. Many, no longer expecting humanity from man, flung themselves into the deepest recesses of the forest, where, though it were with the wild beasts, they might find peace. Others took refuge upon some frightful rocks that lay in the midst of a great Lake nearly four hundred leagues in circumference,—choosing rather to find death in the waters, or from the cliffs, than by the fires of the Iroquois. A goodly number having cast in their lot with the people of the Neutral Nation, and with those living on the Mountain heights, whom we call the Tobacco Nation, the most prominent of those who remained invited us to join them, rather than to flee so far away,—trusting that God would espouse their cause when it should have become our own, and would be mindful of their protection, provided they took care to serve him. With this in view, they promised us that they would all become Christians, and be true to the faith till the death came which they saw prepared on every side for their destruction.

This was exactly what God was requiring of us,—that, in times of dire distress, we should flee with the fleeing, accompanying them everywhere, whithersoever their faith should follow them; and that we should lose sight of none of these Christians, although it might be expedient to detain the bulk of our forces wherever the main body of fugitives might decide to settle down. This was the conclusion we came to, after having commended the matter to God.

We told off certain of our Fathers, to make some itinerant Missions,—some, in a small bark canoe, for voyaging along the coasts, and visiting the more distant islands of the great Lake, at sixty, eighty, and a hundred leagues from us; others to journey by land, making their way through forest-depths, and scaling the summits of mountains. Go which way we might, since God was our guide, our defense, our hope, and our all, what was there to fear for us?

But on each of us lay the necessity of bidding farewell to that old home of sainte Marie,—to its structures, which, though plain, seemed, to the eyes of our poor Savages, master-works of art; and to its cultivated lands, which were promising us an abundant harvest. That spot must be forsaken, which I may call our second Fatherland, our home of innocent delights, since it had been the cradle of this Christian church; since it was the temple of God, and the home of the servants of Jesus Christ. Moreover, for fear that our enemies, only too wicked, should profane the sacred place, and derive from it an advantage, we ourselves set fire to it, and beheld burn before our eyes, in less than one hour, our work of nine or ten years.

7. A Layman's View of Canada, 1664

THE SMALL secular society which emerged in Canada in the 1640's and 1650's had aims of its own for the colony. Unlike the Jesuits, who emphasized the need to convert the Indians, the laymen stressed economic development and material well-being.

The most articulate member of this group was Pierre Boucher (1622–1717), who came to Canada from Normandy in 1635. He learned the Huron language, served as interpreter for the Quebec garrison, and was employed for a time by the One Hundred Associates. He became governor of Trois Rivières in 1653, received letters of nobility in 1661, and obtained a seigneury in 1667. In 1661, the Canadians chose him to go to France to sollicit military aid against the Iroquois. The True and Genuine Description of New France Commonly Called Canada, from which this extract is taken, was written by Boucher following his return to the colony and was published in Paris in 1664.

SOURCE: Pierre Boucher, *True and Genuine Description of New France Commonly Called Canada* (Paris, 1664), translated by E. L. Montizambert under the title, *Canada in the Seventeenth Century* (Montreal, 1883), pp. 73–81.

CHAPTER XIII
ANSWERS TO QUESTIONS PUT TO THE AUTHOR WHEN HE WAS IN FRANCE

. . . But how can we make money there? What can we get out of it all? This is a question that has often been put to me, and that gave me an inclination to laugh every time it was put to me; I seemed to see people who wanted to reap a harvest before they had sowed any thing. After having said that the country is a good one, capable of producing all sorts of things, like France, that it is healthy, that population only is wanting, that the country is very extensive, and that without doubt there are great riches in it which we have not been able to bring to light, because we have an enemy who keeps us pent up in a little corner and prevents us from going about and making discoveries; and so he will have to be destroyed, and many people will have to come into this country, and then we shall know the riches of it; but some one will have to defray the cost of all this; and who shall do it if not our good King? He has shown an inclination to do it, and may God be pleased to keep him still of the same mind.

Our neighbours, the English, laid out a great deal of money at the outset on the settlements they made; they threw great numbers of people into them; so that now there are computed to be in them fifty thousand men capable of bearing arms; it is a wonder to see their country now; one finds all sorts of things there, the same as in Europe, and for half the price. They build numbers of ships, of all sorts and sizes; they work iron mines; they have beautiful cities; they have stage-coaches and mails from one to the other; they have carriages like those in France; those who laid out money there, are now getting good returns from it; that country is not different from this; what has been done there could be done here. . . .

It seems to me that I hear some one say: "you have told us much about the advantages of New France but you have not shown us its disadvantages, nor its inconveniences, yet we know well that there is not a country in the world however good it may be, in which something that is disagreeable is not met with." I answer that you are right. It has been my study all along to make these things known to you; but in order to enable you to understand them more clearly, I shall here specify in detail what I consider the most troublesome and disagreeable things. . . .

The first is that our enemies, the Iroquois keep us so closely pent up that they hinder us from enjoying the advantages of the country. We cannot go to hunt or fish without danger of being killed or taken prisoners by those rascals; and we cannot even plough out fields, much less make hay, without continual risk: They lie in ambush on all sides, and any little thicket suffices for six or seven of those barbarians to put themselves under cover in, or more correctly speaking in an ambush, from which they throw themselves upon you suddenly when you are at your work, or going to it or coming from it. They never attack but when they are the strongest; if they are the weakest they do not say a word; if by accident they are discovered they fly, leaving every thing behind them; and as they are fleet of foot it is difficult to catch them; so you see we are always in dread, and a poor fellow does not work in safety if he has to go ever so little a way off to his work. Wives are always uneasy lest their husbands, who have gone away to their work in the morning, should be killed or taken prisoners and they should never see them again; and these Indians are the cause of the greater number of our settlers being poor, not only through our not being able to enjoy the advantages of the country as I have just said, but because they often kill cattle, sometimes hinder the gathering in of the harvest, and at other times burn and plunder houses when they can take people by surprise. This is a great evil, but it is not beyond remedy, and we expect one from the benevolence of our good King, who has told me that he wishes to deliver us from it. It would not be very difficult to do so, for there are not among them more than eight hundred or nine hundred men capable of bearing arms. It is true they are warlike men, and very dexterous at fighting in the woods; they have given proof of this to our Commanders from France who despised them; some of these were killed and others were forced to admit that one must not neglect to take precautions when one goes to war with them, that they understand the business, and that on this score they are not barbarians; but after all, a thousand or twelve hundred men well led would give occasion for its being said "they were but they are not;" and to have exterminated a tribe that has caused so many others to perish and is the terror of all these countries, would raise the reputation of the French very high throughout New France. . . .

Here is another set of questions that have been put to me, namely: how we live in this country whether justice is administered, if there is not great debauchery, seeing that numbers of worthless fellows and bad girls come here, it is said.

I will answer all these questions one after the other, beginning with the last. It is not true that those sort of girls come hither, and those who say so have made a great mistake, and have taken the Islands of Saint Christophe and Martinique for New France; if any of them come here, they are not known for such; for before any can be taken on board ship to come here some of their relations or friends must certify that they have always been well-behaved; if by chance there are found among those who have, some who are in disrepute, or who are said to have misconducted themselves on the voyage out, they are sent back to France.

As for the scapegraces, if any come over it is only because they are not known for what they are, and when they are in the country they have to live like decent people, otherwise they would have a bad time of it; we know how to hang people in this country as well as they do elsewhere, and we have proved it to some who have not been well behaved.

Justice is administered here, and there are Judges; and those who are not satisfied with their decisions can appeal to the Governor and the Sovereign Council, appointed by the King, and sitting at Quebec.

Hitherto we have lived pleasantly enough, for it has pleased God to give us Governors who have all been good men, and besides we have had the Jesuit Fathers who take great pains to teach the people what is right so that all goes on peaceably; we live much in the fear of God, and nothing scandalous takes place without its being put to rights immediately; there is great religious devotion throughout the country.

Chapter XIV.
Continuation of the Same Subject

Several persons after having heard me speak of New France, whether they felt inclined to come to it or not, have put these questions to me: "Do you think I would be fit for that country? What would have to be done in order to get there? If I took four or five thousand francs with me, could I with such a sum make myself tolerably comfortable?" And after these several other questions which I shall mention after having answered these.

You ask me in the first place whether you are fit for this country. The answer I make you is that this country is not yet fit for people of rank who are extremely rich, because such people would not find in it all the luxuries they enjoy in France; such persons must wait until this country has more inhabitants, unless they are persons who wish to retire from the world in order to lead a pleasant and quiet life free from fuss, or who are inclined to immortalize themselves by building cities or by other great works in this new world.

The people best fitted for this country are those who can work with their own hands in making clearings, putting up buildings and otherwise; for as men's wages are very high here, a man who does not take care and practice economy will be ruined; but the best way is always to begin by clearing land and making a good farm, and to attend to other things only after that has been done, and not to do like some whom I have seen, who paid out all their money for the erection of fine buildings which they had to sell afterwards for less than the cost.

I am supposing myself to be speaking to persons who would

come to settle in this country with a view to making a living out of it, and not to trade.

It would be well for a man coming to settle, to bring provisions with him for at least a year or two years if possible, especially flour which he could get for much less in France and could not even be sure of being always able to get for any money here; for if many people should come from France in any year without bringing any flour with them and the grain crops should be bad here that year, which God forbid, they would find themselves much straitened.

It would be well also to bring a supply of clothes, for they cost twice as much here as they do in France.

Money is also much dearer; its value increases one third, so that a coin of fifteen *sous* is worth twenty, and so on in proportion.

I would advise a man having money enough to bring two labouring men with him, or even more if he has the means, to clear his land; this is in answer to the question whether a person having three thousand or four thousand francs to employ here could do so with advantage; such a person could get himself into very easy circumstances in three or four years if he choose to practice economy, as I have already said.

Most of our settlers are persons who came over in the capacity of servants, and who, after serving their masters for three years, set up for themselves. They had not worked for more than a year before they had cleared land on which they got in more than enough grain for their food. They have but little, generally when they set up for themselves, and marry wives who are no better off than they are; yet if they are fairly hard working people you see them in four or five years in easy circumstances and well fitted out for persons of their condition in life.

Poor people would be much better off here than they are in France, provided they are not lazy; they could not fail to get employment and could not say, as they do in France, that they are obliged to beg for their living because they cannot find any one to give them work; in one word, no people are wanted, either men or women, who cannot turn their hands to some work, unless they are very rich.

Women's work consists of household work and of feeding and caring for the cattle; for there are few female servants; so that wives are obliged to do their own house work; nevertheless those who have the means employ valets who do the work of maidservants.

II

The Royal Régime

8. Paternalism

PATERNALISM, according to which the king and his representatives must behave as the father of their people, was the basic philosophy of government during the Ancien Régime. This tradition was so well established in France that there was no need to explain its nature to the colonial administrators. Brief reminders, however, such as those given below, were frequently inserted in the annual dispatches to the governor and the intendant.

Further Reading: W. J. Eccles, Canada Under Louis XIV, 1663–1701 (Toronto, 1964) and G. Lanctot, A History of Canada, Vol. II, From the Royal Régime to the Treaty of Utrecht, 1663–1713 (Toronto, 1964) provide the history of the period covered in this chapter.
    On the government of New France see R. Dubois Cahall, The Sovereign Council of New France (New York, 1915); W. J. Eccles, The Government of New France (Ottawa: Canadian Historical Association Booklets, 1965); G. Lanctot, L'Administration de la Nouvelle France (Paris, 1929); A. G. Reid, "Representative Assemblies in New France," Canadian Historical Review, XXVII (1946), 19–26.

SOURCES: Document A: Memoir of the King to Serve as Instruction to Sr. Talon Proceeding to New France as Intendant of Justice, Police and Finance, March 27, 1665, in E. B. O'Callaghan (ed.), Documents Relative to the Colonial History of the State of New York (15 vols., Albany, N.Y., 1853–87), IX, 27–28. Document B: Jérome de Pontchartrain, minister of marine, to Philippe de Rigaud de Vaudreuil, governor of Canada, June 18, 1712, Archives nationales, colonies (Paris), série B, vol. 34, f. 28. Document C: King's memoir to Philippe de Rigaud de Vaudreuil, governor of New France, and to Guillaume Chazel, intendant, May 15, 1725, Archives nationales, colonies (Paris), série B, vol. 48, ff. 784–785. Documents B and C translated by the editor.

A. Memoir of the King to Intendant Talon, 1665

The King considering all his Canadian subjects, from the highest to the lowest, in the light almost of his own children, and wishing to satisfy the obligation he is under to make them sensible, equally with those in the heart of France, of the mildness and happiness of his reign, Sieur Talon will study solely to solace them in all things, and to encourage them to industry and commerce which alone can attract abundance into the country, and render families of easy circumstances. And inasmuch as nothing can better contribute thereunto than entering into the details of their little affairs and of their household, it will not be mal-a-propos if, after being established, he visit all their settlements, the one after the other, to understand their true state, and afterwards provide as much as possible for the necessities he will have noticed there, so that in performing the duty of a good master of a household, he may expedite for them the means of realizing some profits and of undertaking the cultivation of the wild lands lying nearest those already placed under tillage.

B. Minister of the Marine to Governor Vaudreuil, 1712

I recommend that you only appoint persons who are acceptable to everyone to the positions of which you dispose. The reputation they have acquired makes them easy to identify and you can never exercise too much care in choosing them well, both for the good of the service and to avoid complaints. You must also strive to win the affection of those under your command and of the people you govern; and the surest way to attain this end is always to do justice, to maintain peace and good order among the households, to enter into private arguments only to end them and not to meddle if you think yourself unable to bring about a reconciliation, never to listen to the speeches of women, never to suffer anyone to speak badly of others in your presence and to avoid such talk yourself in order not to offend feelings. . . .

C. King's Memoir to Governor Vaudreuil and Intendant Chazel, 1725

. . . The sieurs de Vaudreuil and Chazel must give [their care and attention] to the increase of population, cultivations, and commerce.

The sieur de Vaudreuil will succeed in this by treating the people gently and kindly, by not permitting them to be vexed or mistreated by the town majors or the captains of militia who command in the countryside, and by preventing these officers from demanding merchandise at special rates from the merchants.

The sieur de Chazel will likewise succeed in this by treating the inhabitants with kindness and goodness, by looking after their needs, by preventing the small inhabitant from being vexed by the mighty, and the officers of justice from using their powers to avoid paying their debts and to harass their neighbors, and by seeing to it that the judges render good and prompt justice. . . .

9. Social and Economic Legislation

PATERNALISM as a philosophy of government did not remain a vague ideal. The impressive amount of socioeconomic legislation it inspired led W. J. Eccles to conclude that New France, from the moment the Crown took it over, became a welfare state. Laws were enacted to provide for the care, by means of state agencies, of the poor, the sick, and illegitimate children; to fix prices, control the volume of exports, and lay down standards of quality for consumer goods. The four police ordonnances that follow give some idea of the manner and spirit in which the colony was administered. The first two were issued by the intendant and Sovereign Council jointly, and the last two by the intendant alone.

SOURCES: Document A: *Jugements et délibérations du Conseil Souverain de la Nouvelle France* (6 vols., Quebec, 1883–85), III, 219–223. Document B: *Ibid.*, vol. V, 233–236. Document C: Archives of the Province of Quebec, Ordonnances of the Intendants of New France, cahier 12A, p. 90. Document D: *Ibid.*, cahier 24, pp. 62–63. All translated by the editor.

A. The Establishment of a Poor Board, 1688

Thursday, April 8, 1688

Upon what has been represented to the Council by the king's attorney general that, notwithstanding orders issued in the past forbidding all persons who claim that they are poor to beg and ask for alms unless they have a certificate of poverty signed by the curé [the parish priest] or local judge, these persons have not kept within these bounds but have persisted in their habit and maintained themselves, their wives, and children in idleness and sloth instead of working to earn their living and upkeep; that this being contrary to the good of the colony and a burden to the public, it has appeared necessary to put a stop to such idleness by means of a new ruling that would prevent fathers and mothers from leading such lives and raising their children in it, by obliging the one and the other to serve usefully; that the matter be settled in such a way, however, that the shameful poor, the elderly, the truly needy, the invalids may be identified so that they may be rescued and not have to beg for any reason whatever, which would relieve both the colony and those who are truly poor. The matter was put to deliberation. The [Sovereign] Council, to provide the poor of Quebec, Trois Rivières, and Ville Marie [Montreal] with the means to subsist, has ordered that a poor board will be established in each of the said places [to be made up as follows:]

The curé, who will inform the shameful poor and the needy. He will seek them out with as much care as possible, without, however, neglecting his other duties.

A director of the poor . . . to whom whose who wish to become eligible for public alms will address themselves. He will thoroughly investigate their state of poverty in order to report to the assembly of the other directors and will seek employment for those who are able to work, both men and women. And since people of this sort, in order to avoid working, frequently demand too much so as to be sent away, this director will agree on a wage with prospective employers, which the poor in question will be obliged to accept.

Of another director who will be commissioned as treasurer. He will receive all the sums donated for the poor at public collections, in church boxes, or in any other manner whatever. This director will keep an exact daily account of the alms delivered to him and of the manner in which they were used following the results of the assemblies. All persons who have made public collections will enter on the treasurer's register the amount they have deposited.

And of another director to act as secretary, who will keep a register of all deliberations and an exact tally of the poor who have been made eligible for charity, together with the day on which they have been assisted.

The curé and the directors will have the right to deliberate [at the assemblies]. None will have any rank above the other and each will have to state his opinion at random. The secretary will count up the votes and the plurality will prevail. The decision will be signed by all the directors in attendance. Meetings will be held at least once a month, as the directors decide, on the day and in the place of their choice. If all are not present at the assembly, two will be enough to settle urgent business.

The secretary will ask two women to alternate each month, or more often if it is deemed appropriate, in taking up collection from each resident of the parish. On these occasions, care must be taken not to be too insistent. Everyone must be left free to practice charity according to his devotion. The women who take up alms will accept everything that is given to them and not only money. They may have someone to follow behind them with a basket to receive the alms, which will be taken to the place agreed upon by the directors.

The directors will draw a distinction between several categories of poor. In some cases, they will only give a little money for the purchase of tools and working implements. In others, the directors will purchase these themselves, lest the money be spent inopportunely by the poor or used for some other purpose. Under pain of an arbitrary fine, the Council forbids innkeepers and all others to purchase from the said poor their tools or their clothes, for these may not be sold for any reason whatever. In yet other cases, the directors will give half a living allowance and will consult together on what is a fitting wage for each one according to the work he is capable of doing.

The directors, according to circumstances, may punish the poor by putting them in prison on bread and water or by depriving them of their provisions for a certain time. The Council grants to the directors the power to act in this manner if the case requires it, saving His Majesty's pleasure. . . .

In the countryside, each parish or seigneury will look after its poor without being allowed to seek help from other parishes or seigneuries. The curé and two persons chosen by the habitants after high mass will serve as directors. The said two directors will have the same powers as those on the boards of the three cities. One will act as treasurer and the other as secretary if he has the ability. Otherwise, he will be replaced by the curé. . . . The seigneur, if he resides on his fief or if he happens to be there, will be invited to the assembly and will have a vote along with the others who make it up.

B. *Regulations for Bakers and Butchers, 1706*

[Monday, February 1, 1706]

Considering the decree rendered in this [Superior] Council on December 1 last, that an assembly of police would be held in the *prévoté* of this city before the lieutenant general and other officials [of this court], where the city's most notable *bourgeois* would be summoned and which would be presided over by Messrs. René Louis Chartier de Lotbinière, first councilor [of the Superior Council], and François Mathieu Martin de Lino, also a councilor, so that the Council may legislate according to their report; the minutes of the assembly held in the *prévoté* on December 5, containing the remonstrances of the *bourgeois*, craftsmen, butchers, and bakers of this city, were presented to the Council by the lieutenant general on the fourteenth of the same month and a decree was rendered on that day ordering that the said minutes be communicated to the attorney general so that an appropriate ordonnance might be issued, based on his conclusions. The attorney general having presented his conclusions, the Council orders:

I

The bakers of this city [Quebec] will always be obliged to have all types of bread on sale in their shops, under pain of a fine of three *livres* for the first offense and of double [this amount] for subsequent ones.

The bread will be of good quality, under pain of confiscation for the benefit of the Hôtel Dieu [hospital] and of an arbitrary fine for the first offense.

From the date of publication of the present ruling, the bakers will only be allowed to sell their bread on the basis of fifty *sols*[1] per *minot*[2] of wheat, at the following rates:

1 The *livre* was divided into twenty *sols* and the *sol* into twelve *deniers*.
2 The *minot* was a measure of volume equal to 1.05 bushels.

Small white loaves weighing fourteen ounces at one *sol marqué*[3] worth twenty *deniers*.

Three pound loaves at five *sols* and six pound loaves at ten *sols*.

Light brown bread at one *sol* per pound.

The bakers will be obliged to mark all their loaves according to their type and weight, under pain of confiscation.

Under pain of a fine of one hundred *livres*, half of it payable to the informer and the other half to the poor of the Hôtel Dieu, all persons are forbidden by the Council to bake biscuits except the bakers, on condition that they will always have a supply of both white and brown for sale, at a price which will be fixed according to that of wheat. All persons are authorized to mill flour for both the colony's internal and external trade.

II

In view of the low cost of livestock, the butchers of this city will in the future sell beef and veal at the rate of three *sols* per pound from Christmas to the Feast of St. John [June 24]; beef at two *sols* six *deniers* per pound and veal at four *sols* per pound from the Feast of St. John to Christmas.

The butchers will be obliged to advise the attorney of the court of *prévoté* of this city, or his delegate, of the date on which they intend to slaughter the animals that are to be placed on sale, so that these officials or their representative may be present to ascertain that the meat is fit for public consumption. The butchers are forbidden to sell any meat that has not been inspected by the attorney or his deputy, under pain of confiscation and a fine of thirty *livres* for the first offense, sixty *livres* for the second, and one hundred *livres* for the third with deprivation for life of the right to practice as a butcher. Half of the fine will be paid to the informer and the other half to the poor of the Hôtel Dieu.

The inhabitants of the country are forbidden to bring calves to sell in this city that are not at least one month old. It is likewise forbidden the butchers to keep such animals therein for purposes of sale, under pain of confiscation in both cases.

The Council likewise forbids all the inhabitants to bring meat to

3 *Sols marqués* were coins whose colonial value was fixed above their French value in order to keep them within the colony.

this city which is not of good quality or that of animals which perished accidentally or which had to be destroyed because of disease, under pain of confiscation of this meat and of a fine of thirty *livres*, payable as above. They are ordered to bring a certificate from the judge or, in places where none is established, from the seigneur, the *curé*, the captain, or other officer of militia. This certificate should state that the livestock was free of disease before being killed and did not perish accidentally as by drowning or poisoning. The inhabitants must present this certificate to the attorney of this city's *prévoté* in order to obtain a permit, which will be issued to them without charge, to place their meat on sale. The butchers at all times will be given the first choice on this meat, for which they will settle in cash at two *sols* six *deniers* from Christmas to the Feast of St. John, at two *sols* from the Feast of St. John to Christmas, and at proportionate rates for veal.

Four butchers' stalls will be erected in this city in the places judged the most convenient. The sale and distribution of meat will take place there on the Tuesdays and Saturdays of every week. The stalls will be equipped with hooks on which to hang the meat and the butchers are ordered to sell it to all cash customers and not to turn them away on the pretext that the meat has been set aside for others.

For each stall the butchers will pay fifty *livres* a year, half payable at Easter and the other half on October 1. They will be obliged to advance this sum forthwith for the building of the stalls.

Henceforth the butchers will be forbidden to sell poultry, eggs, butter, and other foodstuffs, under pain of confiscation and an arbitrary fine.

To prevent infections and stench in the area of the slaughterhouse, the butchers will be obliged to remove at low tide the entrails and manure of the animals they have slaughtered and to wash away the blood and refuse, under pain of a fine of ten *livres*.

C. Rules for a Billiard Room, 1727

Upon the request made to us by Henry Caen, called Lataille, who lives in a house of which he is the proprietor on Montcarmel Street, to open a billiard game, we have granted him the permission to have this billiard game in the said house on the [following] conditions:

That no liquor be sold or given to the players or others to be drunk on the premises or taken away, in any quantity whatsoever, under pain of confiscation of the liquor and of the billiard game; on condition also that he not allow playing on Sundays and holy days in the forenoon and after dinner before four o'clock, under pain of a fine of thirty *livres* for the first offense and of confiscation of the billiard game in case of relapse. He is forbidden to allow workmen and laborers to play on working days, under pain of a fine of ten *livres* for each workman found on the premises. He is also forbidden to accept furniture, food, and clothing in payment for the use of his game from *fils de famille*,[4] soldiers, and servants, and likewise to prevent these persons from wagering such articles between themselves, under pain of being held personally accountable for such actions. We also enjoin him to prevent players from cursing and blaspheming, under pain of a fine of fifty *livres* to be paid jointly by him and the players. We order him to post a copy of this permit in his billiard room.

Done at our residence in Quebec, May 29, 1727

Dupuy

D. The Care of Illegitimate Children, 1736

By his ordonnance of February 6, 1722, concerning women who become pregnant by illicit means, Michel Bégon, formerly intendant of this country, ordered among other things that until provisions were made to support the children born of these women, they would be placed in the care of wet nurses chosen by the king's attorney or, in places where there are no officers of justice, by the parish priest. The wet nurse was to be paid by the farmer of the western domain,[5] according to the orders transmitted to him, the sum of forty-five *livres* in advance for the food and sustenance of the children during the first three months or first quarter, the sum of thirty *livres* also in advance for the second quarter, and a like sum of thirty *livres* payable in advance for each of the subsequent quarters. It was also forbidden, under pain of a fine of three

4 In the present context, *fils de famille* probably designated sons of well-to-do families who had been deported to the colonies under *lettres de cachet* at the request of their parents.

5 The western domain consisted of several taxes and commercial privileges consolidated into one unit by the Crown. This unit, or farm, was periodically leased out to private interests.

hundred *livres* for the first offense and of a more severe penalty in case of relapse, to give the children or have them given to the Indians.

The disorders having increased since the passing of this ordonnance with the result that the cost of feeding and supporting the children has become much greater than it originally was, and orders having been received that it would be fitting to reduce expenses once the children are weaned in view of the low price at which food has been for a long time, we order that beginning next July 1 the amount paid to wet nurses by the king's attorney for feeding and supporting illegitimate children will be reduced to seven *livres* per month from the time they reach the age of eighteen months until they are indentured. We call upon the king's attorney to indenture the children as soon as they reach the age of four and sooner if possible. For the care of children until they reach the age of eighteen months, M. Bégon's ordonnance will apply. . . .

Done at Quebec, June 9, 1736

HOCQUART

10. The Church

THE 1660's were very important years in the religious history of New France. Under the leadership of Bishop Laval, who hoped to establish a purified Christianity in the colony closely attuned to the spirit of the Catholic Reformation, the Church was reorganized around the seminary of Quebec, whose constitution (Document A) was inspired by the decrees of the Council of Trent. Bishop Laval also opposed the sale of intoxicants to the Indians with such vigor that in 1678 the king ordered Governor Frontenac to summon an assembly of Canadian notables to give its opinion on the subject (extracts from the minutes of this assembly are given in Document B). Although a majority of the twenty persons who participated in this so-called Brandy Parliament were against placing any restrictions on the brandy trade, the monarch issued a compromise edict the following year. Carrying liquor to the Indian villages, where the worst abuses took place, was prohibited, but its sale in moderate quantities was authorized in the French settlements. In another domain, Laval and his successor St. Vallier strove to eliminate moral abuse by upholding a sternly puritanical code of personal conduct. Its basic principles are well illustrated by the advice Bishop St. Vallier gave to Governor Denonville and his wife in 1686 (Document C).

It was also in the 1660's with the establishment of the royal régime, that the Church became subordinated to the state. The consequences of this development were twofold. On the one hand, the Church could look to the state to enforce orthodoxy and to punish with temporal penalties offenses such as blasphemy, failure to fast during Lent, and misbehavior in church (Document D); on the other, the Church's liberty of action was severely hindered, as is shown by the limitation of its right to own property (Document E).

Further Reading: M. Eastman, Church and State in Early Canada (Edinburgh, 1915); G. Lanctot, "Servitudes de l'Eglise sous le régime français," in Une Nouvelle France inconnue (Montreal, 1955); A Vachon, "L'eau-de-vie dans la société indienne," Canadian Historical Association Report (1960), pp. 22–32; H. H. Walsh, The Church in the French Era (Toronto, 1966).

SOURCES: Document A: H. Têtu and C. O. Gagnon (eds.), Mandements, lettres pastorales et circulaires des Evêques de Québec, 1659–1887 (6 vols., Quebec, 1887–90), I, 44–46. Document B: Archives nationales, colonies (Paris); série F³, vol. 5, ff. 76–77; 81–83. Document C: Têtu and Gagnon (eds.), op. cit., 169–173. Document D: Archives of the Province of Quebec, Ordonnances of the Intendants, cahier IV, pp. 39–40. Document E: W. B. Lindsay (ed.), Edits, ordonnances royaux, déclarations et arrêts du Conseil d'État du Roi concernant le Canada (3 vols., Quebec, 1854–56), I, 576–579. All were translated by the editor.

A. Patents Establishing the Seminary and the Clergy, 1663

The holy councils, and those of Trent particularly, found that they could do nothing more useful for the effective restoration of ecclesiastical discipline to its pristine vigor than to order the reestablishment of the ancient practice of seminaries, where clerics are instructed in the virtues and sciences appropriate to their state. The excellence of this decree can be observed in a tangible experiment, since the great St. Charles Borromeo, who was the first to execute it soon after the Council [of Trent], and many bishops who followed his example began to restore the clergy to its original splendor, particularly in France. This method having-proved so effective in restoring ecclesiastical behavior in places where it had become lax, we have judged that introducing it in new places would prove no less useful than it was in the first centuries of

Christendom. For these reasons, considering that it has pleased Divine Providence to entrust us with the care of the newly born Church of Canada, called New France, and considering the extreme importance of giving the clergy from the very beginning the best possible training in order to have workers capable of tending this new vine of the Lord, by virtue of the authority invested in us, we have erected and erect now and for always a seminary to provide the new Church with a clergy, to be administered and governed by superiors appointed by us or the bishops of New France our successors, according to the rules we shall draw up for that purpose. In it, young clerics who appear qualified for the divine service will be taught and trained in the ways of administering the sacraments well, in the methods of catechizing and apostolic preaching, in moral theology, in Gregorian plain chant, and in other matters that relate to the duties of a good ecclesiastic; so that furthermore a chapter may be formed with ecclesiastics of the said seminary, whose members will be chosen by us and the bishops of New France our successors, when the king will have the goodness to found such an institution and when the seminary, by God's grace, will have the means of supporting it.

We wish this seminary to be a school of virtue and a reserve from which we may draw pious and able subjects and send them forth anywhere, in parishes or any other part of this country, to take up parochial functions or other duties for which they have been intended and from which they may be withdrawn whenever we will judge it suitable. We have kept for ourselves, our successors, and the seminary forever the right to recall, whenever it shall be judged necessary, all the clerics assigned to parishes and other places, for we do not want them to be attached to any particular parish but desire, on the contrary, that they may be moved, revoked, and dismissed according to the will of the bishops and seminary following the practice of early centuries, which is still observed in certain dioceses of this realm.

And since it is absolutely necessary to provide the seminary and clergy with a revenue, to enable it to meet the expenses it will be obliged to incur, we have assigned to it now and for always all the tithes, whatever the nature and the manner of their collection, to be owned and administered by the seminary according to our orders and under our authority and that of our successors, on condition that it support all the clerics who will be delegated to the parishes and other places of this country, who will always be removable at the will of the bishop and seminary; that it maintain all evangelical workers in sickness and in health, whether they are exercising their functions or are living in the community; that it bear the cost of their journeys to and from France. To avoid litigation and disorders, all these sums will be paid according to the rates fixed by us and our successors. And since it is necessary to build several churches for the divine service and the convenience of the faithful, we order . . . that what sums remain after the seminary has attended to annual expenses will be used to build churches, or for alms and other good works for the glory of God and the good of the Church, according to the orders of the bishop. However, neither we nor our successors will be entitled to make a private use of these funds and we even deprive ourselves of the right to alienate any seminary property, even in case of necessity, without the express consent of four of its members, to wit: the superior, his two assistants, and the procurator.

In testimony of which we have signed these letters and placed our seal thereon.

Given at Paris, March 26, 1663

FRANÇOIS, Bishop of Petraea

B. The Sale of Liquor to the Indians, 1678

MINUTES OF THE ASSEMBLY
HELD AT THE CHATEAU ST. LOUIS OF QUEBEC
ON OCTOBER 10, 1678 AND DAYS FOLLOWING
ABOUT THE INTOXICATING DRINKS
THAT ARE TRADED TO THE INDIANS

THE SR. DU GUÉ—that the brandy trade is absolutely necessary to attract the Indians to the French colonies and to prevent them from taking their pelts to foreigners. This can in no way prejudice the conversion of the Indians or the increase of religion. On the contrary, if this permission is not granted, the Indians, who can find spirits elsewhere, will not come back to the French but go to the English and Dutch, who instead of instructing them in the Gospel will make them fall into heresy or leave them in their state of superstition. He knows that over three hundred Iroquois who were hunting at the Long Sault on the [Ottawa] river, thirty lieues[1]

1 The lieue corresponded to approximately 3 miles.

from Montreal, took their furs to foreigners because no spirits had been given to them.

THE SRS. DE REPENTIGNY AND DE BÉCANCOURT—that trading liquor to the Indians is necessary and must be permitted on condition of preventing *coureurs de bois* and vagabonds from taking it to the places where the Indians hunt, under pain of very severe penalties. It is very important for the establishment of commerce and religion that we give them drink; for if we refuse they will assuredly draw away from us and go to the Dutch and the English, taking their pelts there and depriving the French inhabitants of the benefits they derive from them. This commerce is the only one which yields some profit, because of the high cost of the other merchandise we trade to the Indians. Furthermore, by going to foreigners, they will remain idolatrous or will be instructed in a false religion. As far as alleged disorders are concerned, they have no knowledge of the murders, incest, and adultery which have supposedly been caused by liquor since [its trade] has been permitted, although there have been such happenings among people who make no use of these drinks. At Sault Ste. Marie, five or six Indians acting purely out of savagery raped a woman and cut off her head. On the missions last fall there was an Ottawa chief named Talon who had seven wives, and a chief of the Pottowatomies who had two sisters as wives. The reserved case[2] has done no good whatever. On the contrary, it has only served to trouble consciences and caused perhaps the damnation of some inhabitants. . . .

THE SR. DUPLESSIS GASTINEAU—that spirits must not be traded to the Indians because this commerce ruins religion. Formerly they prayed assiduously and received the sacraments. Now, they live like heathens and commit all sorts of crimes as a consequence of their continuous state of drunkenness. This barter is a cause of damnation for the French, because of the manner in which they despise the orders of the Church, and for the Indians, because they only drink to get drunk. It is ruinous for commerce because the Indians, in order to drink, contract debts on all sides and spend more on intoxicants in two months than they would in two years to support their families.

2 The sale of spirits to the Indians became a "reserved case" in 1660. In that year Bishop Laval declared that anyone guilty of this act incurred excommunication and reserved to himself the right to lift this penalty.

THE SR. JOLLIET—that going into the woods with liquor to meet the Indians coming to trade with the French must be prohibited under pain of death, and the Indians must likewise be forbidden to take it back with them. But the inhabitants should be allowed to give them something to drink in their homes and places of trade, with moderation and without making them drunk, and they should be punished in case of disorder. It is not true to say that all Indians get drunk. A few, like those who live among us, use liquor properly. Others use it as an object of trade. They buy it in our habitations and take it into the woods to exchange it for beaver. . . . It is true, however, that there are not many of these, not three in two hundred.

THE SR. LE BERT—that the liberty to trade spirits in houses with moderation could be granted, but that the French and the Indians should be forbidden to take it into the woods or to the native villages. As for the allegation that trading liquor to the Indians is a way of bringing them to the faith, he maintains on the contrary that it is rather an obstacle. Where commerce is concerned, whether [spirits] are traded or not, the result is always the same and their pelts will always fall into the hands of the inhabitants.

AND THE SR. DOMBOURG—that if the trade of liquor is prohibited, disorders will disappear, the Indians will live in tranquillity, and there will no longer be attempts to extort their pelts for a little liquor. The French will apply themselves to cultivating the land, which will cause the country to flourish, while if the said trade is permitted the country, far from increasing, will decline, and God will be very badly served, for the Indians only drink to get drunk and in that state commit incest and many other crimes. Sons kill their fathers and rape their sisters. Mothers kill their children and women prostitute themselves for a pint of spirits. If this trade is permitted, *coureurs de bois* will spring up everywhere to engage in it. It is a great sin to give spirits worth twenty *sols* in exchange for beaver worth six to seven francs [i.e., *livres*]. When the Indians have drunk they sell everything they own and sometimes give away a gun for a half *sétier* of spirits. Indians are not seen in as great numbers as before since they began to barter for liquor, for they drink so much of it that they kill themselves. This passion for drink prevents their conversion, for having become accustomed to this habit they will do nothing else nor hear God spoken of.

C. Advice to the Governor and His Wife
on Their Obligation
to Set a Good Example for the People,
c. 1686

CONCERNING FEASTS

1. When the governor and his wife honor someone by accepting [an invitation] to dine at his home, it is fitting that it be for dinner and not for supper so as to avoid late entertainments, dangerous pastimes, and other unseemly happenings that usually occur at nocturnal banquets and gatherings.

2. They should declare themselves unhappy, offended, and forever dismissed, if the meals they are served are too sumptuous. Thus, they will find themselves at tables where frugality is observed and little by little will accustom the people to avoid those sumptuous repasts which inconvenience households as much as they oppose the rule of temperance and offend Christian modesty and decency.

3. They should never suffer these feasts to be accompanied by balls and dances and many other dangerous and licentious recreations; their presence at such entertainments would be the cause of an evil that experience has long shown to be one of the gravest in Quebec.

CONCERNING BALLS AND DANCES

Although balls and dances are harmless by nature, they are nonetheless so dangerous because of the environment they provide and the harmful consequences they almost invariably entail that, according to St. Francis de Sales, one must state of them, as a doctor of mushrooms, that the best are worthless. This saint, who undertook to make devotion pleasant and easy to persons of our century, nevertheless could not suffer that anyone be present at a ball or a dance unless it could not be otherwise; in which case he wished this recreation to be tempered by such modesty, good intention, dignity, Christian thoughts, and pious sentiments that the participant would be preserved from the corruption that almost always steals into consciences as a result of this amusement. . . .

This being so, it is of great importance for the glory of God and the salvation of souls that the governor and his wife, on whose conduct most people will pattern their own, not only firmly refuse to enter houses where people are gathered for balls and dances, but also close their own to this sort of entertainment. . . .

However, since their daughter stands in need of recreation on account of her age and vivacity, she may be permitted a few decent and moderate dances, but only with persons of her own sex and in the presence of her mother as a safeguard against indecent words and songs; but not [in the presence of] men and boys since, to speak frankly, this mixing of the sexes is the cause of the disorders occasioned by balls and dances. . . .

Concerning Plays and Other Declamations

But we do not believe that it would be in keeping with her [the daughter's] Christian profession to permit her to hold the part of a character in a play and appear before the public as an actress reciting verse, no matter how holy the contents may be; and we believe that we should be even less tolerant of boys and girls reciting together, for this would renew unintentionally in this country the practice of theater and plays, which are equally, and perhaps more, dangerous than balls and dances and which have been inveighed against with vehemence because of the disorders they have caused in the past.

Concerning Luxurious Clothes and Nudities

Luxury and vanity in the dress of women and girls being one of the principal disorders, which has long been noticed here, and one which has the most vexatious consequences, it is most desirable that the governor and his wife act zealously on this point by expressing in both word and deed the indignation they feel for such an abuse and by warning and even privately reprimanding those who appear dressed in ostentatious clothes.

Ostentation in clothing appears first of all in the rich and showy fabrics which are worn by [women and girls] and which exceed by far their condition and their means. It appears also in the excessive garb which they put on, in the extraordinary way in which they dress their hair, which they fill with bodkins and leave uncovered, in those immodest curls which are so expressly forbidden by the Epistles of St. Peter and St. Paul and by all the doctors of the Church and which God has often severely punished, as may be seen by the example of the unhappy Pretextate. According to St. Jerome, who knew her, her hand was withered and five months later she died suddenly and was dashed into Hell, as an angel from God had warned her, because on the command of her husband she had curled and mundanely dressed her niece.

But what render luxury in the clothes of women and girls infinitely pernicious are scandalously indecent and immodest dresses, baring the neck and shoulders, which are thus left exposed or covered with a transparent veil. This is absolutely forbidden and must never be tolerated since it is a cause of perdition for an infinite number of souls. The Holy Ghost and Holy Scripture warn us to turn our eyes away from an indecently clad woman because many have perished under the seducement of her vain and pompous appearance.

This profligacy begins at an early age when little girls, even those of lowly birth, are dressed and adorned like dolls and appear with bare shoulders and necks. They continue in this practice when they grow older and even after they are married. As an inevitable consequence, lewdness and a great number of other sins are perpetuated in this country, to the great prejudice of this new Christianity.

JEAN, Bishop of Quebec

D. A Police Ordonnance
Commanding the People
to be Respectful in Church,
1710

Since coming to this country we have made every effort to inspire in the people the sentiments of religion and respect which must be theirs when they attend divine service. However, we learn with sorrow that in spite of the ordonnances we have rendered on this subject, which were meant to explain the commands of the Church and the orders we had received from His Majesty, the scandal continues, there being people who are so bold, or rather so impious, as not to keep in church the respect which is becoming in a place where our holy mysteries are celebrated, and who hold in scorn the word of God, making ready to leave when their priests begin to announce it to them. Were such behavior to continue, it could bring the anger of God down upon us and this country, if we were so weak as not to oppose it with all our might when we have the means of repressing it. We are also informed that the greatest disorder comes from some young men who, either because they lack education or because they are not restrained by their fathers and mothers, often cause all the scandal, pushing their impudence to the point of smoking near the church after leaving it to avoid hearing the instructions that are meant for them, and going about neighboring houses threatening to molest those who might report their misbehavior.

To correct all these disorders, we order that our previous ordonnances will be executed and by virtue of these forbid all persons, whatever their rank and condition, to chat in church or to lack in other ways the respect that is due in such a holy place; to smoke at the doors or near them; to leave the church when the priests are delivering their sermons except in case of great necessity, under pain of a fine of ten *livres* against the offenders, payable even by the fathers for their children, and of a jail sentence in case of relapse. The fine will be payable to the vestry of the parish where the offense was committed. We call upon the priests of the parishes in question to publish the present ordonnance, to renew it every year at Easter and Christmas, and to advise us of violations of it. We call upon the captains of militia to see that it is enforced. . . .

Given at Quebec, March 22, 1710,

[Signed] RAUDOT [intendant of New France]

E. Declaration of the King
Concerning Religious Orders and People of Mortmain[3] Established in the French Colonies, 1744

Louis, by the grace of God king of France and Navarre, to all those who will see these present letters, GREETING. The progress of religion has always been the principal object of the cares taken and the expenses incurred by the kings our predecessors for the establishment of colonies in America. For this reason, they considered that they could never grant too many privileges to those who had dedicated themselves to bringing the light of faith to the colonies.

3 According to canon law, Church lands were legally inalienable. They were said to be held in mortmain, or deadhand, because they could never be sold, transferred, or given, and hence were forever lost to lay society.

Since our advent to the throne we have spared nothing to support and quicken the zeal of the ecclesiastical communities and religious orders established in these colonies, and we have the satisfaction of seeing that our subjects find there in regard to religion all the assistance that they could expect at the heart of our realm. But on the other hand, because the use these communities and religious orders made of their privileges and exemptions enabled them to acquire considerable estates, the late king . . . judged that certain limitations had become necessary. He ruled in 1703 that none of the religious orders established in the islands [i.e., the West Indies] would be allowed to expand their plantations beyond an area employing one hundred Negroes; and since this regulation was not carried out, we ordered by our letters patent of August, 1721, that in the future religious orders would not be allowed to acquire any new properties, whether in land or buildings, without our express permission in writing, under pain of forfeiting them to the royal domain. The present state of our colonies requires that we make still more extensive arrangements concerning this matter. Whatever favor establishments founded for motives of religion and charity may deserve, it is time that we took effective precautions not only to prevent the formation of new ones but also a multiplication of acquisitions by the existing ones. These withdraw from commerce a considerable part of the wealth of our colonies and can only be regarded as contrary to the common good of society. For these reasons, we have resolved to promulgate an exact law . . .

ARTICLE I—In accordance with the ordonnances and regulations made for the interior of our kingdom, we forbid the foundation or establishment in our American colonies of any new religious communities, hospitals, poorhouses, congregations, brotherhoods, colleges, or other corporations and communities, either ecclesiastical or secular, without our express permission given in our letters patent and registered by the Superior Councils of our colonies in the form that will be prescribed hereafter.

ARTICLE II—We expressly forbid, under pain of invalidation, the making of provisions in a last will and testament for the founding of a new establishment of the kind mentioned in the preceding article, or the favoring of persons who would be charged with forming such an establishment. . . .

ARTICLE III—Those who might wish to make a foundation or establishment of the type already described, by donations *inter vivos*, will first of all be obliged to present to our governors, lieutenants general, and intendants, or to the under-governors and *ordonnateurs* in the colonies, the draft of the act by which they intend to make the said foundation or establishment, so that a description of it may be sent to us. If we find it pleasing, letters patent will be issued, but always with the express clause that the plans may not be added to or changed in any way after the registration of the said letters by our Superior Councils. . . .

ARTICLE IV—We will only issue letters patent authorizing a new foundation or establishment after receiving an account of its usefulness, of the nature, value, and quality of the goods with which it will be endowed, and after having taken the advice of our governors, lieutenants general, and intendants, or of the under-governors and *ordonnateurs*, and even after having received the consent of the communities and hospitals and of the other interested parties already established in the colony where the foundation is planned.

ARTICLE V—Express mention will be made in our letters patent of the goods with which the establishment will be endowed and none other may be added by donation, acquisition, or otherwise without obtaining our letters of permission. . . .

ARTICLE IX—We declare null and void all the establishments of the kind mentioned in the first article which have not been authorized by our letters patent registered by our Superior Councils and all provisions and acts made either directly or indirectly in their favor. . . . As for the establishments which have existed peaceably and against which no demand of invalidation has been made before the present declaration, we reserve the right to take appropriate action after receiving a report on their object and nature.

[Signed] Louis

Registered . . . at Quebec, October 5, 1744

11. The Seigneurial System

THE SEIGNEURIAL régime in New France was a system of land tenure designed to assure the colony's internal development. The Crown made land grants to seigneurs who, in turn, divided part of their estates into farms known as *rotures*, which they conceded to ordinary habitants. The whole system was based on the fulfillment of the rights and obligations listed in the title deed. The deed to the seigneury of Saurel (*Document*

A) and to a roture in the seigneury of Beaupré (Document B) show what these rights and obligations were in the case of a seigneur and roturier respectively.

The two arrêts of Marly, named after the place in France where the king issued them on July 6, 1711, represent the most important effort to eliminate the abuses which had crept into the seigneurial system and to oblige delinquent seigneurs and roturiers to develop their estates. Before these arrêts, the seigneur was under no obligation to subgrant land within his seigneury; afterward, he became a mere agent of the Crown whose function was to concede land to whoever applied for it in return for customary dues. (Documents C and D give these two edicts, the first relating to the seigneur, the second to the roturier.)

Toward 1710, a French military officer and engineer named Gédéon de Catalogne was commissioned by the colonial authorities to conduct a survey of all the Canadian seigneuries. His findings and recommendations (extracts are given in Document E) may have been largely responsible for the policy decision made by the royal government in 1715 to suspend further seigneurial grants so as to enable existing ones to increase their population. Only in the 1730's was the practice of granting seigneuries resumed on a regular basis. From Catalogne's report the reader will note the uneven rate of development of different seigneuries and the varied social background of the seigneurs.

Further Reading: E. R. Adair, "The French Canadian Seigneury," Canadian Historical Review, XXXV (1954), 187–207; S. Diamond, "An Experiment in 'Feudalism': French Canada in the Seventeenth Century," William and Mary Quarterly, 3rd series, XVIII (1961), 3–34; W. B. Munro, The Seigniorial System in Canada, A Study in French Colonial Policy (New York, 1907); R. C. Harris, The Seigneurial System in Early Canada, A Geographical Study (Madison, Wis., 1966).

SOURCES: Document A: Title deed of the Seigneury of Saurel, granted to Pierre de Saurel, office of the Carignan-Salières Regiment, October 29, 1672, in W. B. Munro (ed.), Documents Relating to the Seigniorial Tenure in Canada, 1598–1854 (Toronto, 1908), pp. 34–36. Reprinted by permission of Champlain Society Publications. Document B: Concession by Charles Aubert de La Chesnaye to Claude Bouchard, called le petit Claude, Quebec Judicial Archives, register of the Notary Guillaume Audouart, April 11, 1662. Document C: Edicts, Ordinances, Declarations and Decrees Relative to the Seigniorial Tenure, Required by an Address of the Legislative Assembly, 1851 (Quebec, 1852), p. 272. Document D: Ibid., p. 273. Document E: Archives Nationales, Colonies (Paris), série C "A vol. 33, pp. 304–

306, 313–314, 331–332, 344–346, 350–351, 359–362, 365 (pagination of the transcripts of the Public Archives of Canada). Documents A, B, and E translated by the editor.

A. *Concession of a Seigneury, 1672*

His Majesty has always sought with the diligence and zeal befitting his just title of eldest son of the Church the means of promoting in the farthest lands the propagation of the faith and the preaching of the Gospel, the glory of God and the Christian name, first and principal reason for the establishment of a French colony in Canada, and secondly to make known in the parts of the earth farthest removed from [civilization] the greatness of his name and the power of his arms. Having estimated that there was no surer way to [attain these ends] than to compose the colony of men who would make worthy occupants by their personal qualities, who would increase it by their labor and their application to the cultivation of the land, and who would support it by a vigorous defense against the insults and attacks to which it could be subjected in the course of time, His Majesty has sent to this country a good number of his loyal subjects, officers of his troops of the regiment of Carignan and others, the majority of whom conform to the great and pious design of His Majesty by agreeing to attach themselves to the country and to form seigneuries of a size proportionate to their means. The sr. de Saurel, captain in the regiment of Carignan, having requested [such a concession], by virtue of the power invested in us and in consideration of the good, useful, and praiseworthy services which he has rendered to His Majesty in different parts of both Old France and the New, where he went by royal orders, we have granted, given, and conceded by the present letters to the said sr. de Saurel an area of two and a half *lieues* frontage on the St. Lawrence River, one and a half *lieue* being below the Richelieu River, by two *lieues* in depth if such there be, with the *iles* St. Ignace, *iles* Ronde, and *iles* de Grace, thus named on our map, to be possessed by him, his heirs, and assigns, subject to the oath of fealty and homage which he will be obliged to render at the Château St. Louis in Quebec, to which he will be subjected according to the customary rights and dues and to the Custom of the *prévoté* and *vicomté* of Paris[1] . . . and on condition that he keep *feu*

1 The Custom of Paris was a codification of French customary law which was in effect in much of northern France and later became the law of Canada.

et lieu[2] on the said seigneury and stipulate in the contracts he will make with his tenants that they will be obliged to reside within the year on the concessions he has granted or will grant them, failing which he will regain full title to the land. The said sr. de Saurel will preserve the oak trees that are fit for naval constructions on the land he has set aside for his domain and on the concessions he has granted to his tenants. He will also give immediate notice to the king or to us of mines and minerals, if any be found within the limits of the fief, and will allow for necessary roads and passages. The whole subject to His Majesty's good pleasure, whose confirmation of these letters he will be obliged to obtain within a year from this day.

In witness whereof we have signed the present letters, set the seal bearing our coat of arms, and our secretary has countersigned.

Done at Quebec, this 29th day of October, 1672.

TALON

B. Concession of a Roture, 1662

Before Guillaume Audouart, secretary of the council established by the king in Quebec and notary in New France, and the undersigned witnesses, appeared Charles Aubert de La Chesnaye. In his own name and as attorney of the seigneurs of Beaupré, by virtue of the procuration passed before the notaries and scriveners of the city of Rouen on [date left blank], which he has shown to me, he has granted in consideration of seigneurial *cens et rentes*,[3] payable annually on All Saints Day, November 1, to Claude Bouchard, called le petit Claude, present and accepting for himself, his heirs, and assigns, an area of three *arpents*[4] of land on the great St. Lawrence River, one and a half *lieues* in depth, the said three *arpents* being bordered on one side by the land belonging to Nicolas Manière and on the other by lands not conceded. This concession is made on the following conditions: the said Bouchard promises and obliges himself to pay each year on All Saints Day the sum of twenty *sols* of nonredeemable *rente* for each *arpent* of

2 To keep home and hearth, that is, to live on the seigneury or have a representative in residence there.
3 The *cens* was a token cash payment made to signify that the land was held *en roture*. The *rente* was the basic ground rent.
4 The *arpent* was roughly equal to one acre.

frontage on the great St. Lawrence River, a *cens* of three *sols* for the entire concession, and three live capons also payable annually and without fraud on All Saints Day at the seigneurial manor of Beaupré or at the place designated by the attorney or representatives of the seigneurs. . . . The said *cens et rentes entail lods et vente,*[5] seizin,[6] and fines, according to the Custom of the city, *prévoté,* and *vicomté* of Paris, which is followed in this country of New France. The lessee will also be obliged to clear his land without delay and to build a house on it within a year from this day at the latest, and to continue to cultivate it in the following years so that the *cens et rentes* may be collected annually. Failing this the seigneur will be entitled to recover full title to the land he has relinquished, without lawsuit in any shape or form and without compensation for the expenses [the lessee] may have incurred. The said Bouchard will also be obliged to allow a road fifteen feet wide along the river for the benefit of navigation and to bring his grain to the seigneurial mill to have it ground there. To maintain friendly relations with his neighbors, he will be obliged to fence in his land as he clears it, failing which he will not be entitled to claim compensation for the damage his neighbors' cattle might cause. He will be obliged to pay the tithe should the case arise.[7] The lessee will enjoy full possession of the concession and will use and dispose of it as he, his heirs and assigns will think fit, for so it has been granted. . . .

C. Edict of Marly Concerning the Seigneurs, 1711

DECREE OF THE KING DIRECTING THAT THE LANDS WHICH HAVE BEEN CONCEDED BE BROUGHT INTO CULTIVATION AND OCCUPIED BY INHABITANTS—JULY 6, 1711

The King being informed that, among the tracts of land which His Majesty has been pleased to grant and concede in seigniory to his subjects in New France, there are some which have not been entirely settled, and others on which there are as yet no settlers to bring them into a state of cultivation, and on which also those to

5 *Lods et ventes* was a tax of one-twelfth of the sale price, which was levied by the seigneur on the sale of a *roture* out of the line of direct succession.
6 Seizin meant that the roturier was placed in immediate possession of the land.
7 The tithe was instituted in 1663, one year after this concession was made.

whom they have been conceded in seigniory have not yet commenced to make clearings for the purpose of establishing their domain thereon;

And His Majesty being also informed that there are some seigniors who refuse, under various pretexts, to concede lands to settlers who apply to them with the hope of being able to sell the same, and at the same time impose upon the purchasers the same dues as are paid by the inhabitants already settled on lands, which is entirely contrary to His Majesty's intentions, and to the clauses and conditions of the concessions, by which they are merely permitted to concede lands at an annual ground rent; whereby very great detriment is done to the new settlers, who find less land open to settlement in the places best adapted to commerce;

For remedy whereof His Majesty, being in his council, has ordained and ordains that, within one year at the farthest from the day on which the present decree shall be published, the inhabitants of New France to whom His Majesty has granted lands in seigniory, who have no domain cleared and who have no settlers on their grants, shall be held to bring them into cultivation and to place settlers thereon, in default of which it is His Majesty's will that the said lands be reunited to his domain after the lapse of the said period, at the diligence of the attorney general of the superior council of Quebec, and on the orders to be given in that behalf by the governor and lieutenant general of His Majesty, and the intendant in the said country;

And His Majesty ordains also, that all the seigniors in the said country of New France shall concede to the settlers the lots of land which they may demand of them in their seigniories, at a ground rent and without exacting from them any sum of money as a consideration for such concessions; otherwise, and in default of their so doing, His Majesty permits the said settlers to demand the said lots of land from them by a formal summons, and in case of their refusal, to make application to the governor and lieutenant general and intendant of the said country, whom His Majesty enjoins to concede to the said settlers the lands demanded by them, in the said seigniories, for the same dues as are laid upon the other conceded lands in the said seigniories, which dues shall be paid by the new settlers into the hands of the receiver of His Majesty's domain, in the city of Quebec, without its being in the power of the seigniors to claim from them any dues of any kind whatever.

And this decree shall be registered in the registry of the superior council of Quebec, and read and published wherever need shall be.

Done in the King's council of state held at Marly, His Majesty being present, the 6th day of July 1711.

[Signed] PHELIPPEAUX [Minister of Marine]

D. Edict of Marly Concerning the Roturiers, 1711

DECREE OF THE KING WHICH DECLARES AGAINST THE SETTLERS A FORFEITURE OF THE RIGHT OF PROPERTY IN THE LANDS WHICH HAVE BEEN CONCEDED TO THEM, IF THEY DO NOT BRING THEM INTO A STATE OF CULTIVATION BY RESIDING THEREON (en y tenant feu [et] lieu) WITHIN A YEAR AND A DAY FROM THE PUBLICATION OF THE SAID DECREE, OF THE SIXTH OF JULY 1711

The King being informed that there are lands conceded to the inhabitants of New France which are neither settled nor cleared, and on which these inhabitants content themselves with cutting down some trees, thinking by this means, and by means of the concessions thereof made to them by those to whom His Majesty has granted tracts of the said lands in seigniory, to secure to themselves the right of property therein, which prevents these lands, being conceded to other and more laborious settlers, who might occupy them and bring them into a state of cultivation, and which is also very prejudicial to the other inhabitants settled in those seigniories:—

Because those who do not reside upon their lands nor bring them into a state of cultivation, do not contribute their share of labor to the public works which are ordered for the good of the country and of the said seigniories, which is quite contrary to the intentions of His Majesty, who only permitted those concessions to be made with a view to the settlement of the country, and on condition that the lands should be settled and brought into a state of cultivation; and it being necessary to remedy such an abuse:—

His Majesty being in his council, has ordained and ordains, that in a year and a day at the furthest from the date of the publication of the present decree, the settlers in New France who do not reside upon the lands which have been conceded to them, shall be held so to reside thereon (d'y tenir feu et lieu) and to bring them into a state of cultivation, in default of which, and after the lapse of the said time, it is His Majesty's will that on the certificates of the curates and of the captains of militia in the settlement (*Capitaines de la Côte*), to the effect that the said settlers have been a year without keeping house and home on their lands, and have not brought them into a state of cultivation, they shall be declared to have forfeited the right of property therein, and the same shall thereupon be reunited to the domains of the respective seigniories, in pursuance of orders to be pronounced by the Sieur Bégon, intendant in the said country of New France, whom His Majesty commands to see to the execution of the present decree, and to cause it to be enregistered in the registry of the superior council of Quebec, and published and posted up wherever need shall be, so that no one may be ignorant thereof.

Done in the King's Council of State, held at Marly, His Majesty being present, the sixth day of July, one thousand seven hundred and eleven.

[Signed] PHELIPPEAUX

E. Extracts from Gédéon de Catalogne's Survey of the Canadian Seigneuries, 1712

The seigneury of La Chesnaye[8] belongs to the heirs and creditors of the late sr. Martel, whose widow married the sr. Bailleul, lieutenant of the troops. This seigneury, together with those of Repentigny, St. Sulpice, and La Valterie, form a single parish which has been entrusted to a priest of the Seminary of Montreal. If the Iroquois had not killed part of the inhabitants and retarded cultivation, each of these parishes would be able to support a priest, for the land is very good and produces wheat and vegetables in abundance. There are several fine meadows and grazing grounds to feed a large number of cattle. Fine wood of all types can be found in places, but fruit trees only grow in a few spots.

The seigneury of Repentigny[9] belongs to the seigneur of that name, captain of the colonial regular troops. The shore line in that area is very pleasant and even, and several islands produce wheat

8 On the north shore of the St. Lawrence, near the northern tip of the island of Montreal.
9 The seigneury after La Chesnaye, going down river.

and grain in quantity. All types of trees grow on the mainland. The Iroquois killed some of the inhabitants and delayed its development for many years. . . .

The seigneury of St. Sulpice[10] belongs to the Gentlemen of the Seminary of Montreal. The Iroquois wars explain why it is not well settled. The land, furthermore, is only good in places, which, however, produce good wheat and vegetables, although not as abundantly as at Repentigny. All types of trees grow in the forest, which is intersected by plains and marshes where beaver and moose formerly abounded.

The seigneury of Longueuil[11] belongs to the baron of that name, lieutenant de roi[12] in Montreal. The parish is administered by a priest from the Seminary of Quebec. The land is only good in places because of rocks and wet plains that are difficult to drain. Nonetheless, the lands along the river are settled by habitants who are well-to-do and in some cases wealthy. This is the result of costly improvements carried out by the seigneur. Ditches have been dug and the rocks have been removed and used to build a fort and fine houses. A road of four and a half lieues connecting with Chambly was even begun and is currently very advanced; but work on it was discontinued because it involved the seigneur in heavy expenses and held out no prospects of future profit. Its completion is necessary, however, to be able to come promptly to the rescue of Chambly in case of attack, for reinforcements sent by water must travel thirty-six lieues. The lands that are cultivated produce good grain and vegetables, but not as abundantly as the neighboring seigneuries. Quantities of medium-size wood for construction can be found on the seigneury. . . .

The seigneury of Yamasca marks the beginning of the government of Trois Rivières on the southeast side [of the river]. It belongs to the sr. Petit, a merchant of Trois Rivières, who acquired it from the late sr. de La Chesnaye. It forms a parish together with St. François. The land is low and flat. The part that is cultivated produces all types of grain and vegetables. Fish and game are plentiful. There are all types of wood, some of which are suited for buildings and construction.

The seigneury of St. François belongs to the heirs of the sr.

10 A part of the island of Montreal.
11 On the south shore of the St. Lawrence, facing the island of Montreal.
12 The title of a position in the government hierarchy.

Crevier. The Jesuit fathers minister to it and to the Abenaki Indians who are settled there. The land is very nice and level, particularly the islands, which are very fertile in all sorts of grain and vegetables. Wood is of all types. Fish and game are plentiful.

The seigneury of Luçeaudière[13] has no *habitants*. Those nearby do not know who the seigneur is. The land seems to be very good. All types of wood grow on it, particularly large pine trees. . . .

The seigneury of Beaupré[14] . . . belongs to the Gentlemen of the Seminary of Quebec. The land is very nice. It includes three parishes, to wit, L'Ange Gardien, Château Riché, and Ste. Anne. The shore line is bordered along its entire length by a height of land, at the base of which are fields at the level of the tidal flats. These have been drained by ditches and made fertile in all sorts of grains and vegetables. Although the height of land is not as fertile, it is moistened by mountain water and is fit to produce all sorts of grains, fruits, and vegetables, not as abundantly as the lowlands but the grain is of better quality. The *habitants* of this shore are reputed to be and are in effect the most hard-working and the richest in all Canada. They have long manufactured linen and cloth. Although the mountains are steep, they provide them with timber and kindling wood. The Daughters of the Congregation [of Notre Dame] have an establishment at Château Riché.

At Cap Tourmente, which is an extension of the seigneury of Beaupré, the Seminary of Quebec has its principal manor house. It is divided into the big farm and the small farm. Students go there for their recreation during their holidays. There are fine buildings and all types of domestic animals. . . .

The seigneury of Platon Ste. Croix[15] belongs to the Ursuline nuns of Quebec. Most of the land is very high and only mediocre. That which is cultivated produces good grain, but not as abundantly as elsewhere. Vegetables grow better, particularly flax and hemp. Eel fishing is better here than in any other place. There are all types of wood, which they sell in the city.

The seigneury of Choret[16] belongs to the seigneur of that name,

13 The seigneury after St. François, going down river.
14 A short distance downriver from Quebec and the last seigneury on the north shore of the St. Lawrence.
15 On the south shore of the St. Lawrence, about halfway between Trois Rivières and Quebec.
16 The seigneury after Platon Ste. Croix, going down river.

a *laboureur*.[17] The land is very high in relation to the river, but quite level. The little of it that is under cultivation produces very good grain and vegetables but is not fit for fruit trees that do not grow in clayey soil. There is eel fishing, but it is not plentiful. There are all types of wood, which are sold at Quebec. . . .

OBSERVATIONS ON THE ESTABLISHMENT

In relation to the great size of the settlement, there is not one-quarter of the workmen required to clear and cultivate the land.

Farmers do not cultivate the land with enough care. It is certain that one *minot* as sown in France would produce more than two as sown in Canada.

Since the seasons are too short and there is much bad weather, it would be desirable that the Church allow the performance of essential works on feast days. There are not ninety working days left from May, when sowing begins, to the end of September, after allowance is made for holy days and bad weather. Yet, the strength of the colony hinges on that period.

It would be necessary to compel neglectful *habitants* to labor on the land by depriving them of the right to go on [fur trading?] voyages, which exempt them from work. They earn thirty or forty écus[18] on a voyage of two or three months but waste the farming season, and land remains fallow as a result. . . .

Oblige the seigneurs, in order to facilitate the establishment of their seigneuries, to give sufficient common land at low prices and to build mills and other public conveniences. Many persons lose up to a third of their time traveling fifteen or twenty *lieues* to mill their flour. . . .

Order the *grand voyer* to apply himself to building the roads and bridges necessary for the public, which is something very essential. . . .

The subordination of the vassal to his seigneur is not observed. This error is the result of seigneuries being granted to commoners, who have not known how to maintain their rights over their tenants. Even the officers of militia, who are their dependents, have for the most part no consideration for their superiority and wish on occasions to be regarded as independent.

17　A wealthy farmer.
18　An écu was worth 3 *livres*.

12. The Birth of a Diversified Economy, 1673

DURING THE early years of the royal régime, Canada enjoyed a period of unprecedented economic growth. One of the architects of this prosperity was the intendant Jean Talon, who ably carried out the plans of Jean-Baptiste Colbert, the minister of marine, for a strong and diversified economy. Shortly after returning to France in 1673, Talon submitted a memoir to the king describing what had been done in the colony since his arrival there in 1665. Extracts from this report are given below.

Further Reading: T. Chapais [Ignotus], Jean Talon, Intendant de la Nouvelle France (1665–1672) (Quebec, 1904).

SOURCE: Memoir of Talon on Canada (1673), in Rapport de l'Archiviste de la Province de Québec, 1930–1931 (Québec, Imprimeur du Roi, 1931), pp. 175–178. Translated by the editor.

. . . It has appeared to me that one of the principal intentions of His Majesty was to form over the years a large and populous colony, full of men suited for all types of professions in the army, the navy, and the fisheries, and strong enough to engage in all types of work.

The girls sent from France by the king and the marriages they contracted with the soldiers who have voluntarily chosen to settle in the colony have so greatly increased the number of settlers that when taking the census in 1671 I found by the birth certificates that seven hundred children had been born in that year. At present I have reason to believe that one hundred marriages between young men and girls born in the colony are possible annually. . . .

His Majesty further intended that the settlers of his colony of New France should enjoy the felicity of his reign to the same degree as his subjects of the old; that the Antilles, in the southern part of America, should be supported by the northern part, which can produce clothing and the necessities of life of which the southern part finds itself deprived by its exposure to the sun and a tropical climate; that stationary fisheries be established, so that the kingdom may not only do without the fish it buys from foreign countries for considerable sums, but also send to the Levant the dried fish that is consumed there in great quantities. The better part of this fish is presently supplied by the colony of Boston and caught off the coast of Acadia which belongs to His Majesty. [Boston] pays a tribute of fifty *livres* per launch in recognition of this proprietary right, which the Governor [of Acadia] at Pentagouet [on the Penobscot River] collects or ought to collect.

He also had in view the support of his navy with the wood that grows in Canada, the iron that could be discovered there, the tar that could be manufactured, and the hemp that could be grown for the making of ships' riggings. With these four products, he would no longer have to obtain from the princes of the Baltic, with an appearance of dependence, what is necessary to sustain his navy, which is such an important element of his glory and of his state's support.

In all this Canada seems to have responded well enough to the hopes of His Majesty. Hemp is being cultivated with success, cloth is being woven, cable and rope are being produced. The tar which has been manufactured has been tested both here and in France and found to be as good as that drawn from the north. Iron has been discovered, which master forgers consider to be suitable for all purposes. Vessels, which have now been sailing for six years, have been built for individuals who opened up the trade of Canada with the islands. At present there is one of 450 tons and forty-two guns being built for the king, which will put to sea next summer, and there is almost enough material in the yards for another. Before leaving, I established two workshops. During the present winter the first, of twenty-eight men, should produce 1,000 to 1,200 pieces of lumber suitable for the construction of a vessel of 600 to 700 tons, of which His Majesty has seen the model; from the labors of the second, we may hope for 25,000 to 30,000 feet of sheathing. . . .

Stationary fisheries, which are so useful since dried cod is consumed almost everywhere in Europe, have been started before my departure by the younger sr. Denis, who settled at Percé Island; by the sr. Marson, an infantry lieutenant, and the *chevalier de* Grandfontaine, who left with his family fifteen days before my departure to settle on the St. John River; and by the sr. Martinon, an old settler of Acadia, who went to live on the shores of that river.

These beginnings can be supported and increased by the company we propose to establish according to the plans submitted to M. Colbert. . . .

Opening a trade between Canada and the Antilles is no longer considered a difficult thing. It was done by me in 1668 with a vessel built in Canada which successfully carried a cargo of this country's products. From there it sailed to Old France with a load of sugar and then returned to the New with the products of the kingdom of which this country stands in need. Every year since, as a result of this example, this commerce has been carried out by two or more vessels. . . .

This commerce is made up of the excess quantities of peas, salmon, salted eels, green and dried cod, planks and cask wood, and will be increased by excess wheat which will be converted into flour. It is estimated that Canada could export 30,000 *minots* each year if the crops are not ruined by bad weather. Peas could amount to 10,000 *minots*, and salted beef and pork will not in the future make up the smaller portion of this trade. Sales in the islands being favorable, I expect that Canada could soon supply pork, since it now does without that of France from which it formerly drew up to 1,200 barrels annually. The inhabitants of Port Royal in Acadia could supply salted beef. I obtained sixty quintals at twenty-two *deniers* a pound from there two years ago, which was as good as that of Ireland.

Beer could also profitably enter into this trade. I can guarantee 2,000 barrels a year for the islands and more if the consumption is greater, without altering the supply to the colonists of New France. It is by these methods that His Majesty will succeed in his aim of destroying the trade of the Dutch with our islands, without depriving his subjects residing there of the support they derived from it.

With all these provisions, which Canada will be able to supply in proportionately greater quantities as she develops, the islands will be provided with the necessities of life and will only lack a few accessories like spices, olive oil, wine, and salt. There is even the possibility of establishing salt works in Acadia if the king judges that it would not be prejudicial to Old France to make this new colony self-sufficient in this respect and to enable it to provide by itself for all its needs. I say all its needs not even excluding clothing which, we may hope, will be manufactured not only for the

Canadians but in a few years for the islanders as well. For crafts have already been established for the fabrication of cloth, linen, and shoes; we already have enough leather to manufacture on the average 8,000 pairs of shoes annually; we will have as much hemp as we will care to grow; and the sheep which His Majesty sent have bred very well and will provide the material for the sheets and other cloths which we have begun to weave.

And all these things taken together will form the essence of a trade that will be useful to all His Majesty's subjects and will make for the happiness of those of New France. Thanks to the king's care and support, they live in peace and no longer suffer from those pressing needs which they felt for almost everything when his troops first landed in the colony.

Potash, which has successfully undergone a series of tests, can be used to wash linen or can be converted into a soft soap for bleaching or for cleaning silks and sheets. It can be produced in Canada in sufficient quantities to enable Paris to do without Spanish sodium, on which it spends a considerable sum. It could also enable Douay, Lille, Tournay, Courtrai, and other cities in Flanders and even in France where cloth is bleached to dispense with the potash of Muscovy and Poland, which increases the trade of the Dutch who accept this product in partial exchange for the beaver and spices they trade in those countries.

Potash should be received all the more favorably in Paris since all laundrywomen know very well that Spanish sodium is very acrid and wears out the cloth, something which potash does not do. . . .

Such, approximately, are the results of His Majesty's first attempt to make of a country that is crude, savage, and pagan the commencements of a province, and perhaps of a kingdom, that is refined, happy, and Christian.

13. The Discovery of the Mississippi, 1673

WHILE WORKING to develop the Canadian economy, Jean Talon also organized several voyages of discovery and exploration which pushed back the frontiers of New France. Of these the most important was the one undertaken in 1673–74 by the Canadian-born Louis Jolliet (1645–1700) and the Jesuit Jacques Marquette (1637–1675), for it resulted in the discovery of the Mississippi River and opened the vast regions of the southwest to French commerce and influence. The following document is extracted from the account of the discovery written at Quebec in 1674 by Father Jacques Dablon, the superior of the Jesuits. It is based on information which Jolliet was forced to supply from memory, all his notes and maps having been lost when the canoe in which he was returning to Canada capsized in the Lachine Rapids near Montreal.

Further Reading: J. Delanglez, Life and Voyages of Louis Jolliet (Chicago, 1948); E. B. Osler, La Salle (Toronto, 1967); J. P. Donnelly, Jacques Marquette (Chicago, 1968).

SOURCE: Thwaites (ed. and trans.), The Jesuit Relations and Allied Documents, LVIII, 93–101.

Relation of the Discovery of Many Countries Situated to the South of New France, Made in 1673

[Quebec, August 1, 1674]

Two years ago, Monsieur the count de Frontenac, our governor, and Monsieur Talon, then our intendant, decided that it was important to undertake the discovery of the Southern Sea, after having accomplished that of the Northern; and, above all, to ascertain into what sea falls the great river, about which the Savages relate so much, and which is 500 leagues from them, beyond the Outaouacs.

For this purpose, they could not have selected a person endowed with better qualities than is sieur Jolliet, who has traveled much in that region, and has acquitted himself in this task with all the ability that could be desired.

On arriving in the Outaouac country, he joined father Marquette, who awaited him for that voyage, and who had long premeditated that undertaking, for they had frequently agreed upon it together. They set out, accordingly, with five other Frenchmen, about the beginning of June, 1673, to enter countries wherein no European had ever set foot.

Their journal stated that—leaving the Bay des Puans,[1] at the latitude of 43 degrees and 40 minutes—at first they voyaged for nearly 60 leagues upon a small river, very smooth and pleasant, running in a west-southwesterly direction. They found a portage which would enable them, by going half a league, to pass from that

1 Green Bay.

river to another, which flowed from the northwest. Upon that stream they embarked, and, after going 40 leagues to the southwest, they found themselves, on the 15th of June, at 42 and one-half degrees of latitude, and successfully entered that famous river called by the Savages Mississipi,—as one might say, "the Great River," because it is, in fact, the most important of all the rivers in this country. It comes from a great distance northward, according to the savages. It is a noble stream, and is usually a quarter of a league wide. Its width is still greater at the places where it is interrupted by islands—which, however, are very few. Its depth is as much as ten brasses of water; and it flows very gently, until it receives the discharge of another great river,[2] which comes from the west and northwest, at about the 38th degree of latitude. Then, swollen with that volume of water, it becomes very rapid; and its current has so much force that, in ascending it, only four or five leagues a day can be accomplished, by paddling from morning to night.

There are forests on both sides, as far as the sea. The most vigorous trees that one sees there are a species of cotton-tree, of extraordinary girth and height. The savages therefore use these trees for making canoes,—all of one piece, fifty feet in length and three in width, in which thirty men with all their baggage can embark. They make them of much more graceful shape than we do ours. They have so great a number of them that in a single village one sees as many as 280 together.

The nations are located near the Great River, or farther inland. Our travelers counted more than 40 villages, most of which consisted of 60 to 80 cabins. Some villages even contained 300 cabins, such as that of the Illinois, which contains over 8,000 souls. All of the Savages who compose it seem to have a gentle nature; they are affable and obliging. Our Frenchmen experienced the effects of this civility at the first village that they entered, for there a present was made them—a pipe-stem for smoking, about three feet long, adorned with feathers of various kinds. This gift has almost a religious meaning among these peoples; because the calumet is, as it were, a passport and safeguard to enable one to go in safety everywhere, no one daring to injure in any manner those who bear this caduceus. . . .

The soil is so fertile that it yields corn three times a year. It produces, naturally, fruits which are unknown to us and are excel-

2 The Missouri River.

lent. Grapes, plums, apples, mulberries, chestnuts, pomegranates, and many others are gathered everywhere, and almost at all times, for winter is only known there by the rains.

The country is equally divided into prairies and forests, and provides fine pastures for the great number of animals with which it abounds. The wild cattle never flee. The Father counted as many as 400 of them in a single herd. Stags, does, and deer are almost everywhere. Turkeys strut about, on all sides. Parroquets fly in flocks of 10 to 12; and quail rise on the prairies at every moment.

Through the midst of this fine country our travelers passed, advancing upon the Great River to the 33rd degree of latitude, and going almost always toward the south. From time to time, they met Savages, by whom they were very well received, through favor of their caduceus or calumet-stem. Toward the end, they learned from the Savages that they were approaching European settlements; that they were only three days, and finally only two days distant from these; that the Europeans were on the left hand; and that they had to proceed but 50 leagues farther, to reach the sea. Then the Father and sieur Jolliet deliberated as to what they should do,—that is, if it were advisable to go on. They felt certain that, if they advanced farther, they would fling themselves into the hands of the Spaniards of Florida, and would expose the French who accompanied them to the manifest danger of losing their lives. Moreover, they would lose the results of their voyage, and could not give any information regarding it, if they were detained as prisoners—as they probably would be, if they fell into the hands of Europeans.

These reasons made them resolve to retrace their steps, after having obtained full information about everything that could be desired on such an occasion. They did not return by exactly the same route; at the end of November, they reached the bay des Puans, by different routes from the former one, and with no other guide than their compasses.

14. The Expansion of the Fur Trade

In the mid-1670's a number of factors combined to undermine the economic system which Colbert and Talon had begun and to turn Canada into a vast fur trading empire. This, in turn, caused a sharp increase in the number of coureurs de bois, Frenchmen who deserted the colony for the west in order to trade with the Indians. The following description of the life of the coureur de bois is taken from a long memoir on the fur trade written in 1705 by Denis Riverin (1650–1717). Riverin had come to Canada in the 1670's and soon become one of the colony's leading citizens. He was keenly interested in economic questions and his numerous memoirs on the fur trade are among the best of the period.

Further Reading: C. W. Alvord, The Illinois Country, 1673–1818 (Springfield, Ill., 1920) and L. P. Kellogg, The French Regime in Wisconsin and the Northwest (Madison, Wis., 1925) are basic accounts of French activities in the west. Also, H. A. Innis, The Fur Trade in Canada (Toronto, 1956); A. L. Burt, "The Frontier in the History of New France," Canadian Historical Association Report (1940), pp. 93–99.

SOURCE: Denis Riverin, Historical Memoir to My Lord the Comte de Pontchartrain on the Harmful Results of Having Placed All the Beaver in the Same Hand, December 12, 1705, Archives nationales, colonies (Paris), série C¹¹A, vol. 22, ff. 362–364. Translated by the editor.

Coureurs de bois are Frenchmen who were either born in Canada or who came to settle there. They are always young men in the prime of life, for old age cannot endure the hardships of this occupation. Some are of good social standing, others are merely habitants or sons of habitants; others, finally, have no occupation and are called volunteers. The profit motive is common to all men.

Some take their own merchandise to the savages and others borrow it from merchants; some are salaried employees and others form partnerships with the merchants.

Since all of Canada is a vast and trackless forest, it is impossible for them to travel by land; they travel by lake and river in canoes ordinarily occupied by three men. These are made of birchbark drawn tautly over a frame of very thin and light cedarwood. In structure they are almost similar to the gondolas of Venice. They are divided into six, seven, or eight places by light wooden crossbars that serve to support the sides and bind them together. These bars are longest at the middle and become shorter as they near the extremities, where the sides come together. Since a canoe cannot be made from a single sheet of bark, several pieces are sown together with pine roots more flexible and lighter than willow. To prevent leaks, the seams are coated with a gum which the Indians extract from pine trees. The Indians, and particularly their wives, are excellent canoe makers; few Frenchmen are successful. These canoes used to cost only twenty *écus*, but since [the French began] to roam the woods their value has risen to as high as four hundred *livres*.

The *coureurs de bois* themselves conduct their canoes using small paddles made of hard, light wood. The man in the stern steers—this is the skill of the trade—the two in front paddle. The strongest are the ones who advance most speedily. A canoe skillfully manned can cover fifteen *lieues* in one day in still waters and more when moving with the current. Progress is slow going upstream and still slower in swift waters and rapids, which can only be crossed by pushing on poles as do the boatmen on the Loire River. When impassable cascades or waterfalls are encountered the men put ashore, unload the bundles, which are of a size and weight to be carried, and transport them with the canoe on their backs and shoulders through the forest for a quarter, a half, or a full *lieue*, and sometimes two or three, until the cascades are left behind and the water once more becomes navigable. This is called a portage. It is not only necessary to get around rapids but also to move from lake to lake and river to river in order to reach one's destination.

A favorable wind is a great help for the canoemen, who can then hoist the sail that is carried in each craft. In the evening, when they put ashore to eat and rest, the sail becomes a tent. This is called *cabaner*[1] because a hut is built with branches, poles, and this sail, which shelters the travelers at night or when contrary winds oblige them to stop for a few days.

It is in such a canoe that these three men embark at Quebec or Montreal to go three hundred, four hundred, and sometimes five hundred *lieues* to search for beaver among Indians whom they have frequently never seen. Their entire provisions consist of a little biscuit, peas, corn, and a few small casks of brandy. They carry as little as possible in order to make room for a few bundles of merchandise and are soon obliged to live from hunting and fishing. For this reason, they always take along good guns, powder, shot, and small nets. If fish and game are scarce, as frequently happens, they are obliged to eat a sort of moss, which they call *tripe*, that grows on rocks. With it they make a broth that is black and loathsome

1 *Cabaner:* from the word *cabane*, meaning hut.

but which they would rather eat than die of starvation. If they have nothing to eat on their return journey or on their travels from one tribe to another they will resort to their moccasins or to a glue they make from the skins they have bartered.

Each canoe carries merchandise valued at approximately 3,500 *livres* in Canada, which means that it costs less than 1,500 *livres* in France. Beaver pelts worth close to 7,000 *livres* were obtained in exchange when prices were higher than they are now and when there were less *coureurs de bois*.

These *coureurs de bois* will frequently commit a thousand base actions to obtain beaver from the Indians. They follow them to their hunting grounds and do not even give them the time to dry and cure their skins. They endure the jeers, the scorn, and sometimes the blows of the Indians, who are constantly amazed by such a sordid display of greed and by Frenchmen who come from so far away at the cost of great hardship and expense to pick up dirty, stinking beaver pelts which they have worn and have discarded.

Since little time is required to carry out this trade, the life of the *coureurs de bois* is spent in idleness and dissolute living. They sleep, smoke, drink brandy whatever its cost, gamble, and debauch the wives and daughters of the Indians. They commit a thousand contemptible deeds. Gambling, drinking, and women often consume all their capital and the profits of their voyages. They live in complete independence and account to no one for their actions. They acknowledge no superior, no judge, no law, no police, no subordination. . . .

15. The Royal Régime in Acadia, 1686

THE COLONY of Acadia on the Atlantic seaboard was far more richly endowed than Canada with natural resources. There were furs north of the Bay of Fundy, excellent harbors on the Atlantic, the world's finest fisheries a short distance away, good farmland, timber, and coal. Yet the colony was neglected by France and soon fell under the influence of nearby New England. In 1685 Jacques de Meulles, intendant of Canada, inspected Acadia and urged the adoption of measures to bring this valuable territory under effective French control. The following extract has been taken from his report of 1686 to Louis XIV.

Further Reading: E. Lauvrière, La Tragédie d'un peuple: histoire du peuple acadien de ses origines à nos jours (*2 vols., Paris, 1924*); E. Rameau de Saint-Père, Une Colonie Féodale en Amérique: l'Acadie (*1604–1881*) (*2 vols., Paris, 1889*).

SOURCE: [Jacques de Meulles], Memoir of 1686 on What Can Be Done in Acadia, Archives nationales, colonies (Paris), série C^{11}D, vol. 2, pp. 72–82 [pagination of the transcripts of the Public Archives of Canada]. Translated by the editor.

In order to succeed in establishing Acadia it would be necessary to build a city of some consequence at Port Royal and a fort at Pentagouet [the Penobscot River] to serve as a barrier against the English and confine them within their boundaries. [Port Royal] would be a secure harbor for the French vessels that come and go along that coast and for those that cruise there by order of Your Majesty. In a very short time respectable families and powerful merchants would settle there, who would trade to all parts of the world with the codfish that would be theirs in great quantity. A large settlement and a store would also be required at La Have. The harbor there is magnificent; it can shelter more than fifteen hundred vessels at any given time. Two similar establishments would also be required at Cape Breton Island and Percé. By making the fisheries free, by fixing the price of fish at six, seven, or eight *livres* per quintal, and by restricting the sale of this fish to the stores above mentioned, fishermen would soon flock there from everywhere. Fine villages and even cities would spring up in less than ten years and a great number of sailors would become available, who could render important services to Your Majesty. . . .

It is certain that the subjects of Your Majesty in that continent, supported by your resources and your authority, would make before long a very beautiful and very rich country and one most becoming to France, which would certainly always profit from it. This land would provide France with an outlet for her wines, spirits, and other products. Codfish will never be found off the French coast and Canada will never produce wine and spirits. France and Acadia seem to have been created for each other.

Your Majesty would derive two considerable advantages from that continent: the sole control of the beaver trade by destroying the Iroquois and of the codfisheries by the establishment of Acadia.

Cod is traded in all parts of the world and may someday become one of the Crown's greatest sources of revenue. At first some money would have to be spent, but we can be sure that it would produce its hundredfold in a short time. . . .

Boston, which is one hundred *lieues* from Port Royal, has become important over the past twenty years as a result of the codfisheries in which its inhabitants engage off shores that belong to Your Majesty. That city is as beautiful and powerful as La Rochelle. The inhabitants of Salem, which is only five *lieues* from Boston, are so eager to fish that they already own eighty boats which make two or three annual voyages to the area of Port Royal. Once they have their quota of cod, they carry it back to Salem to dry it. These fishing operations could be carried out much more readily by Frenchmen settled in Acadia. The English of Salem have to travel nearly one hundred *lieues*, while the French, being settled in the vicinity of these shores, would find many more conveniences to salt and dry their catch. . . .

Acadia presently amounts to very little, for France neither supports nor maintains it. As a result of frequent contacts and transactions with the English and of the devastation wrought by the corsairs who often raid this coast and plunder the inhabitants whenever they have undertaken something, the latter have abandoned these shores to settle in the vicinity of Boston. I speak from knowledge, for I know of many families who had made some constructions which they used for fishing and who were plundered in 1683. . . . Most of those who have withdrawn among the English would certainly return if they thought they could find security at Port Royal and on the Acadian coast. During my journey I assured the people who are settled there that Your Majesty would look after them and that you had surely not been informed of all these things. The inclination the people of Acadia feel for the English is excusable, for they receive almost no news and no help whatever from France. The English alone bring them their annual supplies. Three or four English barks come every spring with everything they need and receive peltries and other goods in exchange. . . .

At Minas, the St. John River, and Port Royal I saw Englishmen who were trading and carrying away all the fruits of this country. They will always do so unless there is a change. Others can be found along the entire length of the Acadian coast, particularly where there are French settlements. Some even put up scaffolds to dry their fish and small houses to be more at their ease. They have even built large stores at Port Royal where they keep shop, a practice I did not forbid, not having received Your Majesty's orders. The English will keep Acadia in misery, for they will prevent Frenchmen who would deprive them of their annual profit from settling there. These same English, however, do not tolerate that we trade in their colonies, particularly not at Boston, where the receipt of French merchandise has been prohibited. This leads me to believe that we should retaliate and forbid all Frenchmen, whatever their condition and their rank, from trading directly or indirectly with foreigners, under pain of very severe penalties. This is already practiced in Canada as a result of orders sent there by Your Majesty two years ago, but such orders in Acadia presuppose the establishment of that colony.

The last remark one can make to Your Majesty on this subject is that if France should one day make war with England, Canada being inland, the English of this continent would find it very easy to make themselves the masters of the St. Lawrence and to reduce in two or three months a colony which represents the labor of many years. The fear of devastation might even induce the French to surrender voluntarily to England and to adopt her customs and religion. But by making establishments with good seaports on the Acadian coast and at Port Royal it would be easy for France completely to destroy Boston and the other English settlements, thereby augmenting the Catholic, Apostolic, and Roman religion and making it flourish in all North America. . . .

III

Intercolonial Rivalry, 1682–1713

16. Conflict on Hudson Bay, 1680's

HUDSON BAY was the earliest scene of Anglo-French rivalry in North America. From 1682 to 1700, the Hudson Bay Company and the Canadian-based compagnie du Nord battled for control of the rich northern fur trade. At times it appeared possible that the French company would succeed in driving its British rival from the Bay, but a weak corporate structure and long and costly lines of communication finally caused its downfall. The following reading has been taken from an anonymous memoir addressed to the marquis de Seignelay, French minister of marine from 1683 to 1690. In it spokesmen for the compagnie du Nord describe their difficulties with the English and ask for royal protection.

Further Reading: E. E. Rich, The History of the Hudson's Bay Company, 1670–1870 (2 vols., London, 1958–59), I, 1670–1763; G. Frégault, Iberville le Conquérant (Montreal, 1944).

SOURCE: Memoir to My Lord the Marquis de Seignelay on the Affairs of the Bay of the North in Canada, collated at Quebec on November 12, 1712, by Governor Vaudreuil and Intendant Bégon, Rapport de l'Archiviste de la Province de Québec, 1947–1948 (Quebec, Imprimeur du Roi, n.d.), pp. 189–192. Translated by the editor.

At first the French did not oppose the English whom des Groseilliers and Radisson had led to Hudson Bay,[1] because for

1 In 1670 a group of prominent London businessmen, influential courtiers, and members of the Royal Society founded the English Hudson Bay Company. They had been interested in the possibilities of the northern fur trade by two French renegades, Pierre Esprit Radisson and Médard Chouart des Groseilliers.

many years they had no knowledge of this enterprise. But as soon as they became aware of it, they sent their memoirs to my lord Colbert on the importance of this encroachment and on the necessity of evicting these Englishmen. The close union then existing between the [French] king and His Britannic Majesty prevented a decision from being taken on these memoirs. On May 15, 1678, my lord Colbert simply wrote to M. Duchesneau, at that time intendant of Canada, that it would be advantageous to the king's service to contest the ownership of Hudson Bay to the English, who claimed possession of it although it was part of the lands under the dominion of the French Crown. But the colony of Canada had gradually become considerable and its inhabitants, who were increasing in numbers every day, considered that the English usurpation of the bay would totally ruin their commerce, since the Indians would find it easy to take their peltries there by the system of lakes and rivers that discharge into it. In 1682, the said inhabitants formed a company to support their trade in the bay of the north. For this purpose they equipped two small vessels and gave command of them to des Groseilliers and Radisson. His Majesty at that time had pardoned their treason and allowed them to return to Canada. They arrived at the bay without mishap and took possession of a river which they called Bourbon or Ste. Thérèse [the Nelson River], where they built a store and fort and began to trade with the Indians they found there. . . .

Groseilliers and Radisson returned to Quebec . . . and still dissatisfied and full of mischief, went to France. My lord Preston, then on a mission to France from England, was advised of this and persuaded his servant, Gaudet, by promising to have him appointed permanent secretary of the English Embassy, to entice Radisson from the French service. This is what Gaudet did. The better to seduce Radisson he promised to give him his daughter in marriage, and they were in fact married in London.[2] A short time later, Radisson gave memoirs to the English concerning the French establishments on the Bourbon River and promised to make them the masters of it. . . . He left London, arrived at the said river, and surprised the Frenchmen guarding this post, all the more easily because they could not guess that he came as an enemy and that

2 Margaret Charlotte Gaudet was Radisson's second wife. They were married in 1685.

the sr. Chouard, their commander, was Groseilliers's son and Radisson's nephew.

While this was taking place, a small vessel sent by the inhabitants of Quebec to continue the trade at the Bourbon River arrived. The crew were very surprised to learn of Radisson's treachery and of the loss of the French establishment, which was worth more than 400,000 *livres*, at which price were estimated 32,000 beaver pelts, six bales of marten, two bales of otter, merchandise, tools, provisions, and ammunition.

This news spread dismay among the inhabitants of Quebec and they decided to avenge themselves on the English. This appeared all the easier since it is only 150 *lieues* by land from Quebec to the bottom of the bay [James Bay], and there was a system of lakes and rivers to facilitate the execution of their design. Thus, when His Majesty conceded the Bourbon River to the inhabitants by an edict of his council of May 20, 1685, a considerable company was formed at Quebec, which resolved to spare nothing to inflict reprisals on the English and to drive them from a country which only the treason of Frenchmen corrupted by money and other means had enabled them to usurp.

In March, 1686, this company equipped from ninety to one hundred men with everything necessary for this expedition. Traveling by lake and river, they reached the bottom of the bay of the north, where they attacked the three forts the English had built after being led there by Groseilliers and Radisson with such spirit that they captured each one. They seized everything they found inside, as well as one hundred fifty Englishmen on duty whom they provided with a small ship and provisions, enabling them to retire where they pleased.

The inhabitants would have reason to be happy with this expedition if the booty taken from the English had been equal to the value of the losses suffered at the Bourbon River. But the three forts only yielded 50,000 *livres* of peltry, 20,000 *livres* of merchandise, plus approximately 20,000 *livres* in equipment, cannons, and barks, which was barely enough to cover the costs of the expedition. Thus, they are far from having recovered the 400,000 *livres* plundered by the English at the Bourbon River the preceding year.

This, my lord, is what the inhabitants humbly represent. They respectfully beseech Your Highness to grant them your protection by compelling the English to surrender not only the 400,000 *livres* of booty taken at the Bourbon River by Radisson's treachery but also the property of the said river in the state in which it was when they settled there; [also] to make His Majesty issue orders for the Quebec company to remain in possession of the three posts taken from the English in 1686 . . . not only because Frenchmen discovered these posts and took possession of them but also because the English only went there by Radisson's treachery, which gives them no proprietary rights.

The said company of Quebec needs the protection of Your Highness all the more since it has exhausted itself by the great expenditures it has been obliged to incur to support the rights of His Majesty to the bay of the north, which would have been lost entirely without the great efforts it made for its preservation.

It also humbly beseeches Your Highness to consider the importance of this bay which, being at the center of the colony of Canada, can draw all the beavers of the Ottawa [Indians] by the lakes and rivers that discharge into it. This beaver cannot fall into English hands without causing Canada's total ruin.

If on the contrary it pleases Your Highness to grant your protection to the company, the colony will become the mistress of all the beavers, and all the nations of Europe which engage in this trade will be obliged to turn to it. This will considerably increase the commerce of His Majesty and the [royal] duties.

17. The Second Iroquois War

WHILE THE FRENCH were attempting to conquer Hudson Bay they also had to stave off a formidable challenge by the Iroquois to win control of the western fur trade. War with the Five Nations having become inevitable by 1682, the new governor, Le Febvre de La Barre, summoned an assembly of Canadian notables to consult with them before formulating a policy. The opinion expressed by this assembly is given in Document A.

The Iroquois war culminated during the second administration of Governor Frontenac (1689–1698). Although he has been traditionally portrayed as the savior of New France, critical reassessment of the evidence has shown that Frontenac was in fact an inferior military leader. His failure to prosecute the war against the Iroquois vigorously, alienated the western allies and almost resulted in the isolation of the colony by the mid-1690's. This situation is described in Document B, which is an abstract of several Canadian dispatches prepared by a clerk of the ministry of marine. Only in 1696 did Frontenac finally launch the great expedition against the Iroquois cantons that broke the back of the Five Nations.

Further Reading: W. J. Eccles, Frontenac, The Courtier Governor (Toronto, 1959); F. Parkman, Count Frontenac and New France Under Louis XIV (Boston, 1884).

SOURCES: Document A: O'Callaghan (ed.), Documents Relative to the Colonial History of the State of New York, IX, 194–195. Document B: Ibid., 633.

A. State of Affairs with the Iroquois, 1682

It is proposed by the Governor that it is easy to infer, from the records Count de Frontenac was pleased to deposit in his hands of what had passed at Montreal on the 12 Sept. last between him and the Iroquois Deputy from Onontagué,[1] that these people are inclined to follow the object of their enterprize, which is to destroy all the Nations in alliance with us, one after the other, whilst they keep us in uncertainty and with folded arms; so that, after having deprived us of the entire fur trade, which they wish to carry on alone with the English and Dutch established at Manate and Orange, they may attack us isolated, and ruin the Colony in obliging it to contract itself and abandon all the detached settlements, and thus arrest the cultivation of the soil, which cannot bear grain nor hay except in quarters where it is of good quality.

As he is not informed in the short time since his arrival from France of the state of these tribes and of the Colony, he requests the gentlemen to acquaint him with all they know of these things, that he may inform his Majesty thereof, and represent the necessities of this Colony, for the purpose as well of averting this war as of terminating and finishing it advantageously, should it be necessary to wage it. Whereupon the Meeting, after being informed by the Rev[d] Jesuit fathers of what had passed during five years among the Iroquois Nations, whence they had recently arrived, and by M. Dollier of what had occurred for some years at Montreal, remained unanimously and all of one accord, that the English have omitted nothing for four years to induce the Iroquois, either by a great

1 Onontagué is the French for Onondaga.

number of presents or by the cheapness of provisions, and especially of guns, powder and lead, to declare war against us, and that the Iroquois have been two or three times ready to commence hostilities; but that having reflected that, should they attack us before they had ruined in fact the allied nations and their neighbors, those would rally, and, uniting together, fall on and destroy their villages whilst they were occupied against us, they judged it wiser to defer, and to amuse us whilst they were attacking those Nations; and having commenced operations, with that view, against the Ilinois last year, they had so great an advantage over them that, besides three or four hundred killed, they took nine hundred prisoners; therefore, should they march this year with a corps of twelve hundred well armed and good warriors, there was no doubt but they would exterminate the Illinois altogether, and attack, on their return, the Miamis and the Kiskakons, and by their defeat render themselves masters of Missilimackina[2] and the Lakes Hérié and Huron, the Bay des Puans, and thereby deprive us of all the trade drawn from that country, by destroying at the same time all the Christian Missions established among those Nations; and therefore it became necessary to make a last effort to prevent them ruining those Nations, as they had formerly the Algonquins, the Andastez, the Loups (Mohegans), the Abenaquis and others, whose remains are dispersed among us at the settlements of Sillery, Laurette, Lake Champlain and elsewhere. . . .

. . . That it is a war which is not to be commenced to be left unfinished, because knowing each other better than seventeen years ago, if it were to be undertaken without completing it, the conservation of the Colony is not to be expected, the Iroquois not being apt to retreat. That the failure of all aid from France had begun to create contempt for us among the said Iroquois, who believed that we were abandoned by the great Onontio, our Master; and if they saw us assisted by him, they would probably change their minds and let our allies be in peace, and consent not to hunt on their grounds, nor bring to the French all the peltries they trade at present with the English at Orange; and thus, by a small aid from his Majesty, we could prevent war and subjugate these fierce and hot spirits, which would be the greatest advantage

2 Missilimackina, or Michilimackinac, at the junction of Lakes Huron and Michigan, was the most important military and trading station held by New France in the western country.

that could be procured for the Country. That, meanwhile, it was important to arm the militia, and in this year of abundant harvest to oblige them to furnish themselves with guns, in order to be put to a good use when occasion required.

B. *State of Affairs with the Iroquois, 1695*

The perpetual deputations of the Iroquois to Mr de Frontenac on the subject of peace which he believed they sincerely desired, kept every thing between the French and them somewhat in suspense and left him in a state of incertitude until the month of October 1694. These negotiations have been continued until the commencement of April 1695, by a final embassy from the Iroquois who, a few days afterwards, recommenced [war] with more cruelty than ever.

These divers parties who came against the Colony have killed a number of persons, and inhumanly massacred and burnt those of whatever age or sex that fell into their hands.

The Iroquois under the direction of the English of New-York, and under favor of those negotiations, which had been preceded by some damages they had received from the war the French had been waging against them, had hunted and raised some provisions wherewith to procure ammunitions and arms; and unknown to and without the participation of the French, were at the same time taking advantage among the Upper Nations, our allies, of the prospect of the peace which was negotiating between the Iroquois and Count de Frontenac. The effect of this was, that the Nations tired of carrying on the war alone, whilst they beheld the French treating of peace with the Iroquois, were apprehensive that it would be concluded and that they would eventually, be left to carry on hostilities alone. Previous to the departure of the vessels, just returned from Quebec, Mr de la Mothe Cadillac, the Commandant at Michilimakinac had sent an express to give notice that the Hurons were in treaty with the Iroquois; that the Outtawas were shaken for the same reason; that two other Nations called the Foxes and Mascoutens, mustering 1200 warriors that had never opposed the French, were, also, designing to join the Iroquois, and to go and settle near them to protect themselves from the Sioux, (another Nation, at a greater distance from the French trade,) who had declared, and made war on them last year, so that no hope could remain of averting this storm from the union of all those Nations of the Continent except by some considerable enterprise against the Iroquois in order to retain the Upper Indians, whose obedience can be expected to be preserved only so long as the French will be the strongest, and those Indians will continue under the impression that we can prevent their destruction by the Iroquois. Wherefore, all efforts must be directed to this point, and to the retrenching as much as possible the expense in the Upper Country, in order to diminish, at the same time, the beaver trade of the French among the more distant nations among whom they have spread themselves.[3]

18. A Plan to Conquer New York, 1689

To WAGE war on New France, the Iroquois were dependent on the arms and ammunition supplied by the English and Dutch traders of Albany. For this reason, many Canadian officials felt that the destruction of Albany or the conquest of New York would soon bring the Iroquois to their knees. In January, 1689, Hector de Callières, governor of Montreal from 1684 to 1698 and governor-general of New France from 1699 until his death in 1703, drew up plans for land and sea operations against New York which he presented to the French court. Louis XIV approved the project, but delays caused by European commitments prevented its execution.

SOURCE: Callières to Seignelay, January, 1689, in O'Callaghan (ed.), Documents Relative to the Colonial History of the State of New York, IX, 404–407.

To MY LORD, THE MARQUIS OF SEIGNELAY

As the recent Revolution in England will change the face of American affairs, it becomes necessary to adopt entirely new measures to secure Canada against the great dangers with which it is threatened. . . .

3 This trade was being carried out largely by Frontenac agents sent into the west under pretext of military necessity. It seriously injured the economic interests of the Ottawa Indians, New France's principal allies, who had hitherto acted as middlemen between the distant tribes and the French.

Chevalier Andros, as well as the whole English Colony, is protestant, so that there is no reason to hope that he will remain faithful to the King of England,[1] and we must expect that he will not only urge the Iroquois to continue the war against us but he will even furnish them with Englishmen to lead them and to seize Niagara, Michilimakinak and other posts proper to render him master of all the Indians our allies, according to the project they have long since formed, and which they began to execute when we declared war against the Iroquois and captured 70 Englishmen who were going to take possession of Michilimakinak, one of the most important posts of Canada; our entrepôt for the Fur Trade and the residence of the Superior of the Reverend Jesuit Fathers who are Missionaries among our Indians, and which belongs, incontestably, to us.

It is to be expected then, that they are about to endeavor to invest the entire of Canada and raise all the Savages against us, in order to wholly deprive us of every sort of Trade and draw it all to themselves by means of the cheap bargains they can give of goods, at nearly at one-half the price our Frenchmen can afford theirs, for reasons to be elsewhere explained, and thus become masters of all the peltries; the trade wherein sustains Canada and constitutes one of the chief benefits that France derives from that Colony.

No sooner will the English have ruined our Indian Trade than, uniting with those Savages, they will be in a position to fall on us, burn and sack our settlements, scattered along the River St. Lawrence as far as Quebec, without our being able to prevent them, having no fortress capable of arresting them.

Things being thus disposed, the only means to avoid these misfortunes is to anticipate them by the expedition to be hereafter explained and which I offer to execute forthwith, if it please His Majesty to confide its direction to me on account of the particular knowledge I have acquired of the affairs of that country during five years that I had the honor to serve His Majesty and to command his troops and Military there, after twenty years' service in the army.

The plan is, to go straight to Orange, the frontier town of New-York, one hundred leagues from Montreal, which I would undertake to carry; and to proceed thence to seize Manathe, the capital of that Colony situated on the sea coast; on condition of being

1 James II.

furnished with supplies necessary for the success of such an expedition. . . .[2]

After we became masters of the town and fort of Manathe I should cause the Inhabitants to be disarmed, and send my Canadians back by the Albany river to Orange on the way to their bateaux and home. I should winter at Manathe with all the troops I would have brought with me except the 200 soldiers left to guard Orange; and as I should have nothing to fear from the land side, being master of the rivers, I would employ the winter in strengthening my position against attacks of the English whilst waiting until His Majesty be pleased to send what may be necessary to secure this important conquest.

It will render His Majesty absolute master of all the Iroquois who derive from that Colony whatever arms and ammunition they have to make war on us, afford us the means to disarm them whenever considered necessary, and thereby to impose on them such laws as His Majesty may please; the town of Boston, the capital of New England being too far from them to derive any aid from it.

Having mastered the Iroquois we shall have equal control of all the other Savages who will come without hesitation and bring us all their peltries. This will cause the trade of our Colony to flourish; considerably augment His Majesty's revenues and eventually diminish the expenses he is obliged to incur for the preservation of Canada.

It will firmly establish the Christian Religion as well among the Iroquois as among the other Savages to whom we shall be able to speak as masters when they are surrounded both on the side of Canada and of New-York.

It will secure and facilitate the Cod fishery which is carried on along our coasts of la Cadie [Acadia] and on the Great Bank.

It will give His Majesty one of the finest harbors in America, accessible at almost all seasons of the year in less than one month of very easy navigation; whilst the voyage from France to Quebec cannot be prosecuted except in summer, on account of the ice that closes the River St Lawrence which is itself long and perilous.

2 Callières asked for 2,000 troops, regulars and militia, and two warships that would blockade New York Harbor and bombard the town while he attacked on land.

It will give his Majesty one of the finest countries of America, in a milder and more fertile climate than that of Canada, from whence a quantity of provisions and produce, useful for his Majesty's subjects, can be derived.

19. The Foundation of Louisiana, C. 1700

WITH THE FOUNDATION of Louisiana, Anglo-French rivalry in America assumed continental proportions. Between 1698 and 1702, Pierre Lemoyne d'Iberville, Canadian-born soldier and sailor who had served brilliantly in Hudson Bay and Newfoundland, made three voyages from France to the Gulf of Mexico. He discovered the mouth of the Mississippi River, which had eluded La Salle in 1685, erected a series of forts along the Gulf coast, and began to weave a network of alliances with the Indian tribes. In 1701, shortly after returning from his second voyage, he submitted a memoir to Jérome de Pontchartrain, minister of marine, in which he explained why it was important for France to occupy this region. This is an important document, for it marks the beginnings of a policy of encirclement of the English settlements which culminated under La Galissonière fifty years later.

Further Reading: M. Giraud, Histoire de la Louisiane française (3 vols., Paris, 1953—), Vol. I, Le Règne de Louis XIV.

SOURCE: Memoir given by the sieur d'Iberville about the coasts England occupies in North America from the St. Matthew River to the St. George River [1701], in P. Margry (ed.), Découvertes et établissements des Français dans l'ouest et dans le sud de l'Amérique septentrionale (6 vols., Paris, 1879–88), IV, 543–548. Translated by the editor.

It is sufficiently known that in these countries [the English colonies] there are presently more than 60,000 families, which are greatly increasing, for the climate is very good. The English trade there occupies more than six hundred vessels every year, to which must be added five hundred colonial vessels [of every type] that trade between the coastal ports and to the Azores, Newfoundland, Madeira, the Canaries, India, and to all the islands of America.

From 30 latitude north to 37, the countries of Carolina, Virginia, and Pennsylvania are separated from the lands of Florida by a mountain range, whose distance from the sea varies between ten, fifteen, and twenty *lieues*. It is very high, and five, six, or ten *lieues* in width. . . . In many places settlers have fully occupied the space between the mountains and the sea and their children will have to go beyond these mountains to find room to settle. Many have already done so in different places and joined up with several Indian tribes. . . .

If we consider for a moment the country that the English occupy on this continent, that which they plan to occupy, the forces which they have in their colonies where there are neither priests nor nuns and where everyone marries, and how they will have grown in thirty or forty years, we cannot doubt that they will occupy the country between themselves and the Mississippi, which is some of the finest in the world. Joined with the Indians, they will be able to raise sufficient forces on land and sea to make themselves masters of all America, or at least of the greater part of Mexico, where the population is not increasing in the same proportion as that of the English colonies. The latter will be able to raise armies of 30,000 and 40,000 men and go where they please before France and Spain, which are poorly informed of what goes on in those colonies, become aware of it.

Although the country presently occupied by the English is not very extensive, this must not be a reason for France to delay the adoption of measures to prevent the complete ruin of the French and Spanish colonies in America, especially Mexico, by planting a fine colony in the area where the Mississippi flows into the gulf, by occupying Mobile, and thus preventing the progress of the English in those lands among the Indian tribes.

The Spaniards have thought that it would suffice to occupy the seaports on that coast, such as Apalachee. They have had a settlement there for several years, but since it is barely populated and lacking in strength it would be easy for the English to make themselves masters of it as well as of St. Augustine, which they have founded to protect their boundaries on the Carolina side. . . .

I am certain that the governor of Pensacola had not considered his interests last year when he objected to the establishments I was making on the Mississippi. For surely the Spaniards must realize very well that they are in no condition to establish a colony powerful enough to oppose such strong neighbors and that it can only be most advantageous for them to have France place itself between them and the English by occupying that country. Thus in wartime they may be rescued by the French, or even by the English against the French, who will always be the weaker along that coast since they have not a single family there as yet.

It seems to me absolutely necessary to plant a colony on the Mississippi near the Mobile River and to join up with the Indians who are quite numerous there in separate villages and nations. We must arm and support them so that they may defend themselves against those who side with the English and force the latter back beyond the mountains, which is easy at present since they are not yet powerful to the west of them. The only considerable nation they have won to their side are the Chickasaws, with whom we are having peace negotiations, and the Shawnees. [The Chickasaws] hope that we can supply them with European products, which we transport by river, more easily and more cheaply than the English, who move them overland by horseback. These are the propositions I sent to them last year and they promised that they would be present at an assembly of the chiefs of all nations to be held at our fort on the Mississippi next spring. It will then be easy to persuade them to make peace [with the other nations] and, in return for a few gifts, to deliver to us the English interpreters who are in their villages and to accept missionaries who will maintain them [the villages] in our interest and win great numbers of them to the faith. All this can be done with little expense, but it will not be easy if we wait until later. The English will fortify themselves and will either reduce the number of nations who are in our interest or will oblige them to come to their side.

20. A Plan to Conquer New France, 1708

MILITANT ANTI-FRENCH sentiments first developed in New England, where Puritan antipathies against Catholic New France were exacerbated by the savage border raids of Franco-Indian war parties. These feelings were most forcefully expressed by Samuel Vetch in his famous report, Canada Survey'd . . . Born in Edinburgh in 1668, Vetch lived in New

York from 1699 to 1702 and then moved to Boston, where he soon won the favors of the governor, Joseph Dudley. Being active in the intercolonial trade, Vetch frequently visited Canada and so gained an extensive first-hand knowledge of the country. Written in 1708, Canada Survey'd so impressed the British government that it immediately stepped up its military assistance to the colonies. British regulars played a leading role in the conquest of Port Royal in 1710. The following year a mighty assault against Canada by land and sea was organized but had to be abandoned following the loss, in the treacherous currents of the lower St. Lawrence, of several units of the fleet sailing against Quebec.

Further Reading: F. H. Hammang, The Marquis de Vaudreuil, New France at the Beginning of the Eighteenth Century (Bruges, 1938); G. M. Waller, Samuel Vetch, Colonial Enterpriser (Chapel Hill, N.C., 1960); Y. F. Zoltvany, "New France and the West, 1701–1713," Canadian Historical Review, XLVI (1965), 301–322.

SOURCE: C. Headlam (ed.), Calendar of State Papers, Colonial Series, America and West Indies, 1708–1709, pp. 41–51.

Canada Survey'd, or the French Dominions upon the Continent of America briefly considered in their situation, strength, trade and number, more particularly how vastly prejudiciall they are to the British interest, and a method proposed of easily removing them.

It cannot but be wondred att by all thinking men who know the valuableness of the Brittish Monarchy in America, both with regard to their power and trade, that a nation so powerfull in shiping, so numerous in subjects, and other ways so wisely jealous of their trade, shou'd so tamely allow such a troublesome neighbour as the French, not only to sitt down peaceably beside them, but with a handfull of people vastly dispersed to possess a country of above 4,000 miles extent, quite encompassing and hemming in betwixt them and the sea, all the Brittish Empire upon the said Continent of America, by which they have already so mightily obstructed the Brittish trade, all America over, and must in time totally ruin the same, unless seasonably prevented, as will appear by the following considerations, (and what renders us intirely inexcusable is, that the half of one year's loss we sustain in trade by them, besides the vast expence both the Crown and Country is att, in maintaining of troops and garrisons upon their frontiers, bribing of the natives for their friendshipps, or indeed, more properly speaking, being tributaries to those inhumane savages for their favour and assistance; the half, I say, of one year's loss we sustain would, if rightly aplyed, wholly dispossess them of the Continent and Newfoundland, and by so doing render H.M. sole and peaceable possessor of all the North Continent of America, large enough to form four kingdoms as bigg as Great Brittain). . . .

[Vetch then describes the colonies of Canada and Acadia, dwelling particularly on the situation and strength of the chief places, the number and disposition of the regular troops, the names of the chief officers, and the products of the country.]

. . . And now that we have made itt evidently appear that the interest of the whole British Empire in America, is inseparably linkt with that of the Continent, itt remains next to consider how much damage the Colony yearly doe the said Brittish Continent, in ruining and obstructing their trade, the expence they occasion the same by the warr, besides the loss of people, every one of whom are vastly valuable, in so new and trading Colonyes. To make this more evidently appear, lett us consider the particular Governments which suffer mostly by them (though indeed all the Brittish Continent doe considerably already, and are ere long like to doe more), but to come to particulars, New York and the Jerseyes have of late, by means of the french seducing over to them a great part of the five Nations (who have so long been in league with the Crown of Brittain), and are known by the names of Senecas, Makuas, Onondagos, Cajugas and Oneidas, the french Missionaryes, who swarm among them, have carryed over, both to the French interest and religion, a great many of them, and with them the furr trade, which was formerly so valuable and profitable to those Colonyes of the Brittish, that merchants now in London, who lived there 20 years agoe, say there used to be exported from thence yearly about £50,000 value in beaver and other furrs, this they have not only almost intirely lost, but are att a vast expence, both of blood and treasure, to defend their frontiers from the insults of those troublesome neighbours. . . .

But to give the finishing stroke to all, and shew unanswerable arguments for reducing Canada at any rate, lett us only consider New England, a country of att least ten times the trade of all forementioned Colonyes, and whose loss doe more then exceed their proportion to the same. New England is so well situate for trade, both with respect to the conveniency of its harbours, the commodityes itt affords for commerce, the healthyness of the climate, which with the genius of the people calculate to improve all those advantages, have rendred itt a place of vast trade and buisiness, for besides that the inland country affords great quantityes of all sorts of provisions, horses, cattell, and lumber, fitt to be transported to the West Indies and elsewhere, the maritime parts affords an immense quantity of timber fitt for shipping, masts and all navall stores, which they have not fail'd to improve to the best advantage, for they yearly build some hundreds of vessells, while their sea costs, which are wonderfully rich in fish of all sorts, affords them advantageous cargos to load them withall. But of late years, the disturbance they have mett withal, in every part of their commerce, from their troublesome neighbours the french, hath been of so fatall consequence, that itt hath almost intirely ruined that Country, and must ere long inevitably doe so, if some remydy be not quickly afforded them. For besides the ravaging the frontiers, burning their uttermost towns and settlements, murdering and carrying away captives ye inhabitants by the french, and their unexpressably savage accomplices, the Indians, who have no compassion on either sex or age, nor are they bounded by any laws of reason or religion, but do exercise all manner of barbarityes upon their prisoners of all sorts, long after quarter is given, those unparalelled hostilityes not only lay waste the uttermost parts of this country, but occasion a constant expence and trouble of keeping a considerable force upon the frontiers, who, after all, are not able to prevent frequent irruptions of the barbarous enemy, who are favoured in their enterprises by the thickness and impassableness of the woods, with which they are well accustomed. These and the like reasons have rendred uninhabited one of the best and most fertile countryes upon all the Continent, commonly called the Eastern Country. . . .

I believe itt will plainly appear to any considering person, that the loss, expence and detriment in trade, (besides the barbarous murthers of many persons) sustain'd by the English upon the Continent in America from the french who inhabitt the same Continent, amounts to severall hundred thousand pounds yearly, and must in time, as the french grow more numerous, be vastly more, for by their situation, the french have sourrounded and hemmed in betwixt them and the sea, all the English Governments upon the Continent, so that in time, when they are fully peopled, as they project in a great measure to be, after the warr is over, by transporting thither (as Monsieur Rodot, the present Intendant of Canada, told me the french King designed), 20,000 men, who will chuse rather to gain their bread by hunting and gunning, then by labouring the ground. Should such a thing happen, they may easily in time be able to make the Brittish find use for their shipping and be forced to transport themselves elsewhere and leave their improvements to their more powerfull neighbours, and though this should never happen, yett posterity will blame us for risking the same while the remedy is so easily in our power, and the expence will not amount to near one half of the yearly loss we sustain from them, as will appear by the following scheame, which the author, who pretends to know that country as well as any subject of the Crown, and who made itt his business to know, with that designe of being capable to serve his country, engages to give his assistance in putting the design in execution.

To effectuate which great enterprise (so vastly advantageous to the honour and interest of the Crown and the people of great Brittain and itts Empire in the west Indies and North America), there would need no more than two battallions of regular Troops from Great Brittain, who would cost the Crown no more expence, excepting their provision and transportation, then they now doe in Scotland, where they are idle, nor more men of warr for their convoy and protection than are ordinarly employed in attending the Colonyes of New York, New England, or conveying home the Virginia fleets, which they might likeways doe in the fall after that expedition was over. With those two battalions and six men of warr joyned from New England with 1000 of their best men, which they will readily furnish and transport by sea to goe directly to Quibeck about the latter end of May, or beginning of June, fitted with bombs, mortars and one or two bomb ketches, while a body of 1500 men from Nework, Jersey and Connecticout, which they would readily furnish, marched by land being joyn'd by our five Nations of Indians directly to Montreal, with which number they would hardly fail of takeing that place, and att least preventing their regular troops, who are mostly quartered thereabouts, from coming to the assistance of Quibeck, which, by cutting off the inhabitants of the Isle of Orleans from joyning them, which might be done by sending two nimble, well mann'd sloops up thither before the fleet came in sight, and as itt is almost humanely impossible the town could hold out, being attacqued att three different places att once upon the side to the water, where itt hath no walls, and could not have any great number to defend itt, while the fireing their houses by the bombs would employ many of them to quench itt, upon taking of which two towns of Quibeck and Montreal, all the rest of their forts and settlemts. would fall of course into the hands of the Crown, and will not only afford a booty to the captors farr exceeding all the expence of the undertaking, but infinitely advance the commerce of the Brittish over all America, and particularly make them sole masters of the furr, fish and navall stores trade over all the Continent, and H.M. sole Soveraign of the North Continent of America, and of hundreds of nations of new subjects, who will become intirely obedient to her laws, when they have no preists to poyson them, nor no rivall Monarch to debauch them from her interest and make Canada a noble Colony, exactly calculate for the constitutions and genius of the most Northern of the North Brittains.

21. The Peace of Utrecht, 1713

THE FIRST period of intercolonial rivalry ended in 1713 with the ratification of the Peace of Utrecht. Britain gained Hudson Bay, Newfoundland, Acadia, and the right to trade with all the western tribes. The peace treaty, however, did not define the Anglo-French boundary in America but called for the formation of a joint commission to deal with the matter. This body met in 1719 and again in 1749. Its inability to reach an agreement on this crucial question made another intercolonial war practically inevitable.

SOURCE: Treaty of Peace and Friendship between the most Serene and most Potent Princess ANNE, by the Grace of God, Queen of Great Britain, France, and Ireland, and the most Serene and most Potent Prince LEWIS the XIVth, the most Christian King, Concluded at Utrecht the 31/11 Day of March/April 1713 (London, 1713), pp. 70–75.

X

The said most Christian King shall restore to the Kingdom and Queen of *Great Britain*, to be possessed in full Right for ever, the Bay and Streights of *Hudson*, together with all Lands, Seas, Sea-

Coasts, Rivers, and Places situate in the said Bay, and Streights, and which belong thereunto, no Tracts of Land or of Sea being excepted, which are at present possessed by the Subjects of France. All which, as well as any Buildings there made, in the Condition they now are, and likewise all Fortresses there erected, either before or since the *French* seized the same, shall, within Six Months from the Ratification of the present Treaty, or sooner, if possible, be well and truly delivered to the *British* Subjects, having Commission from the Queen of *Great Britain* to demand and receive the same. . . . But it is agreed on both sides, to determine within a Year, by Commissaries to be forthwith named by each Party, the Limits which are to be fixed between the said Bay of *Hudson,* and the Places appertaining to the *French;* which Limits both the *British* and *French* Subjects shall be wholly forbid to pass over, or thereby to go to each other by Sea or by Land. The same Commissaries shall also have Orders to describe and settle in like manner the Boundaries between the other *British* and *French* colonies in those parts. . . .

XII

The most Christian King shall take care to have delivered to the Queen of *Great Britain,* on the same Day that the Ratifications of this Treaty shall be exchanged, Solemn and Authentick Letters, or Instruments, by virtue whereof it shall appear that . . . all *Nova Scotia* or *Accadie,* with its ancient Boundaries, as also the City of *Port Royal,* now called *Annapolis Royal,* and all other things in those Parts, which depend on the said Lands and Islands, together with the Dominion, Propriety, and Possession of the said Islands, Lands, and Places, and all Right whatsoever, by Treaties, or by any other way obtained, which the most Christian King, the Crown of *France,* or any the Subjects thereof, have hitherto had to the said Islands, Lands, and Places, and the Inhabitants of the same, are yielded and made over to the Queen of *Great Britain,* and to Her Crown for ever, as the most Christian King doth at present yield and make over all the particulars abovesaid; and that in such ample manner and form, that the Subjects of the most Christian King shall hereafter be excluded from all kind of Fishing in the said Seas, Bays, and other Places, on the Coasts of *Nova Scotia,* that is to say, on those which lye towards the East, within 30 Leagues, beginning from the Island commonly called *Sable,* inclusively, and thence stretching along towards the South-West.

XIII

The Island called *Newfoundland*, with the adjacent Islands, shall from this time forward, belong of Right wholly to *Britain*; and to that end the Town and Fortress of *Placentia*, and what ever other Places in the said Island, are in the Possession of the *French*, shall be yielded and given up, within Seven Months from the Exchange of the Ratifications of this Treaty, or sooner, if possible, by the most Christian King to those who have a Commission from the Queen of *Great Britain*, for that purpose. . . . But it shall be allowed to the Subjects of *France*, to catch Fish, and to Dry them on Land, in that Part only, and in no other besides that, of the said Island of *Newfoundland*, which stretches from the Place called Cape *Bonavista*, to the Northern Point of the said Island, and from thence running down by the Westernside, reaches as far as the Place called *Point Riche*. But the Island called *Cape Breton*, as also all others, both in the Mouth of the River of St. *Lawrence*, and in the Gulph of the same Name, shall hereafter belong of Right to the *French*; and the most Christian King shall have all manner of Liberty to Fortifie any Place, or Places there.

XIV

It is expresly provided, that in all the said Places and Colonies to be yielded and restored by the most Christian King, in pursuance of this Treaty, the Subjects of the said King may have Liberty to remove themselves within a Year to any other Place, as they shall think fit, together with all their moveable Effects. But those who are willing to remain there, and to be subject to the Kingdom of *Great Britain*, are to enjoy the Free exercise of their Religion, according to the usage of the Church of *Rome*, as far as the Laws of *Great Britain* do allow the same.

XV

The Subjects of *France* inhabiting *Canada*, and others, shall hereafter give no Hindrance or Molestation to the Five Nations or Cantons of *Indians*, subject to the Dominion of *Great Britain*, nor to the other Natives of *America*, who are Friends to the same. In like manner the Subjects of *Great Britain*, shall behave themselves Peaceably towards the *Americans*, who are Subjects or Friends to *France*; and on both sides they shall enjoy full Liberty of going and

coming on account of Trade. As also the Natives of those Countries shall, with the same Liberty, resort, as they please, to the
British and *French* Colonies, for Promoting Trade on one side, and
the other, without any Molestation or Hindrance, either on the
Part of the *British* Subjects, or of the *French*. But it to be exactly
and distinctly settled by Commissaries, who are, and who ought to
be accounted the Subjects and Friends of *Britain* or of *France*.

IV

The French Empire at Its Height, 1713–1754

22. The Foundation of Ile Royale

UNDER THE TERMS of the Peace of Utrecht, France had been deprived of all her possessions on the North Atlantic coast except Cape Breton Island. In order to maintain themselves on the strategical seaboard, the French, soon after 1713, began to build the fortress of Louisbourg on this desolate piece of land, which they renamed Ile Royale. As early as 1706, Antoine-Denis Raudot, co-intendant of Canada with his father Jacques from 1705 to 1711, had recommended placing a settlement on Cape Breton Island. With remarkable accuracy, he had foreseen the role such a colony might play in the French empire as a military base, fishing station, and commercial center.

Further Reading: J. S. McLennan, Louisbourg from Its Foundation to Its Fall, 1713–1759 (London, 1918).

SOURCE: [A. D. Raudot], Memoir to My Lord the Comte de Pont-chartrain on the Establishment of a Colony on Cape Breton Island, November 30, 1706, Archives nationales, colonies (Paris), série C¹¹B, vol. I, pp. 427–428, 472–474, 478–482, 496 [pagination of the Public Archives of Canada transcripts]. Translated by the editor.

Reasons for Making This Establishment

Colonies are necessary only insofar as they are useful to the founding states; they are only useful if they procure these states with new benefits and assured means of increasing their commerce.

Following these principles, the French colonies in South America are necessary because they produce sugar, indigo, cotton, and other objects that France would be obliged to purchase from foreigners and because this commerce occupies a great number of her vessels that consume her merchandise and foodstuffs and pay substantial duties to the [tax] farmers of His Majesty.

For the same reasons, the colony of Canada is necessary, although it is a minor object, because it produces beaver pelts, moosehides, and sundry furs, which France would be obliged to buy from foreigners, who would lay down the law, particularly in regards to beaver, which supports a large hatmaking industry in the kingdom. . . .

The colony [Ile Royale] whose foundation we propose is not only necessary because of the codfish which can only be caught off the Canadian coast, but also because it will enable us to bring all the fisheries under French control and deprive the English of them, who until now have usurped their principal benefits. No one can deny that the fisheries are one of the world's great commercial assets. They provide an outlet for salt, occupy a great number of vessels, are a nursery for seamen, draw money from foreign countries into France, and pay substantial taxes to His Majesty. . . .

First Advantage

. . . No matter the season when vessels sail for the fishing grounds, they have a long and difficult crossing before reaching the Canadian coast or the Grand Banks. No one is unaware that the winds for these voyages are almost always contrary. The vessels which engage in dry fishing remain almost four months off the coast, and the entire voyage takes nearly eight months. Those that salt their catch are not so long at sea, but they are greatly exposed. Thus, these voyages are always long and cost a great deal to the merchants who, far from making profits, are often quite happy to salvage part of their investment. . . .

All these inconveniences would cease if the fisheries became stationary, and this commerce would then flourish in both war and peace. The merchants would no longer have to advance money and, should they do so, would hardly run any risks. Being assured of finding all the fishing done by the inhabitants of the settlement, vessels would no longer sail at the equinox of March but in May, June, and July. In such a fine season they would not risk losing their salt, provisions, and merchandise, nor be forced to turn back.

The navigation being easy, they would take on no extra crew and only the quantity of provisions necessary to reach the settlement. Instead of launches and other fishing apparatus they would load cargoes of merchandise and fishing implements, not for their own use as in the past but to trade with the merchants of the settlement, who would give processed fish in return. The trip from France to the settlement would take forty days. They would only spend there the time necessary to load and unload and would return to France in twenty days. The entire trip would take three months and they could make two a year. . . .

Third Advantage

If we consider attentively the progress of the English in their colony of New England, we will rightly tremble for the safety of Canada. . . . These people, in a few years, will be numerous and formidable, and the population of Canada will not be much greater than it is today. Whether it be the climate, which favors the cultivation of their land and the raising of their cattle and enables them to navigate in all seasons, or their industry, it is certain that their colonies are established in that area as England herself. There is still time to foresee and prevent the inevitable consequences of English superiority which, we must not doubt, will finally inspire in them the idea of becoming masters of Canada and by this method of all North America. The loss of Canada will not appear very important to those who are not thoroughly familiar with it, but it is nonetheless certain that along with this country France would lose the beaver trade, which is sizable and necessary by its extent, and that of moose and other peltries for which outlets exist in the kingdom and in foreign lands. . . . To these reasons we may add that it pertains to the king's glory and piety not to let such a great country fall into the hands of an heretical nation, which is jealous of the commerce of the French and which would stifle in their hearts and those of the Indians the seeds of religion.

In losing Canada, France would also lose the codfisheries. The English, to control these, would fortify themselves in all favorable places. Their vessels would cover the Grand Banks and close the navigation of those seas to the French. The number of sailors in the kingdom would be reduced by half. We would be obliged to buy codfish from the English. We would also lose a market for salt and fishing gear, and the king, the taxes he reaps from this great commerce. The harm would be too great for His Majesty to endure, but it would only be by prodigious expenses and open war that we could recover possession of what we can easily retain by fortifying Cape Breton Island. This island is the key to Canada and to all the coasts of New France. If we fortify it, the English will be unable to undertake anything in that area. They will never venture into the depths of the St. Lawrence River to reach Quebec as long as they have a post of such importance behind them. . . .

Fourth Advantage

All the vessels returning from the islands of America, and from Peru, Mexico, the South Seas, and even the Indies, are compelled by prevailing winds to sail near the upper reaches of the Canadian coast and off the southern tip of the Grand Banks of Newfoundland in order to return to Europe. Frequently, many of these ships are short of rations, water, and wood, have broken their masts, sprung leaks, or carry sick crew. Nearly seven hundred *lieues* remain before they reach France and they are in no condition to travel that distance without being assisted. The establishment on Cape Breton Island would be a very necessary and very useful shelter for these vessels in distress. They would not have to sail more than one hundred *lieues* to reach it from the tip of the Grand Banks. The healthy climate of that country and good food would cure their sick; they would obtain masts, water, wood, provisions, and everything necessary for refitting; they might even take on new crew in case of necessity.

It would be a harbor and place of rendezvous in wartime, where fleets carrying silver bullion and other costly merchandise could receive intelligence of the situation in Europe. If necessary they could send light craft to France, which could travel the distance in sixteen to eighteen days, to ask for escorts. While awaiting their arrival these fleets would refit at the island. A stopover of two months is not a great delay when treasures are at stake. . . .

Conclusion

The proposed establishment places all the fisheries under French control and completely excludes the English from them; it protects the colonies of Canada, Acadia, and Newfoundland against English enterprises and prevents them from becoming the masters of all these vast countries and of all the fisheries as a consequence; it undermines their settlement of Boston without making war; it becomes a place of refuge for damaged vessels which sail these seas on fishing expeditions or on voyages to Canada; it becomes a meeting point for ships from the Indies, the islands of America, and New Spain; it increases the number of sailors, facilitates the trade with Canada, and favors the marketing of that colony's grain and foodstuffs; it provides His Majesty's shipyards with masts, yardarms, sheathings, planks, pitch, tar, fish oils, coal, and plaster. Foreigners who have become accustomed to supplying all these goods will no longer carry away the king's money. It enhances the domination of His Majesty, the commerce of his subjects, the duties paid to his tax farms, and the consumption of the kingdom's salt and other products.

23. The Importance of Louisiana, 1714

LOUISIANA LAY practically abandoned during the War of the Spanish Succession, but a serious attempt was made to develop this colony following the return of peace. In 1712, because of the bankrupt condition of the royal treasury, it was ceded to Antoine Crozat, one of the richest men in France. Although Crozat's colonization effort ended in failure, he or persons of his entourage wrote several important memoirs that stressed Louisiana's economic and strategic value. Reports like the one given below, which was submitted to the government in 1714 might explain why John Law made the Mississippi colony the foundation stone of his giant Company of the Occident in 1717. Unfortunately this company collapsed five years later, ruining many Frenchmen who had heavily invested in it. The bursting of the "Mississippi bubble" severely discredited Louisiana in French public opinion.

Further Reading: M. Giraud, Histoire de la Louisiane française, Vol. I, Le Règne de Louis XIV, Vol. II, Années de transition, 1715–1717, Vol. III, L'Epoque de John Law, 1717–1720; P. Heinrich, La Louisiane sous la Compagnie des Indes (Paris, 1908).

SOURCE: [Anonymous], Memoir to Make Known the Necessity of Sending Settlers to the Colony of Louisiana, 1714, Archives nationales, colonies (Paris), série C¹³A, vol. 3, ff. 655–664. Translated by the editor.

The first discovery of the country of Louisiana, located in North America, was made in 1683, but this enterprise was not followed up as a result of the death of the sr. de La Salle, who had gone there with a very small number of men. After the peace of Ryswick, the king sent there the sr. d'Iberville, who laid the first foundation of the colony; but the war which had just ended having started again a short time later, affairs did not permit His Majesty to send the help that would have been necessary to secure this establishment. At present, as a result, there are not two hundred inhabitants scattered in a land of very vast extent. That such a small number of men, overwhelmed by miseries, have maintained themselves is a miracle which can only be attributed to the more urgent matters that occupied the English in Europe. But now that His Majesty has made peace with all the powers with which he was at war, it seems in the interest of the state that this new colony be helped in proportion to its needs, of which the most essential is to strengthen it with settlers.

Until now this new colony has been regarded quite indifferently, because it does not yet produce anything. But if we pay attention to the advantages that can be derived from it subsequently, it will be agreed that there is none whose preservation and increase is so important to the state.

At present the kingdom's maritime commerce has almost been reduced to nothing. However, the navigation of merchant vessels in peacetime turns out the trained seamen the king uses in his naval forces when war is declared. Thus, in general, it is important to increase navigation. Various settlements can be made in Louisiana if we work at them seriously and the commerce of that colony will occupy a great number of vessels in a few years.

The establishment of the colony of Louisiana has three objectives: the commerce of the goods it can produce, that which can be carried out with the Spaniards, and the need to limit the English, who are already too powerful in that part of America.

In order to understand this system, we must begin by examining what is called Louisiana. It is an area of land of more than four hundred *lieues*, from the Nation of the Illinois—which is allied to Canada—to the Gulf of Mexico, through which flows the Mississippi River, today called St. Louis, more than eight hundred *lieues* in length. The rights of the king and his possession of such a vast country are only upheld by two infantry companies not amounting to sixty men, who are stationed in a mean wooden fort on the Mobile River, some twelve to fifteen *lieues* from the Gulf, from which they dare not venture, and by approximately two hundred inhabitants who are so dispersed that there is no post where forty could be assembled.

This country is in the middle of the interior and separates New Mexico and New Biscay from the English colonies. The latter occupy the entire coast of that part of America from Placentia [Newfoundland], which was ceded to them, to Florida, which belongs to the Spaniards, who only have two weak forts there, the one being St. Augustine on the English side, the other Pensacola on ours. The English, who are very numerous in that country, are spread out toward the interior. They occupy the Upper Wabash and the headwaters of almost all the other rivers that flow into the Mississippi and nearly reach our fort of Mobile.

It is easy to understand from such a situation that if we do not fortify ourselves on the Mississippi River the English, who are very powerful in their colonies, will reach it by means of the rivers on which they are presently located. Afterwards, they will not only expel us from the weak forts we occupy on the lower river but also in a very short time penetrate New Mexico and New Biscay. From there they will easily expel the Spaniards and seize their mines, a matter which cannot be regarded as irrelevant to the affairs of Europe. There is still more. If they establish themselves on the Mississippi and Wabash rivers, they will soon conclude alliances with the Indian nations of the [Great] lakes and Canada will be lost. This is all the more certain since the surrender of Placentia and Acadia would make it nearly impossible to send reinforcements in wartime, and the English would become the masters of all North America. Only a strong establishment in Louisiana can prevent this. If that colony were sufficiently populated, different posts could be established on the Mississippi and Wabash rivers. These, plus the alliances we have made with the Indian nations, would form a line of communication with Canada and a barrier against the English colonies. The English are fully aware of the importance of Louisiana. One need only ask the marquis d'Huxelles what he overheard at Utrecht about our Mississippi establishment.

The commerce that can be carried out in Louisiana is easy to appreciate. It is, so to speak, a store in the midst of the Spanish Indies, to which we can hope to draw much silver specie, either by trading in the Spanish ports or by finding a way to enter New

Mexico via the rivers that flow into the Mississippi. This matter is now receiving attention. Louisiana is presently the only colony which can enable France to obtain some of the silver from the Spanish mines.

The trade this colony can produce is altogether different from that of the other French colonies, none of which have the resources that can be found here. We can extract excellent red copper, lead, saltpeter, silk, buffalo hides, nut oil, not to mention all types of pelts as in Canada. At present we draw all this merchandise from foreign countries, for which we pay immense sums of money. . . .

If a little attention is paid to all the reasons explained above, it will be impossible to deny the great importance of sending settlers to Louisiana forthwith. This is all the easier in the present circumstances since the reduction of the army will produce a great number of useless subjects who will emigrate to foreign countries for the most part. It will be sufficient for the king to send out five to six hundred men, because other settlers will go there voluntarily afterwards. At the moment, no one wants to emigrate to an abandoned land where there is no security.

24. Integrating Canada into the Imperial Economy, 1729

DURING THE TENURE of Frédéric de Maurepas as minister of marine from 1723 to 1749, the French colonial empire in America reached the peak of its development. Maurepas's policy, inspired by classical mercantilist doctrine, was to integrate mother country and colonies into a self-sufficient economic unit from which all foreign trade would be excluded. Although this ideal was never fully achieved—large numbers of vessels from New England called at Louisbourg annually and the contraband fur trade between Montreal and Albany continued unabated—Maurepas's policy did stimulate many sectors of the Canadian economy. In the following passage, the minister outlines his program for Canada to Gilles Hocquart, the newly appointed intendant of that colony.

Further Reading: M. Filion, Maurepas, ministre de Louis XV (1715–1749) (Montreal, 1967); G. Lanctot, A History of Canada, Vol. III, From the Treaty of Utrecht, 1713, to the Peace of Paris, 1763 (Toronto, 1965).

SOURCE: Memoir of the King to Serve as Instructions for the Sr. Hocquart, Commissary General of the Marine and *Ordonnateur* in New France, March 22, 1729, Archives nationales, colonies (Paris), série B, vol. 53 ff. 476–479. Translated by the editor.

Since the colony of Canada is valuable only insofar as it is useful to the kingdom, the sr. Hocquart must discover ways that can contribute to this end.

One of the greatest benefits that the Canadians can procure for France can come from the establishment of fisheries. Those of porpoises and seals that have been started in different places can provide the kingdom with an abundant quantity of fish oils, which are always in great demand but which for the most part are supplied by the Dutch. This commerce is likely to become very extensive and can never be too greatly encouraged. Besides oils it also provides sealskins, which can be used in a number of ways. In every respect, then, this commerce can only be most advantageous.

There are also masts and lumber to be drawn from Canada, not only for the royal shipyards, but also for private enterprise. In 1724, His Majesty sent the sr. de Tilly, a naval lieutenant, and a carpenter to Canada to inspect the forests and prepare wood for masts. This enterprise was beset by great difficulties and their efforts met with little success. The wood that was cut was of poor quality or wasted before being placed aboard the ships. As a result, there appeared reason to believe that obtaining masts from Canada would have to be deferred until the colony was more densely populated. The sr. Hocquart, however, must persist in the project in order to report on what can be done to render it feasible. . . .

Various crops can also be grown in Canada that will be of great utility to France, such as flax and hemp, which must be purchased in the north for considerable sums. In the past, His Majesty sent both types of seed to Quebec. The *habitants*, who were already in the habit of growing hemp, began to cultivate flax seven or eight years ago. In order to encourage them to increase this cultivation, His Majesty had set its price at sixty *livres* per quintal up to September 14 of last year and at forty *livres* after that date. He had ruled that this price would be maintained during the present year and lowered to twenty-five *livres* beginning on January 1, 1730, which is still higher than its cost in France. However, since this is a sizable reduction, which might induce the *habitants* to discontinue this crop, His Majesty will approve if the sr. Hocquart sets the price at thirty-five *livres* or even at forty *livres* in 1730 if he thinks it [advisable]. His Majesty is prepared to incur this expense because of the future utility of this crop, but it would be in vain if the *habitants* continued to prepare their hemp as badly as they have done until now. Every year complaints have been received. . . . The sr. Hocquart will do what he can to remedy this situation and will inform the *habitants* that His Majesty will not buy their hemp at any price if they are not more careful. . . .

Tar is also made in Canada from the pine trees that grow there in quantity. His Majesty recommends that he maintain the *habitants* in this habit so that in the future this product may be available for the shipyards. . . .

His Majesty has been informed that sheep in Canada grow a good type of wool. Since there is a great consumption of this product in the kingdom, His Majesty wishes him to encourage as much as he can those who own suitable pastures to raise sheep. Eventually, this can procure considerable wealth for the colony and a more comfortable life for the *habitants*.

His Majesty recommends that he increase as much as possible the vegetable crops that have already been started in the colony. These not only procure abundance for the *habitants* but also give rise to a profitable trade with Ile Royale and the West Indies, consisting of shipments of wheat, biscuit, and peas.

By his letters patent of October, 1727, His Majesty has forbidden foreigners from engaging in any type of trade with the island colonies of France. At the same time measures were taken to assure that the island colonies of America, particularly the Windwards, would obtain from French merchants the supplies that Englishmen formerly brought there as the result of a tolerance most prejudicial to the commerce of the kingdom. These measures taken by His Majesty have met with the success which had been expected, for all foreign trade has been banished from the islands. French merchants have supplied them abundantly with salt beef, flour, and other foodstuffs, while cod, salted fish, and oils have been sent from Ile Royale. But French commerce has been unable to replace the cattle, horses, planks, staves, and shingles which New England had supplied in quantity. His Majesty gave orders to the sr. de Beauharnois [the governor] and Dupuy, formerly intendant of New France, to find out how this part of the trade could be made up of shipments from Canada to Martinique, which would be very beneficial to both colonies, by using Ile Royale as a clearinghouse, particularly for the horses and cattle. Upon his arrival, the sr. Hocquart . . . will obtain information on the state of this commerce and will do what he can to develop it. His Majesty recommends that he work at it, for it is one of the most important services he can render.

Before concluding this article on cultivations, His Majesty will observe to him that the Canadians have not until now realized the progress that could have been expected. Long wars, verily, have hindered the growth of the colony. The *habitants* became accustomed to wielding weapons and to going on expeditions and felt no inclination to remain on the land after the return of peace, although this is what is most enduring and can best contribute to the concentration of strength which the colony requires as protection against the hostile enterprises of its neighbors. With this in mind, the sr. Hocquart must encourage and favor cultivation and the increase of the population as matters most important for the safety of the colony.

It is very important to prevent all manner of trade between the inhabitants of Canada and the English, since the latter would necessarily supply merchandise that can be drawn from the kingdom. For this reason, he will rigorously enforce the letters patent of October, 1727. . . .

25. The French Canadian *Bourgeoisie*

SINCE THE BEGINNING of the royal régime in 1663, the state, not private enterprise, had been the chief agency of colonization. Gilles Hocquart, intendant from 1729 to 1748, believed that the colony's growth would be more rapid if Canadian entrepreneurs took charge of its economic development. Soon after his arrival in Canada he concluded that these men were lacking, and he tried to formulate a policy that would favor the formation of such an entrepreneurial group. Although the Crown refused to accept his suggestion to restrict the Canadian operations of French merchants (Document A), it did make a substantial cash loan to enable some Canadians to establish ironworks near Trois Rivières (Document B).

Further Reading: J. N. Fauteux, *Essai sur l'industrie au Canada sous le régime français* (2 vols., Quebec, 1927); A. G. Reid, "Intercolonial Trade during the French Regime," Canadian Historical Review, XXXII (1951), 236–251 and "General Trade between Quebec and France during the French Regime," Canadian Historical Review, XXXIV (1953), 18–32; J. Lunn, "The Illegal Fur Trade out of New France, 1713–1760," Canadian Historical Association Report (1939), pp. 61–76.

SOURCES: Document A: Hocquart to the comte de Maurepas, October 27, 1732, Archives nationales, colonies (Paris), série C^{11}A, vol. 58, pp. 71–72 [pagination of the Public Archives of Canada transcripts]. Document B: Hocquart to Maurepas, October 26, 1735, ibid., vol. 63, pp. 98–102, 104–105. Both translated by the editor.

A. *The Absence of Wealthy Entrepreneurs, 1732*

It is very true that a large number of merchants owe considerable sums in France. . . . Without being venturesome, I could say that these amount to more than 250,000 *livres.* Presently, the Canadian merchants do not profit from half the commerce that is carried out here. It is the merchants of La Rochelle and Rouen who send their factors with great quantities of merchandise here and accept bills of exchange and peltries in return. This reduces the commerce of the domiciled merchants and probably prevents them from paying off their old debts. After considering these remarks, perhaps you will find that the reasons the Canadians often give for excluding the transients from the retail trade are well founded. It is for you to decide, my lord, if it would not be preferable in this case to further the interests of the domiciled merchants rather than those of the transients. It is true that freedom of trade favors all the inhabitants of the colony because it results in cheap and abundant goods. But on the other hand, it would be desirable to have wealthy merchants in this country, even if they were not numerous, because they would be in a position to begin and develop enterprises that their limited means do not even permit them to attempt at the present.

The cultivation of the land provides the inhabitants of the countryside with a comfortable sustenance and industry does the same for the artisans of the towns. Only the domiciled merchants remain to be protected. They have always considered that the trade of the transients harmed them and perhaps you will find, my lord, that they are somewhat justified. In any event, we will not change the current practice without your orders.

B. Launching the St. Maurice Ironworks, 1735

From the plans, my lord, you will see that since it will cost 36,003 *livres* 6 *sols* 8 *deniers* to make the establishment [the St. Maurice ironworks], and 61,250 *livres* to operate it, an advance of nearly 100,000 *livres* is required to begin this enterprise. The plans also show that the value of the annual production will be 116,000 *livres*. Thus, initial expenses will be reimbursed in the very first year and a profit of 16,000 *livres* will remain. In subsequent years, the profit should be 60,000 *livres*, from which 10,000 *livres* should be deducted to cover the cost of moving the iron and other unforeseen expenditures. Even if costs were much higher, there would still remain a sizable annual profit. Thus, this enterprise can only be very useful, both to those who will undertake it and to the entire colony which will derive new export products from it. . . .

Notwithstanding these obvious advantages, the persons who started this enterprise with the sr. de Francheville are unable to pursue it because they lack the necessary cash resources. They have already spent 22,000 *livres*, according to the accounts received from the sr. de Francheville and from his widow since his death. This expenditure can be written off as a complete loss, because the buildings and other things that were done by order of the sr. de Francheville cannot be integrated into the establishment proposed . . . except for the house built to lodge the workers, and even that may have to be moved.

No one else can be found in the colony to pay in cash the sums required for this establishment. To undertake it on credit would be to expose it to failure, because everything would then be much costlier. Only three solutions remain, so as not to deprive the colony of the advantages this enterprise would procure.

The first would be that His Majesty take it over and reimburse the persons who have spent money on it. The second would be to form a company in France that would provide the necessary funds. The third would be for His Majesty to lend the sums required to the persons who began the establishment in order to enable them to complete it. . . .

It does not appear fitting for His Majesty to exploit these iron mines for his own account, since the costs would be much greater for him than for private parties who watch over every item of expenditure and whose principal concern is economy. Furthermore, the accounting procedure to be followed for this type of exploitation would be costly and difficult. Persons could probably be found in Paris to take charge of the enterprise; but since it is your intention, my lord, to favor the inhabitants of this colony, your views would be better served by a company formed in Canada. . . .

After examining the reports M. Hocquart sends annually on the state of commerce, you have decided that the colony needs export products. Iron would assuredly be one, and this enterprise might result in the foundation of others of a similar nature, since iron mines can be found in three or four different places in the colony. If the profits of those of the St. Maurice are as sizable as the sr. Olivier [the master of the forges] assures, these establishments would account for an important part of the colony's commerce and of the royal customs revenue, if it pleased His Majesty to tax Canadian iron. . . .

26. The Opening of the Far West, 1733

PIERRE GAULTIER DE VARENNES, sr. de La Vérendrye (1685–1749) was the foremost French North American explorer of the eighteenth century. Born in Trois Rivières, he had originally opted for a military career. During the War of the Spanish Succession he had fought on the frontiers of New England and in Newfoundland before sailing for France to join the armies of Louis XIV. At Malplaquet in 1709 he was wounded nine times and left for dead on the field of battle.

Following his return to Canada he became interested in the fur trade and in 1726 was granted command of a post on Lake Nipigon, north of Lake Superior. In 1730, the court commissioned him to undertake the discovery of the western sea but declined to subsidize the venture. This obliged La Vérendrye to seek financial support from Canadian merchants who were interested in the commercial possibilities of the project.

La Vérendrye's career during the next fifteen years was beset by all sorts of difficulties and hardships. He was frequently criticized by the court because of the slowness of his progress through the West, harassed by his Montreal creditors, and exposed to the hostility of some of the Indian tribes. He had not succeeded in reaching the Pacific when he asked to be relieved of his command in 1745. He had, however, pushed nearly as far as the Rockies and established a chain of posts across the western prairie which enabled New France to reconstruct a fur trading network that had been shattered by the loss of Hudson Bay in 1713.

The following document is a report on La Vérendrye's progress, written by Governor Beauharnois in 1733. It illustrates the multiple dimensions of the undertaking.

Further Reading: N. M. Crouse, La Vérendrye, Fur Trader and Explorer (Ithaca, N.Y., 1956); A. S. Morton, "La Vérendrye. Commandant, Fur trader, and Explorer," Canadian Historical Review, IX (1928), 284–298.

SOURCE: L. P. Burpee (ed. and trans.), Journals and Letters of Pierre Gaultier de Varennes de La Vérendrye and His Sons (Toronto: Champlain Society Publications, 1927), pp. 102–109. Reprinted with the permission of the publisher.

September 28, 1733

The Sieur de la Vérendrye who has undertaken this discovery has made an establishment on Lake Tecamamiouen where he has built a fort with two gates on opposite sides. The interior length of the side is fifty feet with two bastions. There are two main buildings each composed of two rooms with double chimneys. Around these buildings is a road seven feet wide; in one of the bastions a storehouse and a powder magazine have been made, and there is a double row of stakes, thirteen feet out of the ground.

He has constructed another fort to the west of the Lake of the Woods, distant sixty leagues from Lake Tecamamiouen. The interior of this fort measures one hundred feet with four bastions. There is a house for the missionary, a church, and another house for the commandant, four main buildings with chimneys, a powder magazine and a storehouse. There are also two gates on opposite sides, and a watch-tower, and the stakes are in double row and are fifteen feet out of the ground.

The last-mentioned establishment is on the lands of the Cree and within reach of the Assiniboin; fish and game are abundant, wild oats grow in great quantity, and as the land there is good the Sieur de la Vérendrye had it burnt over to clear it. The wild oats which are abundant enabled him to save the wheat he had brought,

and he will not be obliged in future to bring any from Michilimackinac.

Moreover this fort will procure this advantage, that the French
will be able to profit by a considerable quantity of peltries that are
now taken to the English on Hudson Bay, for if the savages find
the French on their passage they will not go in search of the
English, whom they apparently neither like nor esteem.

All the savages of these districts are much given to war. In 1732
he [the Sieur de la Vérendrye] had prevented them from going to
war, but in 1733 he had been obliged to let them march, on condition, however, that they should not go against the Sioux of the
Rivers, of which they gave him their promise.

Towards the end of last winter he had sent his son with the Sieur
de la Jemeraye, his nephew, to construct a fort at Winnipeg. They
reached a point about fifteen or twenty leagues from the lake of
that name, according to what the savages told them, but could not
get there on account of the ice. The younger Sieur de la Vérendrye
remained in that place so as to proceed on his way as soon as the
weather should permit, and the Sieur de la Jemeraye started for
Montreal, where he arrived on the twentieth of September.

He handed to Monsieur de Beauharnois two collars which the
Cree had sent him, the one as a pledge of their submission and
fidelity and of the care they were taking to keep the road open for
the French and their allies; the other in sign of their joy in having
Frenchmen upon their lands and in forming only one body with
them. He reported to him that the chief of the Cree intended to
remain with the elders of his people near the French fort all the
summer, and that he was even going to raise wheat, the seed for
which had been supplied to him by the Sieur de la Vérendrye.

As regards the Assiniboin, none of them came to the fort of the
Lake of the Woods, because they had been scared by being told
that the French wanted to eat them, and that for that purpose they
were to be followed by Sioux and Saulteur;[1] but their fear has now
been dispelled, and the chief of the Cree begged the Sieur de la
Vérendrye to count these savages, who are allies of his nation,
among his children, and assured him that they would shortly come
and join him.

The Sieur de la Jemeraye is to start again, as soon as the ice

1 Chippewa, or Ojibway.

melts, for the Lake of the Woods, where he expects to arrive in the month of August; and in September he will leave that place to go and winter one hundred and fifty leagues further. After that wintering he will leave in the spring of the following year in order to go to the country of the Ouachipouennes, otherwise called "the Sioux who go Underground."[2]

This nation is on the River of the West[3] three hundred leagues or thereabouts from the Lake of the Woods according to the report of the Cree who have been there in war. They say that the Ouachipouennes have eight villages established there, fields of Indian corn, melons, pumpkins, beans, horses, cats and dwellings constructed of wood and earth and built like French houses, that they are of the same height as other savages, that some of them have light hair, some red and some black, that they speak a language which has some resemblance to French but is quite unlike English, that they are dressed in ox-hide, that they use earthen pots and have some large axes all worn away by use, that they never make war on any tribe, but that they are always on their guard and defend themselves bravely when attacked.

The Cree and the Assiniboin have constantly made war upon them and have captured several children from them. The Sieur de la Jemeraye bought three of them which he took to Montreal. He says that he has seen these children playing together, that in their games they neigh like horses, and that when they saw cats and horses they said they had animals of the same kind at home.

The Cree and the Assiniboin have made peace with that tribe, and the former have promised the Sieur de la Jemeraye and the son of La Vérendrye to conduct them thither, where they can get information as to how to get down to the Western Sea in which to all appearance that great river discharges.

The Sieur de la Jemeraye adds that the prevailing winds at the Lake of the Woods are westerly and very rainy, which leads him to conjecture that they come from the sea, and he declares that he has spoken to twenty Cree savages separately in private and at different times to see if their stories would agree, and that they have always told him the same thing; if their accounts have not agreed it has been in the matter of differences in certain animals they have seen in their travels.

2 The Mandans.
3 The Missouri River.

27. Canadian Society,
Early 1720's

THE ABLEST description of Canadian society during the French régime was written by the Jesuit historian F. X. de Charlevoix (1682–1761). A teacher at the College of Quebec from 1705 to 1709, Charlevoix returned to America in 1720 by order of the Prince Regent to gather information on ways of reaching the western sea. This mission took Charlevoix from Quebec to New Orleans by the inland route and lasted three years. Beside preparing his report to the Prince Regent, Charlevoix also wrote an account of his voyage in the form of thirty-six letters addressed to the Duchess de Lesdiguières. These letters were published in 1744 as Volume III of the famous Histoire et description générale de la Nouvelle France, the first noteworthy history of the French colony.

The first extract, taken from Letter III, is a description of Quebec society; the second, taken from Letter X and bearing a Montreal dateline, is more general in scope.

Further Reading: G. Frégault, Canadian Society in the French Regime (Ottawa: Canadian Historical Association Booklet, 1962); W. J. Eccles, Canadian Society During the French Regime (Montreal, 1968); J. Hamelin, Economie et société en Nouvelle France (Quebec: Cahiers de l'Institut d'Histoire de l'Université Laval, 1960); F. Parkman, The Old Régime in Canada (Boston, 1887).

SOURCE: F. X. de Charlevoix, Journal of a Voyage to North America Undertaken by Order of the French King Containing the Geographical Description and Natural History of that Country, particularly Canada. Together with an Account of the Customs, Characters, Religion, Manners and Traditions of the Original Inhabitants. In a Series of Letters to the Duchess of Lesdiguières. Translated from the French of P. de Charlevoix (2 vols., London, 1761), I, 111–114, 263–268.

Letter III

. . . I have already said, that they reckon no more than seven thousand souls at Quebec; yet you find in it a small number of the best company, where nothing is wanting that can possibly contribute to form an agreeable society. A governor-general, with an *état-major*, a noblesse, officers, and troops, an intendant, with a superior council, and subaltern jurisdictions, a commissary of the marine, a grand provost, and surveyor of the highways, with a grand master of the water and forests, whose jurisdiction is certainly the most extensive in the world; rich merchants, or such as live as if they were so; a bishop and numerous seminary; the recollects and jesuits, three communities of women well educated, assemblies, full as brilliant as anywhere, at the lady Governess's, and lady Intendants. Enough, in my opinion, to enable all sorts of persons whatever to pass their time very agreeably.

They accordingly do so, every one contributing all in his power to make life agreeable and chearful. They play at cards, or go abroad on parties of pleasure in the summer-time in calashes or canoes, in winter, in sledges upon the snow, or on skaits upon the ice. Hunting is a great exercise amongst them, and there are a number of gentlemen who have no other way of providing handsomely for their subsistence. The current news consist of a very few articles, and those of Europe arrive all at once, though they supply matter of discourse for great part of the year. They reason like politicians on what is past, and form conjectures on what is likely to happen; the sciences and fine arts have also their part, so that the conversation never flags for want of matter. The Canadians, that is to say, the Creoles of Canada draw in with their native breath an air of freedom, which renders them very agreeable in the commerce of life, and no where in the world is our language spoken in greater purity. There is not even the smallest foreign accent remarked in their pronunciation.

You meet with no rich men in this country, and it is really great pity, every one endeavouring to put as good a face on it as possible, and nobody scarce thinking of laying up wealth. They make good cheer, provided they are also able to be at the expence of fine cloaths; if not, they retrench in the article of the table to be able to appear well dressed. And indeed, we must allow, that dress becomes our Creolians extremely well. They are all here of very advantageous stature, and both sexes have the finest complexion in the world; a gay and sprightly behaviour, with great sweetness and politeness of manners are common to all of them; and the least rusticity, either in language or behaviour, is utterly unknown even in the remotest and most distant parts.

The case is very different as I am informed with respect to our English neighbours, and to judge of the two colonies by the way of life, behaviour, and speech of the inhabitants, nobody would hesitate to say that ours were the most flourishing. In New England and the other provinces of the continent of America, subject to the British empire, there prevails an opulence which they are utterly at a loss how to use; and in New France, a poverty hid by an air of being in easy circumstances, which seems not at all studied. Trade, and the cultivation of their plantations strengthen the first, whereas the second is supported by the industry of its inhabitants, and the taste of the nation diffuses over it something infinitely pleasing. The English planter amasses wealth, and never makes any superfluous expence; the French inhabitant again enjoys what he has acquired, and often makes a parade of what he is not possessed of. That labours for his posterity; this again leaves his offspring involved in the same necessities he was in himself at his first setting out, and to extricate themselves as they can. The English Americans are averse to war, because they have a great deal to lose; they take no care to manage the Indians from a belief that they stand in no need of them. The French youth, for very different reasons, abominate the thoughts of peace, and live well with the natives, whose esteem they easily gain in time of war, and their friendship at all times. I might carry the parallel a great way farther, but I am obliged to conclude; the King's ship is just going to set sail, and the merchantmen are making ready to follow her, so that, perhaps, in three days time, there will not be so much as a single vessel of any sort in the road.

Letter X

. . . Thus it appears, Madam, that every one here is possessed of the necessaries of life; but there is little paid to the King; the inhabitant is not acquainted with taxes; bread is cheap; fish and flesh are not dear; but wine, stuffs, and all French commodities are very expensive. Gentlemen, and those officers who have nothing but their pay, and are besides encumbered with families, have the greatest reason to complain. The women have a great deal of spirit and good nature, are extremely agreeable, and excellent breeders; and these good qualities are for the most part all the fortune they bring their husbands; but God has blessed the marriages in this country in the same manner he formerly blessed those of the Patriarchs. In order to support such numerous families, they ought likewise to lead the lives of Patriarchs, but the time for this is past. There are a greater number of noblesse in New France than in all the other colonies put together.

The King maintains here eight and twenty companies of marines, and three *états-majors*. Many families have been ennobled here, and there still remain several officers of the regiment of Carignan-Salières, who have peopled this country with gentlemen who are not in extraordinary good circumstances, and would be still less so, were not commerce allowed them, and the right of hunting and fishing, which is common to everyone.

After all, it is a little their own fault if they are ever exposed to want; the land is good almost everywhere, and agriculture does not in the least derogate from their quality. How many gentlemen throughout all our provinces would envy the lot of the simple inhabitants of Canada, did they but know it? And can those who languish here in a shameful indigence, be excused for refusing to embrace a profession, which the corruption of manners and the most salutary maxims has alone degraded from its ancient dignity? There is not in the world a more wholesome climate than this; no particular distemper is epidemical here, the fields and woods are full of simples of a wonderful efficacy, and the trees distill balms of an excellent quality. These advantages ought at least to engage those whose birth providence has cast in this country to remain in it; but inconstancy, aversion to a regular and assiduous labour, and a spirit of independence, have ever carried a great many young people out of it, and prevented the colony from being peopled.

These, Madam, are the defects with which the French Canadians are, with the greatest justice, reproached. The same may likewise be said of the Indians. One would imagine that the air they breathe in this immense continent contributes to it; but the example and frequent intercourse with its natural inhabitants are more than sufficient to constitute this character. Our Creoles are likewise accused of great avidity in amassing, and indeed they do things with this view, which could hardly be believed if they were not seen. The journeys they undertake; the fatigues they undergo; the dangers to which they expose themselves, and the efforts they make, surpass all imagination. There are however few less interested, who dissipate with greater facility what has cost them so much pains to acquire, or who testify less regret at having lost it. Thus there is some room to imagine that they commonly undertake such painful and dangerous journeys out of a taste they have contracted for them. They love to breathe a free air, they are early accustomed to a wandering life; it has charms for them, which make them forget past dangers and fatigues, and they place their glory in encountering them often. They have a great deal of wit, especially the fair sex, in whom it is brilliant and easy; they are, besides, constant and resolute, fertile in resources, courageous, and capable of managing the greatest affairs. You, Madam, are acquainted with more than one of this character, and have often declared your surprise at it to me. I can assure you such are frequent in this country, and are to be found in all ranks and conditions of life.

I know not whether I ought to reckon amongst the defects of our Canadians the good opinion they entertain of themselves. It is at least certain that it inspires them with a confidence, which leads them to undertake and execute what would appear impossible to many others. It must however be confessed they have excellent qualities. There is not a province in the kingdom where the people have a finer complexion, a more advantageous stature, or a body better proportioned. The strength of their constitution is not always answerable, and if the Canadians live to any age, they soon look old and decrepid. This is not entirely their own fault, it is likewise that of their parents, who are not sufficiently watchful over their children to prevent their ruining their health at a time of life, when if it suffers it is seldom or never recovered. Their agility and address are unequalled; the most expert Indians themselves are not better marksmen, or manage their canoes in the most dangerous rapids with greater skill.

Many are of opinion that they are unfit for the sciences, which require any great degree of application, and a continued study. I am not able to say whether this prejudice is well founded, for as yet we have seen no Canadian who has endeavoured to remove it, which is perhaps owing to the dissipation in which they are brought up. But nobody can deny them an excellent genius for mechanics; they have hardly any occasion for the assistance of a master in order to excel in this science; and some are every day to be met with who have succeeded in all trades, without ever having served an apprenticeship.

Some people tax them with ingratitude, nevertheless they seem to me to have a pretty good disposition; but their natural inconstancy often prevents their attending to the duties required by gratitude. It is alleged they make bad servants, which is owing to their great haughtiness of spirit, and to their loving liberty too much to subject themselves willingly to servitude. They are however good masters, which is the reverse of what is said of those from whom the greatest part of them are descended. They would have been perfect in character, if to their own virtues they had added those of their ancestors. Their inconstancy in friendship has sometimes been complained of; but this complaint can hardly be general, and in those who have given occasion for it, it proceeds from their not being accustomed to constraint, even in their own affairs. If they are not easily disciplin'd, this likewise proceeds from the same principle, or from their having a discipline peculiar to themselves, which they believe is better adapted for carrying on war against the Indians, in which they are not entirely to blame. Moreover, they appear to me to be unable to govern a certain impetuosity, which renders them fitter for sudden surprises or hasty expeditions, than the regular and continued operations of a campaign. It has likewise been observed, that amongst a great number of brave men who distinguished themselves in the last wars, there were very few found capable of bearing a superior. This is perhaps owing to their not having sufficiently learned to obey. It is however true, that when they are well conducted, there is nothing which they will not accomplish, whether by sea or land, but in order to do this they must entertain a great opinion of their commander. The late M. d'Iberville, who had all the good qualities of his countrymen without any of their defects, could have led them to the end of the world.

There is one thing with respect to which they are not easily to be excused, and that is the little natural affection most of them shew to their parents, who for their part display a tenderness for them, which is not extremely well managed. The Indians fall into the same defect, and it produces amongst them the same consequences. But what above all things ought to make the Canadians be held in much esteem, is the great fund they have of piety and religion, and that nothing is wanting to their education upon this article. It is likewise true, that when they are out of their own country they hardly retain any of their defects. As with all this they are extremely brave and active, they might be of great service in war, in the marine and in the arts; and I am opinion that it would redound greatly to the advantage of the state, were they to be much more numerous than they are at present. Men constitute the principal riches of the Sovereign, and Canada, should it be of no other use to France, would still be, were it well peopled, one of the most important of all our colonies.

28. The Growth of Louisiana

FOLLOWING THE collapse of John Law's Company of the Occident, Louisiana became the property of the Company of the Indies. This corporation did little to develop the colony and eventually returned it to the Crown in 1731. Under the royal regime, Louisiana finally began to acquire shape and form.

Territorially, the colony was divided in two regions: Lower Louisiana, consisting approximately of the southern portions of the present states of Louisiana, Mississippi, and Alabama; and Upper Louisiana, usually referred to as le pays des Illinois by the French, made up roughly of present day Missouri and Illinois. The economy of Upper Louisiana was based chiefly on wheat and furs, that of the lower colony on indigo, tobacco, sugar, cotton, and rice.

The population of Louisiana in 1746 was 8,830, of whom approximately 4,000 were white and the balance Negroes and Mulattoes. These people lived in some twenty different settlements linked together by the drainage system of the Mississippi basin. New Orleans, the capital, was almost a small world in itself. It featured comfortable homes and a small but brilliant court at the Governor's residence. Carriages rolled along its streets which, unlike the narrow and crooked ones of Quebec, were neatly laid out at right angles to one another.

In the following document, Honoré Michel de La Rouvillière, commissaire ordonnateur of Louisiana—the equivalent of the Canadian Intendant—describes the state of the colony to the minister of marine, Antoine-Louis Rouillé, comte de Jouy.

Further Reading: G. Frégault, Le Grand Marquis: Pierre de Rigaud de Vaudreuil et la Louisiane (Montréal, 1952). Vaudreuil was governor of Louisiana from 1742 to 1754. In that year he became governor of Canada; E. Lauvrière, Histoire de la Louisiane française (Baton Rouge, La., 1940); Nancy M. M. Surrey, The Commerce of Louisiana during the French Régime (New York, 1916).

SOURCE: Honoré Michel de La Rouvillière to Antoine-Louis Rouillé, comte de Jouy, minister of marine, September 23, 1752, Archives nationales, colonies (Paris) série C^{13}A, vol. 36, ff. 269–275. Translated by the editor.

Permit me to present a precis of the colony with regard to its establishments, its products and its commerce. I will begin with the latter.

The vessels arrived very late this year, with the result that all types of merchandise were scarce and expensive during the first six months. Prices went down when these vessels, numbering fifteen in all, arrived almost all at the same time. The convoy for the Illinois which left at that time, the Situade of Pensacola which docked here to gather supplies, and four Spanish vessels loaded with tobacco and logwood, provided a quite considerable outlet and maintained the price of the merchandise at a reasonable level. Thus, the merchant vessels will not have journeyed here in vain, and they will find for their return trip wood of all types in quantity; bunched and powdered tobacco which, I hope, will be abundant this year; logwood; indigo in the same amount at least as in the past; and much more peltries than in preceeding years since more than usual was shipped from the Illinois country and that of the Choctaw Indians. The punctual care I take to have bills of exchange delivered to the shipowners twice a year and to have them honored by the inhabitants means that [the former] leave no [unsettled accounts] in the country.[1] This commerce must be lucrative to the shipowners, advantageous to the trade of France and America, and of great benefit to the colony which sustains itself quite well by this means.

The crops of rice and corn will be quite plentiful in the interior of the colony. Indigo will not be as abundant because we had heavy rains and frequent storms all summer, but this deficit will be made up by the number of inhabitants who began to grow the plant this year and who succeeded tolerably well. The Illinois country produced much flour, that is to say, more than usual. Already, enough has come down to supply all the posts along the route [the Mis-

1 This statement of de La Rouvillière is not accurate. In 1752 the inhabitants of Louisiana owed some 3,917,119 livres to the Company of the Indies.

sissippi] and even the Natchitoches [on the Red River]. This puts me somewhat at ease about servicing the interior parts of the colony and will enable me to wait patiently for further assistance from France and the Illinois. I hope that in a very short time this establishment [in the Illinois country], as we continue to place settlers there, will produce enough provisions so that shipments from France can be sizably reduced.

A few individuals started plantations of wax trees in the interior of the colony and were wonderfully successful. The sr. Dubreuil alone produced 6,000 pounds of wax, and other persons produced in proportion. Many have explored the woods toward the sea to find wax trees. The population here uses no other product for its lighting needs and part of [this wax] has gone into our trade with France and America.

A few persons have established cotton plantations with perfect success. I visited a few and found the cotton magnificent. I am sending some to M. de La Galissonière who requested it, together with the seeds, which are rather difficult to detach. The sr. Dubreuil has just patented a spinning wheel which, by means of two joined cylinders of copper, iron, or hardwood, that spin against each other as those of sugar mills, detach the cotton seeds with enough speed to give them commercial value.

All the other products [of the soil] grow perfectly. Each season is very distinctive and makes itself felt in the proper way. The climate is magnificent. The summer, frankly speaking, is a little too hot and stormy, but this is precisely the time when the river reaches its highest level. Its waters can be used as one wishes with neither trouble nor expense, and at the same time one can irrigate land and fertilize it by means of the deposits the waters leave behind. In truth, My Lord, this is the best soil in the world and the finest colony the King can own. His Majesty will later have reason to repent not to have profited from the considerable advantages which he could have derived from it. A small expense made opportunely would produce great benefits to the state. You know, My Lord, that to reap one must sow, and in relation to the results the outlay would not be great. It is only a question of sending inhabitants who know the soil and Negroes to be distributed [to the settlers] on credit.

For some time, the public has awakened to the spirit of emulation. The inhabitants, touched by His Majesty's early kindnesses, have emerged from their lethargy. They are all asking for Negroes and cannot in fact succeed without them. Things are proceeding apace, the colony is increasing daily by its own strength, and spurring it, so to speak, is all that is required. Since the three years I have been here, forty handsome brick homes have been built in New Orleans and many fine estates have been established in the country. Sawmills have been erected. A number of inhabitants have settled on new lands where they are living quite miserably while waiting for the Negroes who will help to clear and extend them. A few of the better sort have given me money so that I may send to San Domingo for Negroes, which I did so as to help them insofar as it is in my power. There is no other way, My Lord, of realizing the benefits which you are entitled to expect from this colony than by sending there good, hard-working peasants, decent people, and a supply of Negroes.

The soldiers recently sent by His Majesty will be an almost total loss for the colony. Most have already deserted or killed themselves with drink, all sorts of debauches, and venereal disease which they mistook for scurvy. . . . I have the sorrow of seeing them all perish after having cost the King a considerable amount. The expenses they occasioned were excessive and bore no fruit since the companies are today down to half their strength. It is necessary, however, that there be a sufficient number of soldiers to strengthen the garrisons and the outposts, where they can even form some establishments. In this manner, the Indians will be kept in awe and will not dare undertake anything against the colony. The inhabitants, not fearing their incursions anymore, will give themselves entirely over to the care of the land. These arrangements, once they are made public, will attract a number of strangers to the colony, who until now have not wished to expose themselves to the fury of the savages. But it would be necessary, My Lord, that the recruits sent here to fill the ranks of the troops be promising young men who can adjust to the climate and who have not ruined their health by debauches.

V

The Fall of New France, 1754–1760

29. An Imperial Vision of New France, 1750

THE WAR of the Austrian Succession, called King George's War in America, was an indecisive round in the final Anglo-French struggle for imperial hegemony. Shortly after the ratification of the Treaty of Aix-la-Chapelle in 1748, which restored the status quo ante bellum, France and England in an ultimate effort to avoid another conflict appointed a joint commission to study the boundary question in America. One of the two French representatives at these meetings was the former interim governor of New France, Roland-Michel Barrin de La Galissonière. Alarmed by the extent of British territorial claims in Acadia, the Ohio Valley, and the Great Lakes country, he wrote his great "Memoir on the French Colonies in America" to impress upon the government the importance of New France. It is interesting to compare this document with the instructions of Maurepas to Hocquart in 1729. While the latter was inspired by purely economic considerations, the former embodies a grand imperial strategy.

Further Reading: R. Lamontagne, La Galissonière et le Canada (Montreal, 1962). For the history of the period covered in this chapter, see G. Frégault, La Guerre de la Conquête (Montreal, 1955); L. H. Gipson, The British Empire Before the American Revolution (13 vols., New York, 1936–), Vol. IV, Zones of International Friction, North America South of the Great Lakes Region 1748–1754; Vol. V, Zones of International Friction, The Great Lakes Frontier, Canada, the West Indies, India, 1748–1754; Vol. VI, The Great War for the Empire, The Years of Defeat, 1754–1757; Vol. VII, The Great War for the Empire, The Victorious Years, 1758–1760; Vol. VIII, The Great War for the Empire, The Culmination, 1760–1763.

SOURCE: La Galissonière, Memoir on the French Colonies in North America, December, 1750, in O'Callaghan (ed.), *Documents Relative to the Colonial History of the State of New York*, X, 220–232.

It may be objected that we must carefully preserve such of the Colonies as are a source of revenue to the State and of wealth to the Kingdom, as St. Domingo, Martinico and the other Tropical Islands; but that those Colonies, which, far from being productive of revenue or wealth, are, like Canada and Louisiana, an expense, ought to be abandoned to themselves.

It is not designed to lessen the weight of this objection. . . .

We shall confine ourselves to regarding Canada as a barren frontier, such as the Alps are to Piedmont, as Luxembourg would be to France, and as it, perhaps, is to the Queen of Hungary. We ask if a country can be abandoned, no matter how bad it may be, or what the amount of expense necessary to sustain it, when by its position it affords a great advantage over its neighbors.

This is precisely the case of Canada: it cannot be denied that this Colony has been always a burthen to France, and it is probable that such will be the case for a long while; but it constitutes, at the same time, the strongest barrier that can be opposed to the ambition of the English.

We may dispense with giving any other proofs of this than the constant efforts they have made, for more than a century, against that Colony.

We will add, however, that it alone is in a position to wage war against them in all their possessions on the Continent of America; possessions which are as dear to them as they are precious in fact, whose power is daily increasing, and which, if means be not found to prevent it, will soon absorb not only all the Colonies located in the neighboring islands of the Tropic, but even all those of the Continent of America.

Long experience has proved that the preservation of the major portion of the settlements in the Tropical islands is not owing so much to their intrinsic strength, as to the difficulty of conveying troops thither from Europe in sufficient numbers to subjugate or keep them, and of supporting such troops there; but if the rapid progress of the English Colonies on the Continent be not arrested, or what amounts to the same thing, if a counterpoise capable of confining them within their limits, and of forcing them to the defensive, be not formed, they will possess, in a short time, such great facilities to construct formidable armaments on the Continent of America, and will require so little time to convey a large force either to St. Domingo or to the Island of Cuba, or to our Windward islands, that it will not be possible to hope to preserve these except at an enormous expense.

This will not be the case if we make a more energetic and generous effort to increase and strengthen Canada and Louisiana, than the English are making in favor of their Colonies; since the French Colonies, despite their destitute condition, have always waged war against the English of the Continent with some advantage, though the latter are, and always have been, more numerous; it is necessary to explain here the causes to which this has been owing.

The first is the great number of alliances that the French keep up with the Indian Nations. These people, who hardly act except from instinct, love us hitherto a little, and fear us a great deal, more than they do the English; but their interest, which some among them begin to understand, is that the strength of the English and French remain nearly equal, so that through the jealousy of these two nations those tribes may live independent of, and draw presents from, both.

The second reason of our superiority over the English is, the number of French Canadians who are accustomed to live in the woods like the Indians, and become thereby not only qualified to lead them to fight the English, but to wage war even against these same Indians when necessity obliges.

Hence 'twill be seen that this superiority of the French in America is in some sort accidental, and if they neglect to maintain it, whilst the English are making every effort to destroy it, 'twill pass into the hands of the latter. There is no doubt but such an event would be followed by the entire destruction of our settlements in that part of the Globe.

This, however serious it may seem, would not be our only loss; it would drag after it that of the superiority which France must claim over England.

If anything can, in fact, destroy the superiority of France in Europe, it is the Naval force of the English; this alone sustained the house of Austria at the commencement of the war of the Spanish succession, as it caused France to lose, at the close of the last war, the fruit of the entire conquest of the Austrian Lower Countries.

We must not flatter ourselves with being able long to sustain an expenditure [for the navy] equal to theirs; no other resource remains then but to attack them in their possessions; that cannot be effected by forces sent from Europe except with little hope of success, and at vast expense, whilst by fortifying ourselves in America and husbanding means in the Colonies themselves, the advantages we possess can be preserved, and even increased at a very trifling expense, in comparison with the cost of expeditions fitted out in Europe.

The utility of Canada is not confined to the preservation of the French Colonies, and to rendering the English apprehensive for theirs; that Colony is not less essential for the conservation of the Spanish possessions in America, especially of Mexico.

So long as that barrier is well secured; so long as the English will be unable to penetrate it; so long as efforts will be made to increase its strength, 'twill serve as a rampart to Louisiana, which hitherto sustains itself only under the shadow of the forces of Canada, and by the connection of the Canadians with the Indians. . . .

Of the French Posts in the Gulf of St. Lawrence; of Ile Royale and Acadia

. . . Nothing is more essential to the preservation of Ile Royale than to secure for it the means of communication with Canada, and to spare no pains to establish entrepôts of provisions, and especially of cattle as well in Ile Royale itself, though they cannot be either considerable or sufficient, as in the Island of St. John [Prince Edward Island] (which is better adapted for that purpose), and in that part of Canada bordering on the Gulf of St. Lawrence.

There is a part of the year when there is no communication between Louisbourg and Canada by the River St. Lawrence, and no route practicable except by way of the River St. John.

This is one of the principal considerations that gives interest to the preservation of that part of Canada, which the English would appropriate under the name of Acadia. Its soil, of itself, is of little fertility; any detachments at all considerable cannot be supported there for a long time to come; but the River St. John, which runs through that country, is the sole available route during six months of the year, between Louisbourg and Quebec; and the only one affording a passage to small detachments, which, dispersed through the woods and sustained by the Indians, are often capable of disconcerting the projects of the English and rendering their execution of them difficult and murderous. Were they masters of this communication, the aid of the Indians would at the same time be lost, Louisbourg would find itself abandoned too often and for too long a time to its own strength, not to succumb to the first hostile attack, and the environs of Quebec would be exposed to the incursions of the enemy by reason of the facilities the latter would possess of reaching that city by ascending the River St. John, which rises in the vicinity of the settlements bordering on the River St. Lawrence. So many powerful reasons show the necessity of attending to the preservation of that part of Canada.

Hence it results that too much precaution cannot be used in arranging the boundaries of Acadia. According to strict construction of the Treaties, and the ancient descriptions of that Province, the cession made to the English terminates at Port Royal and its liberty (banlieue), and at the part of the coasts which extends from the extremity of the Bay of Fundy unto Cape Canso.[1] They must not possess anything on the Bay of St. Lawrence nor towards the Isthmus, nor towards what is called Minas, the inhabitants of which are French and Catholics. If, nevertheless, for the sake of peace, it be determined to cede to them a portion of the Peninsula, which doth not appertain to them, it seems that it ought not to be done, except in return for some advantages, and that it could not be done with safety but by attaching some conditions thereto, without which it would be better perhaps that the claims on both sides remain, with the resolution to maintain them by force in case the English should employ any to extend their possessions beyond what is legitimately their right. . . .

1 According to this interpretation of the Peace of Utrecht Acadia, as defined in Article XII, only designated the town of Port Royal with its vicinity and the coastline of the southern portion of the Nova Scotian peninsula.

Of the Canadian Posts Inland

. . . This post [Oswego], located on ground, and on the borders of a lake, always in the possession of the French, has not been erected by the English until a number of years after the Treaty of Utrecht, and in a period of profound peace. The Governor of Canada then confined himself to protests, and the post has continued, and remains, when it ought to have been pulled down in the beginning by force. . . .

We shall not enter here into any lengthy discussion on the point of right; but we must not omit observing that this post, which has been almost regarded as an object of trifling importance, is capable of causing the entire ruin of Canada, and has already inflicted on it the greatest injury.

There it is that the French often carry on a fraudulent trade which transmits to England profits the most unquestionable, that Canada ought to afford to France.

There it is that the English scatter rum among the Indians, the use of which had been forbidden them by the King's Ordinances, because it set them crazy.

In fine, it is there that the English entice all the Indian Nations, and endeavor by force of presents, not only to debauch them, but also to induce them to assassinate the French traders dispersed throughout the vast extent of the forests of New France.

As long as the English will possess Chouaguen [Oswego] there will be a perpetual distrust of Indians the most loyal to the French; twice more troops than the state of the Colony requires, or comports with its condition, will have to be maintained in times of the most profound peace; forts will have to be established and kept in an infinite number of places, and very numerous and very expensive detachments sent almost every year, to restrain the different Nations of Indians. The navigation of the lakes will be always exposed to be disturbed; agriculture will not advance, except very slowly, and cannot be pursued except in the heart of the Colony; in fine, matters will be always in a situation possessing all the inconveniences of war, even without any of its advantages.

Nothing, then, must be left undone to destroy this dangerous post, on the first occasion for reprisals the English will offer by some of those hostilities they are but too much accustomed to commit in time of peace; supposing that its cession, by common consent, cannot be obtained, for some equivalent.

What has been observed already in the course of this Memoir, when treating of the utility of Canada in regard to the preservation of Mexico, shows the absolute necessity of the free and certain communication from Canada to the Mississipi. This chain, once broken, would leave an opening of which the English would doubtless take advantage to get nearer the silver mines (*la source de l'argent*). Many of their writings are full of this project, which will never amount to anything but a chimera, if France retain her Canadian possessions.

That of the River Oyo [Ohio], otherwise called the Beautiful river, is the most interesting in this relation. It rises near the country at present partly occupied by the Iroquois, runs southwardly, falls into the Ouabache, and with that river into the Mississipi.

This last has been discovered by Sieur De la Salle; who took possession of it in the King's name; and it would perhaps to-day be full of French settlements, had not the Governors of Canada been deterred from establishing permanent posts there by the apprehension that a counterband trade between the French traders and the English would be the consequence.

Neither have the English any posts there, nor did they come to that quarter to trade, except clandestinely, until the last war, when the revolt of some neighboring nations against the French, encouraged them to come more boldly.

They have been summoned since the peace, to retire, and if they do not do so, there is no doubt but the Governor of Canada will constrain them thereto by force, otherwise the case would be the same as at Choueguen, and this misfortune would be still more disastrous, for a post on the Beautiful river would possess more opportunities to do damage than Chouaguen alone.

1st They would have much greater opportunities there than at Chouaguen to seduce the Indian nations.

2nd They would possess more facilities to interrupt the communication between Canada and Louisiana, for the Beautiful river affords almost the only route for the conveyance from Canada to the River Mississipi, of detachments capable of securing that still feeble Colony against the incursions of the neighboring Indians of

Carolina, whom the English are unceasingly exciting against the French.

3ᵈ If the English ever become strong enough in America to dare attempt the conquest of Mexico, it will be by this Beautiful river, which they must necessarily descend.

4ᵗʰ By it alone will they also be able to attack, with any considerable force, and any hope of success, the Illinois posts and all those which will be established along the River St. Louis, otherwise, Mississipi.

5ᵗʰ It is, moreover, by that route that they can attack the post of the Miamis, which, again, cuts off one of our best communications with the River Mississipi, and involves the loss of Detroit, an important post whereof mention will be made hereafter.

The establishment of some posts on the Beautiful river is considered, then, one of the most urgent expenses. . . .

Conclusion

. . . In fine, nothing must be spared to strengthen these Colonies, since they may, and are to be considered as the bulwark of America, against the attacks of the English; since they alone can make up for the want of Naval forces, and the outlay they will occasion will save more considerable expense whereof the effects are much less certain, especially if we allow ourselves to be reduced to the necessity of having to transport reinforcements thither from France, in order to preserve these Colonies in time of war; and since they cannot be abandoned to their actual strength alone, without being delivered over in some sort to the English, who, by the wealth they would draw thence, to the exclusion of other Nations, would most certainly acquire the superiority in Europe.

30. Instructions to Governor Vaudreuil, 1755

IN 1754, the two empires stood once more on the brink of war. The French had established positions in the Ohio Valley and clashed with a corps of Virginians commanded by George Washington which had tried unsuccessfully to drive them out. The following year a French naval squadron carrying reinforcements to Canada was attacked by British warships off Newfoundland. France's policy at this critical moment reflects the influence of La Galissonière. The new governor of Canada, Pierre de Rigaud de Vaudreuil, was told in his instructions to remain on the defensive but to treat any British "usurpation" in Acadia, the Ohio Valley, and the Great Lakes country as an act of war.

SOURCE: Private instructions for Mr. de Vaudreuil regarding the conduct he is to observe toward the English, April 1, 1755, in O'Callaghan (ed.), *Documents Relative to the Colonial History of the State of New York*, X, 291–294.

As yet, the Commissioners have not entered upon the limits of Canada further than what regards Acadia. The demands the British Commissioners have made on that subject, have laid bare the ambition and unjust views of their nation. Under pretext of the cession which has been made to England of Acadia, by Article 12 of the Treaty of Utrecht, they have claimed not only all the Peninsula in which Acadia happens to be situated, but moreover that the cession included on the one side, all the territory extending up to the South shore of the River St. Lawrence, and embraced on the other side the territory which touches the frontiers of New England. But it has not been difficult for his Majesty's Commissioners to destroy ideas so chimerical, and they have shown that the cession of Acadia ought to include only a part of the Peninsula. . . .

He is informed of what has occurred in the direction of the Beautiful river [the Ohio], which the English will now include within the dependencies of Virginia. But he is not aware that, not content with endeavoring to penetrate in that direction, into the interior of the country, and there cut off the communication between Canada and Louisiana, they pretend, further, to have the right to resort to the lakes of Canada, and that the lands which are to the south of Lake Erie and of Lake Ontario belong to them.

They have not yet explained themselves respecting the extent they propose giving their Hudson bay boundaries. But it is to be expected that they will wish to stretch them to the centre of the Colony of Canada, in order to inclose it in all sides. . . .

His Majesty's intention is, in fact, that he confine himself to a strict defensive, so long as the English will not make any attack, which is to be regarded as a rupture on their part.

If, to insure this defensive, he considers it necessary to make the Indians act offensively against the English, he will be at liberty to have recourse to that expedient. But his Majesty desires that he do not determine on that course, except so far as the conduct of the English will render it indispensable for the safety and tranquillity of his government.

Supposing, in the mean time, that, notwithstanding what ought to be naturally expected from the equitable and pacific dispositions, whereof the King of Great Britain does not cease to give assurances, hostilities on the part of the English should reach the point that they must be regarded as a rupture, he should not, in that case, confine himself to a simple defensive; and his Majesty wills that, in such contingency, he make use of all the powers that have been confided to him for the operations which will be best adapted to the good of his service and the glory of his arms.

As these operations must depend on circumstances, his Majesty relies on Sieur de Vaudreuil's zeal, prudence and experience for undertaking those that will appear to him the most advantageous and the most honorable. He recommends to him only to observe, in the selection of those that he will think he can undertake, to give the preference to such as will have for object the English posts that can be wholly destroyed, such as that of Choueguen and even Fort Beaubassin, or will deserve to be preserved after he shall have become master of them, either for the purpose of increasing the Colony of Canada, as would be the case with Acadia, or of being used for exchange, according to the circumstances which will possibly occur or happen, whenever there will be question of a peace, and such would be the capture of Hudson's bay.

But before coming thus to operations of an open war, his Majesty desires that Sieur de Vaudreuil do assure himself that the English will have in fact committed absolute hostilities either against the French settlements or forts of Canada, or against some other Colonies, or at sea.

In this category may be regarded the usurpations they will possibly attempt on the unsettled lands of Canada, and on which they have undertaken to set up unfounded pretensions. His Majesty's intention meanwhile is, that so long as they will confine themselves to operations of that sort, Sieur de Vaudreuil do content himself with opposing them, and even employ force for that purpose only after he has protested and made the summons which time and circumstances will have possibly permitted. And in this regard his Majesty is very glad to enter into a fuller explanation of the pretensions of the English, in order to enable Sieur de Vaudreuil to act more understandingly on occasions relative thereto.

Independent of the Hudson bay boundary, of which there has, as yet, been no question with the English, their pretensions, as has been already observed, have for object to extend the limits of Acadia on one side as far as the South shore of the River St. Lawrence, and on the other, as far as the frontiers of New England; to include in those of Virginia the lands that reach to Lake Erie, and those of the Beautiful river; and to penetrate into the Lakes of Canada; so that in this system they would wrest from the French all the posts the latter possess south of the River St. Lawrence, and the Colony of Canada would find itself reduced to those they have on the north of that river, and wherein it would be soon crippled in consequence of the extension the English will not fail to desire to give the Hudson bay boundary. . . .

3 observations are to be made respecting the frontiers of New England.

First, that in strictness and agreeably to the titles even of the English, his Majesty might claim that they are bounded by the River Sagadahock, but he consents that they extend as far as the River St. George, and possibly he will consent to extending them even as far as the River Pentagouet [the Penobscot], according as the English will lend themselves to a conciliatory arrangement.

Secondly, that in regard to the boundary of New England inland, his Majesty is disposed to agree that it be fixed at what is called the Water shed [the Appalachians], that is to say, the heads of the rivers emptying into the sea.

And thirdly, that Sieur de Vaudreuil must keep secret his Majesty's dispositions, both on this latter article and on that of the River Pentagouet, his Majesty communicating it to him only that he do not undertake anything contrary thereunto until new orders from him.

In respect to the limits of Virginia, they have been acknowledged from all time to be the mountains which bound that Colony on the west. It is only since the last war that the English have set up claims to the territory on the Beautiful river, the possession whereof had never been disputed to the French, who have always resorted that river since it was discovered by Sieur de La Salle. The

English have not yet alleged either title or reasons in support of their pretension. They have only given to understand that they founded it on the rights of the Iroquois; rights which they were in a position to establish, either by title of acquisition or of sovereignty over these Indians. But, 1st, the Iroquois have themselves no rights to these lands; for, besides the Iroquois having set foot on a territory being insufficient to give that Nation a title to it, 'tis certain that we were in possession of the Beautiful river before these Indians had resorted thither.

2^d Title by acquisition would conflict with that by sovereignty, inasmuch as the pretended sovereignty would render the acquisition useless.

3^d That sovereignty is a chimera. The English desire to establish it on the 15th Article of the Treaty of Utrecht, which states that *the inhabitants of Canada will not molest the Five Nations or cantons of Indians subjects of Great Britain.*

But such an enunciation, inserted in a treaty foreign to the Iroquois, can so much the less decide their condition, inasmuch as, besides their not being named in it, the same Article adds, that the respective Commissioners will explain, distinctly, which are the Indians who are or ought to be reputed subjects or friends of the one or the other Nation.

And besides, Sieur de Vandreuil knows well that the Iroquois are very far from acknowledging any Sovereign.

It is, nevertheless, from this chimerical sovereignty that the English desire still to derive their pretended right to the territory extending from the mountains which shut in their Colonies to Lake Erie, as having belonged to the Iroquois. But this pretension destroys itself by the same reasons as that which regards the territory of the Beautiful river.

Finally, the English have not been more fortunate in their explanation of the right of resorting the lakes of Canada. They will pretend, perhaps, to support it on the same Article 15 of the Treaty of Utrecht, which states, speaking of the subjects of France, of the subjects of Great Britain and of the American subjects or friends of the two Crowns, that *the one and the other will enjoy full liberty of going and coming for the good of trade.*

But this disposition has never been understood to mean liberty of trade between the French and English. The general law that is established in all the European Colonies of America against all foreign trade, is enforced in Canada and the adjoining English Colonies. That trade is carried on there only fraudulently; and the liberty stipulated in the Article of the Treaty of Utrecht has never regarded any but the Indians; that is to say, that the Indian allies of France may go to the English to trade, as those who are allies of England may come to the French; but this is the extent of that liberty; for the Indians, allies of France and located on its territory, cannot receive the English in their villages (chez eux) in the same manner as those who are allies of England and settled on English soil, cannot admit the French among them.

31. The Deportation of the Acadians

FOLLOWING the transfer of Acadia to Britain in 1713, the French inhabitants had been given one year to leave the province if they desired to do so. They had chosen to stay, despite the urgings of the French government to move to Ile Royale, but had refused to take the oath of allegiance to the British Crown. A promise of neutrality was the greatest concession they were willing to make.

With the renewal of hostilities between France and Britain their position became an untenable one. The government of Nova Scotia considered that the Acadians were a threat to the smaller British population and to the naval base of Halifax. These feelings of mistrust were not entirely unjustified. French missionaries living among the Acadians were in touch with the authorities at Quebec and frequently doubled as political agents. Evidence mounted that the Acadians were assisting French and Indian war parties by supplying them with provisions and information, and on occasions by joining forces with them. In 1755, after the Acadians had once more declined to take the oath of allegiance, they were deported to various points in the Thirteen Colonies by order of Governor Charles Lawrence and his council, without the previous knowledge or consent of the British government.

In the following document Jonathan Belcher, son of a governor of Massachusetts and New Jersey and chief justice of Nova Scotia from 1754 to 1756, presents the case for deportation to the Lords of Trade.

Further Reading: E. Lauvrière, La Tragédie d'un peuple: Histoire du peuple acadien de ses origines à nos jours (2 vols., Paris, 1924).

SOURCE: Enclosure in letter dated April 14, 1756, Lords of Trade to Henry Fox, Public Archives of Canada, Nova Scotia A series, vol. 58, 1755, pp. 38–48.

The Question now depending before the Governor and Council, as to the Residence or removal of the French Inhabitants from the Province of Nova Scotia, is of the highest moment to the Honour of the Crown and the Settlement of the Colony, and as such a Juncture as the present may never occur for considering this question to any effect, I esteem it my duty to offer my reasons against receiving any of the French Inhabitants to take the Oaths and for their not being permitted to remain in the Province.

1. By their conduct from the Treaty of Utrecht to this day they have appeared in no other light than that of Rebels to His Majesty, whose Subjects they became by virtue of the Cession of the Province and the Inhabitants of it under that Treaty.

2. That it will be contrary to the Letter and Spirit of His Majesty's Instruction to Governor Cornwallis[1] & in my humble Apprehension, would incur the displeasure of the Crown and the Parliament.

3. That it will defeat the intent of the Expedition to Beau Sejour.[2]

4. That it will put a total stop to the Progress of the Settlement and disappoint the expectations from the vast Expence of Great Britain on the Province.

5. That when they return to their Perfidy and Treacheries as they unquestionably will, and with more rancour than before, on the removal of the Fleet and Troops,[3] the Province will be in no condition to drive them out of their Possessions.

1. As to their conduct since the Treaty of Utrecht in 1713 tho it was stipulated that they should remain on their lands on Condition of their taking the Oaths within a year from the date of the Treaty, they not only yet refused to take the Oath but continued in Acts of Hostility against the British Garrison. . . .

In 1744 under Le Loutre[4] 300 Indians supported by these Neutral French marched thro all their districts, and lodged within a quarter of a mile of that Garrison, and no Inhabitants gave any intelligence to the Government.

1 The governor of Nova Scotia from 1749 to 1752.
2 Beauséjour was a fort built by the French on the isthmus of Chignecto. It was captured by an Anglo-American force in June, 1755.
3 These were the forces brought into Nova Scotia for the capture of Fort Beauséjour. They were to leave the province at the onset of winter.
4 Jean-Louis Le Loutre was a missionary among the Micmac Indians and a powerful agent of French influence among the Acadians.

They in like manner supported & maintained in the same year Mr. Devivier[5] who had near surprized the Garrison & only one Inhabitant gave Intelligence which put them on their Guard and prevented it.

In 1746 they maintained 1700 Canadians in their districts the whole Summer waiting for the Arrival of Duke D'anviles Fleet[6] and when part of the Forces came before the Fort, they assisted them, and made all their Fascines,[7] and were to have joined in the attempt, being all Armed by the French.

The Winter following when the English with about 500 Troops were Canton'd at Mines, by advice of the situation of the English Troops given by the French Inhabitants to the French Troops, they drew them to attack the English, and even brought the French Officers into the English Quarter before the Attack was made, and they joined with the French in the Attack, whereby 70 of His Majesty's Subjects lost their lives, above two thirds of whom were sick Persons and were murder'd by the French Inhabitants. This was attested by some of the Soldiers who escaped. They were afterwards before the Capitulation in Arms, and kept Guard over the English Prisoners, and Treated them with more severity than the French King's Subjects themselves did.

They very frequently afterwards Received and maintain'd different Parties of the French during the Continuance of the War.

When the English first made the Settlement at Halifax [1749] and ever since they have spirited up the Indians to commit Hostilities against the English, always maintaining supporting and giving Intelligence to them, where they might distress the Settlement to the best Advantage, it having been always noted that before any Indian Attempts, a Number of the French Inhabitants have been found hovering about those places.

They have constantly since the Settlement obstinately refused to take the Oath of Allegiance, and have induced many of our Foreign Settlers to desert over to the French, and have always

5 Joseph Du Pont Du Vivier led a French force from Ile Royale into Acadia in 1744. They took Canso and made an unsuccessful attempt to capture Port Royal.

6 The duc d'Anville was given command of a large fleet in 1746 whose mission was to conquer Acadia and Newfoundland and reconquer Ile Royale, captured by New England the previous year. The expedition was plagued by misfortune and failed in all three objectives.

7 Fascines were sticks used to strengthen the sides of a trench.

Supplied the French Troops who have intruded upon this Province with Provisions, giving them a constant intelligence of all the Motions of the English, and have thereby forced the English to live in Garrison Towns, and they were unable to cultivate and improve lands at any distance which has been the Principal cause of the great expence to the British Nation and a means of more than half the Inhabitants who came here with an intent to Settle, quitting the Province and settling in other Plantations, where they might get their Bread without risquing their lives.

From such a Series of Facts for more than 40 years, it was evident that the French Inhabitants are so far from being disposed to become good Subjects that they are more and more discovering their inveterate enmity to the English and their affection to the French, of which we have recent Instances in their Insolence to Captain Murrey [sic] hiding the best of their Arms and Surrendering only their useless Musquets, and in their present absolute refusal to take the Oaths of Allegiance.

Under these circumstances, I think it cannot consist with the Honour of the Government, or the safety and prosperity of this Province, to permit any of the Inhabitants now to take the Oaths.

2. It will be contrary to the letter and Spirit of His Majesty's Instructions. . . .

Governor Cornwallis according to this Instruction summoned the French Inhabitants to swear Allegiance, and as they then refused, the Instruction seems to be no longer in Force, and that therefore the Government now have no power to tender the oaths as the French Inhabitants had by their non-compliance with the condition of the Treaty of Utrecht forfeited their Possessions to the Crown.

I would put the case. That His Majesty had required the Answer of the French Inhabitants to be transmitted to the Secretary of State to be subject to His Majesty's further pleasure, and the present Answer of all the French Inhabitants should be accordingly transmitted, "That they would not take the Oath unless they were permitted not to bear Arms against the King of France, and that otherwise they desired Six Months to remove themselves and their effects to Canada, and that they openly desired to serve the French King that they might have Priests." It is to be presumed that instead of examining the Instruction, orders and possibly a force would be immediately sent for banishing such Insolent and dangerous Inhabitants from the Province.

As to the consequences of permitting them to take the Oaths after their refusal.

3. It must defeat the Intention of the Expedition to Beau Sejour.

The Advantages from the success of that Expedition are the weakening the power of the Indians and curbing the Insolence of the French Inhabitants, but if after our late reduction of the French Forts and while the Troops are in their Borders and the British Fleet in our Harbour, and even in the presence of His Majesty's Admirals and to the highest contempt of the Governor and Council they presume to refuse allegiance to His Majesty, and shall yet be received and trusted as Subjects, we seem to give up all the advantages designed by the Victory. If this be their Language while the Fleet and Troops are with us, I know not what will be their style, and the event of their insolence and Hostilities when they are gone.

4. It may retard the Progress of the Settlement and possibly be a means of breaking it up.

The Proportion of French to English Inhabitants is deemed to be as follows

At Annapolis 200 Families at 5 in each Family is	1000
Mines . . . 300 at 5	1500
Piziquid . . . 300	1500
Chignectoo . . . 800	4000
	8000[8]
600 English Families at 5	3000
Ballance of the French against the English Inhabitants	5000

Besides the French at Lunenburgh and the Lunenburghers themselves who are more disposed to the French than to the English.

Such a Superiority of Numbers and of Persons who have avowed that they will not be Subject to the King will not only distress the present Settlers but deter others from coming as adventurers into the Province, for if they should take the Oaths, it is well known that they will not be influenced by them after a Dispensation.

5. As no Expedient can be found for removing them out of the Province when the present Armament is withdrawn, as will be

8 In 1755, the French population of Nova Scotia was closer to 11,000 persons. Of this number, approximately 7,000 were deported in 1755 and smaller groups in the years that followed.

inevitably requisite, for they will unquestionably resume their Perfidy and Treacheries and with more arts and rancour than before.

And as the residence of the French Inhabitants in the Province attached to France[9] occasions all the Schemes of the French King, and his attempts for acquiring the Province.

I think myself obliged for these Reasons and from the highest necessity which is *Lex temporis*, to the interests of His Majesty in the Province, humbly to advise that all the French Inhabitants may be removed from the Province.

[signed] JONATHAN BELCHER

Halifax, 28th July 1755

32. The Capture of Oswego, 1756

WHILE THE BRITISH were striking their great blow in Acadia, the French were winning important victories in the interior of the continent. In 1755, with the aid of Indian allies, they cut to pieces the army of General James Braddock as it advanced through the wilderness against Fort Duquesne, where Pittsburgh now stands. The next year, in their first offensive campaign of the war, the French captured the post of Oswego built by New York on Lake Ontario in 1727. The Canadians had long yearned for the destruction of Oswego, which had thrust English commerce and diplomacy deeply into their network of Indian alliances, and news of its downfall set off an explosion of joy in the colony. An anonymous composer wrote the following song to celebrate the event.

SOURCE: Bibliothèque nationale (Paris), Fonds français, vol. 12506, pp. 4–5. Translated by the editor.

> Amis chantons la gloire
> De nos braves Français
> Célébrons leur victoire
> Célébrons leur exploit
> Qu'en pensera le prince
> Quand Machault[1] lui dira
> Sire entre vos provinces
> Vive le Canada

9 The author must have meant England.
1 Minister of marine from 1754 to 1757.

Vaudreuil par sa prudence
Y prévient le hasard
Bigot par prévoyance
Y fournit les remparts
Le soldat, la milice
Soumis au général
Pour le bien du service
Vole au premier signal

De la Neuve Angleterre
Un des forts boulevards
Mis à niveau de terre
Tirer ses étendards
Toute l'artillerie
Ses vivres, ses vaisseaux
Et son infanterie
Respectent nos drapeaux

D'Ontario les ondes
Sont dans l'étonnement,
De voir que tant de monde
Se rendent en ce moment
Cessez votre surprise
Sachez que nos guerriers
Sur l'eau de la Tamise
Remportent des lauriers.

Friends sing the glory
Of our brave Frenchmen
Celebrate their victory
Celebrate their exploit
What will the prince think
When Machault will tell him
Sire among your provinces
Long live Canada

Vaudreuil by his prudence
Prevents accidents

Bigot by foresight
Provides the ramparts
The soldier, the militia
Obedient to the general
For the good of the service
Fly at the first signal

Of New England
One of the strong bulwarks
Razed to the ground
Its standards pulled down
All its artillery
Its supplies, its vessels
And its infantry
Respect our banners

The waves of Lake Ontario
Are astonished
To see so many people
Surrender at this moment
Cease being surprised
Know that our warriors
On the waters of the Thames
Are conquering laurels.

33. The War Economy

IN THE 1750's the Canadian economy was severely weakened. One reason
for this was the war effort, which absorbed the greater part of the colony's human and financial resources; another was François Bigot,
commissaire ordonnateur of Ile Royale from 1739 to 1745 and intendant
of Canada from 1748 to 1760. Perhaps even more than the conquest,
his highly developed system of war profiteering struck a ruinous blow
at the Canadian business community.

The following passage describes the formation and some of the activities of the triumvirate, as the inner core of the Bigot clique was known.
It is taken from the anonymous Mémoire du Canada, written toward
1770 by a person who was obviously well acquainted with the state of
the colony during the Seven Years' War. During the French Revolution

this memoir and a quantity of other papers from the French archives were purchased by Pierre Dubrowski, an attaché of the Russian Embassy, and placed in the Imperial Library of St. Petersburg.

Further Reading: G. Frégault, François Bigot, administrateur français (2 vols., Montreal, 1948).

SOURCE: [Anonymous], *Mémoire du Canada,* in Rapport de l'Archiviste de la Province de Québec, 1924–1925 (Quebec, Imprimeur du Roi, 1925), pp. 117–119, 127. Translated by the editor.

[Joseph Brassard Deschenaux] was the son of a cobbler who had been taught to write by a notary who lodged at his father's. He had a quick and discerning mind and progressed sufficiently to enter the intendant's service. M. Hocquart, who filled the position at the time, recognized his aptitudes and employed him during the final years of his administration. He once stated, however, that it was necessary to keep a firm hand on the reins with this young man; to slacken them might entail fatal consequences. On M. Hocquart's good recommendation, M. Bigot took Deschenaux into his service upon his arrival in Canada. Never was a man more skillful at dissimulation. He was hard-working and, knowing that he could only acquire and preserve his master's confidence by his knowledge of [the colony's] affairs, spent all his time studying them. Very soon he became indispensable. . . . With his perfect knowledge of affairs came the skill that enabled him to favor the triumvirate without his master noticing it. From that time the commerce of Canada fell into the hands of these three men. A store was even built near the intendancy, where all sorts of merchandise was sold at retail or wholesale prices. With just derision, the people called it *la friponne* [the knave]. There were many reasons for establishing this store. One was to supply the king [i.e., the state-owned store] with all his needs in general; the other was to ruin the merchants by taking over their trade. . . .

Like Deschenaux, [Joseph] Cadet was of lowly birth, but unlike him had never had the least education. In his youth he had minded cattle. But as surprising as this may seem, there was never a man more industrious, more active, and better versed in business matters. He was the instrument of his own fortune and that of the triumvirate, buying up the wheat and flour for this group and making all its transactions. He always appeared to act alone, but it was the triumvirate, nevertheless, which contributed to his ascension. The manners of this man were uncouth, but he was also generous and wasteful to excess.

Hughes Péan was the son of an assistant town major of Quebec, who later obtained this position for himself. The court had received such strong complaints against him before the arrival of M. de la Jonquière that this governor was ordered not to deliver his commission of assistant town major before being fully informed of the nature of the charges made against him; and not only to withhold it but even to place him on trial if they should be founded. Péan, however, found a way to clear himself, or rather the intendant looked after this. All [of Péan's] qualities resided in the charms of his wife. The woman he had married was young, very witty, with a sweet and gracious disposition, and loved to please. The intendant had been won by her gay looks more than by her beauty, for she only had glitter. He had not even been attracted to her upon his arrival; but the coldness of a few belles or the annoyance of husbands obliged him to turn to her. Having learned that his passions were a cause of laughter, he announced that he would so greatly favor her that people would envy her fortune. This is what happened in effect.

Her husband was favored in everything. Among other things he was commissioned to buy wheat and was advanced money from the treasury to make his purchases. He bought wheat cheaply, and the intendant afterward issued an ordonnance setting incomparably higher prices than those paid by Péan. The latter then sold his wheat to the king according to these rates and made a considerable profit. After such fine beginnings, a most brilliant future could be foreseen for Péan. He was dealing with such a kind and generous intendant! . . .

The triumvirate had resolved to seize all the commerce. Cadet looked after the external trade and Deschenaux protected him. These two tasks could not have been in better hands to ruin the king and the colony, as will be seen subsequently. Cadet was industrious, as I stated previously. He went about the countryside buying flour, wheat, and cattle. They then provisioned the posts, and the surplus was shipped outside the country. Because Péan owned a seigneury a few miles below Quebec, where a mill and several sheds had been built, vessels went there to load, and this scheme was kept from the people for a time.

The triumvirate realized its greatest coup when the wheat crop failed. Cadet, who had been recommended to the intendant, was chosen to requisition wheat to supply the posts. An estimate was made of how much the *habitants* required to satisfy their needs, and Cadet was ordered to requisition whatever exceeded this amount. However, he took a great deal more, and the people were reduced to fighting for bread at the bakery doors. Mothers, with none to give to their children, ran to M. Bigot in despair. They implored his aid and beseeched him to intervene, but all was in vain for he barely listened to them. The *habitant*, for his part, crushed by requisitions, tried unsuccessfully to make remonstrances. He was told to speak to the secretary [Deschenaux], who mistreated him and threatened to throw him in jail. If he still insisted on speaking to the intendant the latter was forewarned and, in connivance with his staff, threatened him some more, with the result that there was no way of obtaining justice. Mistreated on every side, the *habitant* sank into a state of extreme misery. Although royal expenditures were increasing, this money was only enriching a few. The intendant himself was connected with many societies that were involved in the upper country and in provisioning the stores. They even had a store in Montreal, but the triumvirate did not have as much scope there as in Quebec, for it was limited by M. [Jean-Victor] Varin, who had done everything he could to take over the provisioning of the royal posts. He was assisted by the storekeeper, [Jean-Baptiste] Martel. Nothing eluded these two men, who were as greedy as the triumvirate; but they were far from exercising as much tyranny in Montreal as the triumvirate in Quebec. The people never complained; only the merchants of Montreal, who were in the same position as those of Quebec. The *voyageurs* particularly had reasons to complain, but about the governors as much as the intendant.

We call *voyageurs* the men who load canoes with various types of merchandise suited for the Indian trade. These people had grown accustomed to buying *congés*, which are permits to trade at a western post issued by the governor. The court, in order to provide a few widows and officers with pensions, had approved this procedure, and the western trade was none the worse for it. But the governors and intendants soon completely seized this commerce. The number of *congés* was gradually reduced until no more were granted. Commandants were placed at the posts who did the governor's sole bidding, and the *voyageurs* were thus deprived of all ways of carrying out their trade. Péan and [François] Le Mercier went one better. The former was sent to the western country to inspect everything in order to favor the enterprises of the new society. . . .

For several years . . . trade had been languishing in this colony. Already, a few Quebec merchants had transferred their funds to France. They had wound up their affairs in order to elude the triumvirate, which had brought everything under its sway and spared only two or three well-known merchants. These were made responsible for buying all the shipments of wine and merchandise that had the good fortune to reach harbor . . . The royal treasury, on which the intendant could draw bills of exchange, was a limitless source of wealth. No more was needed to overrun the trade of a whole colony. Thus, the society used the king's money to keep all merchants away from the colony, even those who would have liked to settle there. . . .

34. The Battle of Quebec, September 13, 1759

THE BATTLE OF QUEBEC lasted barely fifteen minutes and was nothing more than a heavy skirmish. Yet, because of its impact on the history of America, it must be considered one of the decisive battles of the modern world.

Document A is Governor Vaudreuil's account of the battle. Although the Canadian-born Vaudreuil was biased against the French general, Montcalm, the criticism he makes of his strategy in this document is essentially sound. Several French officers were also critical of their superior for attacking with only 3,000 men instead of waiting for the arrival of nearby contingents that would have increased the size of his army to 10,000 men.

The short Document B is an extract from Montcalm's journal which explains the controversial decision to attack. Written by a Montcalm aide following the death of the French general from wounds suffered during the battle, it describes a short conversation between the two men just before the encounter.

Further Reading: T. Chapais, *Le Marquis de Montcalm, 1712–1759* (Quebec, 1911); C. P. Stacey, *Quebec, 1759; the Siege and the Battle* (Toronto, 1959). F. Parkman, *Montcalm and Wolfe* (2 vols., Boston, 1885).

SOURCES: Document A: Pierre de Rigaud de Vaudreuil to Nicolas René Berryer, minister of marine, October 5, 1759, Archives nationales, colonies (Paris), série F³, vol. 15, ff. 285–287. Document B: H. P. Casgrain (ed.), *Journal du marquis de Montcalm durant ses campagnes en Canada de 1756 à 1759* (Quebec, 1895), p. 612. Both documents translated by the editor.

A. Governor Vaudreuil's Account

I kept the army in bivouac on the night of September 12 to 13. I was counting very much on the battalion of Guienne, which I still believed to be on the city heights, but M. le marquis de Montcalm had recalled it at nightfall without advising me.[1]

On that night our sentry posts had been warned to make as little noise as possible, for the supplies we had been obliged to send for were expected to come by water. General Wolfe was informed of this arrangement by two deserters from [the battalion of] Royal Rousillon and he made use of it to attempt his landing.

M. Douglas [a French sentry] saw boats go by within pistol range. When he challenged them, they replied: "Supplies, be still." He did not reconnoiter them. Toward midnight the English landed between a picket of [the batallion of] Languedoc at St. Michel and a detachment of colonial regulars and militia at Ance au Foulon [Wolfe's Cove]. At daybreak they surrounded and attacked the posts of Foulon and Ance des Mères, which were obliged to yield to superior numbers.

M. le marquis de Montcalm was the first to be informed of this venture, and he took whatever measures he deemed appropriate without telling me of them or even seeing me.[2] It was only from a note sent to me at a quarter of six by the chevalier Bernetz that I was informed of the enemy landing at Foulon.

1 Who issued the order directing the batallion of Guienne to withdraw from the Quebec heights is not known for certain. Persons close to Montcalm claimed that the order came from Vaudreuil.
2 Both Vaudreuil and Montcalm were guarding the Beauport shore on the other side of the city when the landing occurred.

I acquainted myself with the measures taken by M. le marquis de Montcalm and learned that the batallion of Guienne, pickets, and then detachments from all the corps, had been moved forward. This had been executed very slowly and with lack of resolution. Meantime, the enemy army of approximately 3,500 men was forming in battle order, leaning its right against the Samos thicket [the river side] and its left against the house of Borgia on the côte of Abraham, [a hill sloping toward the St. Charles River] facing Quebec.

I ordered the army to march . . . I notified M. de Montcalm that the advantage the English had obtained by forcing our sentry posts must be the cause of their defeat but that it was in our interest not to act prematurely, that the English must be attacked simultaneously by our army, 1,500 men who could be easily ordered out of the city, and by the corps of M. de Bougainville.[3] In this manner, the English would be completely surrounded with only their left as an avenue of retreat, where their defeat would also be certain.

This letter was delivered by an orderly, and I then left to join M. le marquis de Montcalm, followed by my *aides de camp.* The small army which he [Montcalm] had assembled numbered 3,000 men at the most and was already in battle order. Part of the Quebec and Montreal militias were on the right, the Trois Rivières militia and some from Montreal on the left. The French regulars were at the center. Several squadrons of colonial regulars, militias, and Indians had been placed between the two armies on the right and left and had been firing successfully for some time.

Such was the state of affairs when M. le marquis de Montcalm received my letter, but hastiness was his sole counsel. He marched against the enemy, unmindful of the fact that he was giving up the heights which his army occupied, putting his soldiers out of breath, and yielding the advantage of terrain to the enemy all at once. Disorder was the inevitable consequence of the hastiness of the march. Our troops fired a general volley, not saving a single shot, and fell back in great confusion. The enemy troops, who were in good order, pursued them as far as the *faubourg* St. Louis. It was at

3 Louis-Antoine de Bougainville, Montcalm's chief *aide de camp*, was patrolling the St. Lawrence shore above Quebec to guard against a possible British landing in that area. He could have brought up 3,000 men in Wolfe's rear, including several élite grenadier companies.

this moment that I arrived on the Quebec heights. At first I thought that I might rally our troops, but there was nothing that could check their flight or overcome their discouragement. The Canadians were more responsive to my voice. I assembled 1,000 to 1,200 of them, who came back on the heights, where they continued to fire for a long time. This facilitated the retreat of our right commanded by M. Dumas, which was still engaged with the enemy's left, which they had thrown back no less than three times. I was momentarily expecting the arrival of the militias I had left behind, but they had been stopped at the bridge [crossing the St. Charles River] by order of the major general [of Quebec] on the pretext that forty boats had been seen before Quebec, as if that mattered! I was therefore obliged to follow our army across the St. Charles River and return to our camp at Beauport.

B. Extract from Montcalm's Journal

I stopped for a moment with M. le marquis de Montcalm who told me: "We cannot avoid battle. The enemy is entrenching himself. He already has two cannons. If we give him the time to become established, we will never be able to attack him with the few troops we have." He added in a sort of shock: "Can it be that Bougainville does not hear this?" He left without giving me the time to say anything except that we were very small.

35. The Articles of Capitulation, September, 1760

ON SEPTEMBER 8, 1760, in the camp before Montreal, Governor Vaudreuil and Jeffery Amherst, the British commander in North America, signed the capitulation which surrendered to Britain the vast area from the Gulf of St. Lawrence to the western Great Lakes. Vaudreuil submitted to the British general a series of requests that aimed to preserve as many as possible of the features of the French régime, but Amherst could hardly be expected to grant all of these. He readily guaranteed security for persons, home, and property, and freedom from religious persecution, but gave negative or equivocal replies to the requests relating to laws and religion.

The capitulation comprises fifty-five articles written in French, the international language of the eighteenth century. The first twenty-six articles are concerned with the laying down of arms—Amherst refused to grant the honors of war to the French troops—the treatment of the wounded, and the evacuation of the French civil and military establishments. Most of the other articles are concerned with the rights of the Canadian population that would remain behind.

SOURCE: A. Shortt and A. G. Doughty, *Documents Relating to the Constitutional History of Canada, 1759–1791* (2 vols., Ottawa, 2nd ed., 1918), I, 30–34.

Article XXVII

The free exercise of the Catholic, Apostolic, and Roman Religion, shall subsist entire, in such manner that all the states and the people of the Towns and countries, places and distant posts, shall continue to assemble in the churches, and to frequent the sacraments as heretofore, without being molested in any manner, directly or indirectly. These people shall be obliged, by the English Government, to pay their Priests the tithes, and all the taxes they were used to pay under the Government of his most Christian Majesty.—"Granted, as to the free exercise of their religion, the obligation of paying the tithes to the Priests will depend on the King's pleasure."

Article XXVIII

The Chapter, Priests, Curates and Missionaries shall continue, with an entire liberty, their exercise and functions of cures, in the parishes of the towns and countries.—"Granted." . . .

Article XXX

If by the treaty of peace, Canada should remain in the power of his Britannic Majesty, his most Christian Majesty shall continue to name the Bishop of the colony, who shall always be of the Roman communion, and under whose authority the people shall exercise the Roman Religion.—"Refused." . . .

Article XXXII

The communities of Nuns shall be preserved in their constitutions and privileges; they shall continue to observe their rules, they shall be exempted from lodging any military; and it shall be forbid to molest them in their religious exercises, or to enter their monasteries: safe-guards shall even be given them, if they desire them.—"Granted."

Article XXXIII

The preceding article shall likewise be executed, with regard to the communities of Jesuits and Recollects and of the house of the priests of St. Sulpice at Montreal; these last, and the Jesuits, shall preserve their right to nominate to certain curacies and missions, as heretofore.—"Refused till the King's pleasure be known."

Article XXXIV

All the communities, and all the priests, shall preserve their moveables, the property and revenues of the Seignories and other estates, which they possess in the colony, of what nature soever they be; and the same estates shall be preserved in their privileges, rights, honours, and exemptions.—"Granted." . . .

Article XXXVI

If by the treaty of Peace, Canada remains to his Britannic Majesty, all the French, Canadians, Acadians, Merchants and other persons who chuse to retire to France, shall have leave to do so from the British General, who shall procure them a passage: and nevertheless, if, from this time to that decision, any French, or Canadian Merchants or other persons, shall desire to go to France; they shall likewise have leave from the British General. Both the one and the other shall take with them their families, servants, and baggage.—"Granted."

Article XXXVII

The Lords of Manors, the Military and Civil officers, the Canadians as well in the Towns as in the country, the French settled, or trading, in the whole extent of the colony of Canada, and all other persons whatsoever, shall preserve the entire peaceable property and possession of the goods, noble and ignoble, moveable and immoveable, merchandizes, furs and other effects, even their ships; they shall not be touched, nor the least damage done to them, on any pretence whatever. They shall have liberty to keep, let or sell them, as well to the French as to the British; to take away the produce of them in Bills of exchange, furs, specie or other returns, whenever they shall judge proper to go to France, paying their freight, as in the XXVIth Article. They shall also have the furs which are in the posts above, and which belong to them, and may be on the way to Montreal; and, for this purpose, they shall have leave to send, this year, or the next, canoes fitted out, to fetch such of the said furs as shall have remained in those posts.—"Granted as in the XXVIth article." . . .

Article XXXIX

None of the Canadians, Acadians or French, who are now in Canada, and on the frontiers of the colony, on the side of Acadia, Detroit, Michillimaquinac, and other places and posts of the countries above, the married and unmarried soldiers, remaining in Canada, shall be carried or transported into the British colonies, or to Great-Britain, and they shall not be troubled for having carried arms—"Granted, except with regard to the Acadians." . . .

Article XLI

The French, Canadians, and Acadians of what state and condition soever, who shall remain in the colony, shall not be forced to take arms against his most Christian Majesty, or his Allies, directly or indirectly, on any occasion whatsoever; the British Government shall only require of them an exact neutrality.—"They become Subjects of the King."

Article XLII

The French and Canadians shall continue to be governed according to the custom of Paris, and the Laws and usages established for this country, and they shall not be subject to any other imposts than those which were established under the French Dominions.— "Answered by the preceding articles, and particularly by the last." . . .

Article XLVI

The inhabitants and Merchants shall enjoy all the privileges of trade, under the same favours and conditions granted to the subjects of his Britannic Majesty, as well as in the countries above, as the interior of the colony.—"Granted."

Article XLVII

The Negroes and panis [Pawnee Indians] of both sexes shall remain, in their quality of slaves, in the possession of the French and Canadians to whom they belong; they shall be at liberty to keep them in their service in the colony or to sell them; and they may also continue to bring them up in the Roman Religion—"Granted, except those who shall have been made prisoners."

VI

The Beginnings of British
Rule, 1760–1810

36. The Treaty of Paris,
1763

THE TREATY OF PARIS, concluded on February 10, 1763, marked the disintegration of the French American empire. Britain, triumphant in America, India, Europe, and on the high seas, obtained Cape Breton Island, Canada, and all the territory east of the Mississippi River. France kept New Orleans and the land west of the river but soon ceded both to Spain to compensate her for the loss of Florida. All that remained of France's once mighty empire after these transfers were the islands of Martinique and Guadeloupe in the West Indies and those of St. Pierre and Miquelon off Newfoundland.

In Canada, some 65,000 French Canadians passed unconditionally under British rule. The only right granted to them was freedom of religion, severely qualified by the phrase "as far as the laws of Great Britain permit."

Further Reading: For the history of the period covered in this chapter, written in many cases from vastly different perspectives, see: M. Brunet, Les Canadiens et les débuts de la domination britannique (Ottawa: Canadian Historical Association Booklet, 1962); A. L. Burt, The Old Province of Quebec (Toronto, 1933); T. Chapais, Cours d'histoire du Canada (8 vols., Quebec, 1919–34), Vol. I, 1760–1791, Vol. II, 1791–1814; D. Creighton, The Empire of the St. Lawrence, 1760–1850 (Toronto, 1956); Hilda Neatby, Quebec, the Revolutionary Age, 1760–1791 (Toronto, 1966); F. Ouellet, Histoire économique et sociale du Québec, 1760–1850 (Montreal, 1966).

SOURCE: Shortt and Doughty, Documents Relating to the Constitutional History of Canada, 1759–1791, I, 115–116.

IV. His Most Christian Majesty renounces all pretensions which he has heretofore formed or might have formed to Nova Scotia or Acadia in all its parts, and guaranties the whole of it, and with all its dependencies, to the King of Great Britain: Moreover, his Most Christian Majesty cedes and guaranties to his said Britannick Majesty, in full right, Canada, with all its dependencies, as well as the Island of Cape Breton, and all the other islands and coasts in the gulph and river of St. Lawrence, and in general, every thing that depends on the said countries, lands, islands, and coasts, with the sovereignty, property, possession, and all rights acquired by treaty, or otherwise, which the Most Christian King and the Crown of France have had till now over the said countries, lands, islands, places, coasts, and their inhabitants, so that the Most Christian King cedes and makes over the whole to the said King, and to the Crown of Great Britain, and that in the most ample manner and form, without restriction, and without any liberty to depart from the said cession and guaranty under any pretence, or to disturb Great Britain in the possessions above mentioned. His Britannick Majesty, on his side, agrees to grant the liberty of the Catholick religion to the inhabitants of Canada: he will, in consequence, give the most precise and most effectual orders, that his new Roman Catholic subjects may profess the worship of their religion according to the rites of the Romish church, as far as the laws of Great Britain permit. His Britannick Majesty farther agrees, that the French inhabitants, or others who had been subjects of the Most Christian King in Canada, may retire with all safety and freedom wherever they shall think proper, and may sell their estates, provided it be to the subjects of his Britannick Majesty, and bring away their effects as well as their persons, without being restrained in their emigration, under any pretence whatsoever, except that of debts or of criminal prosecutions: The term limited for this emigration shall be fixed to the space of eighteen months, to be computed from the day of the exchange of the ratification of the present treaty.

V. The subjects of France shall have the liberty of fishing and drying on a part of the coasts of the island of Newfoundland, such as it is specified in the XIIIth article of the treaty of Utrecht; which article is renewed and confirmed by the present treaty, (except what relates to the island of Cape Breton, as well as to the other islands and coasts in the mouth and in the gulph of St.

Lawrence:) And his Britannick Majesty consents to leave to the subjects of the Most Christian King the liberty of fishing in the gulph of St. Lawrence, on condition that the subjects of France do not exercise the said fishery but at the distance of three leagues from all the coasts belonging to Great Britain. . . .

VI. The King of Great Britain cedes the islands of St. Pierre and Macquelon, [sic] in full right, to his Most Christian Majesty, to serve as a shelter to the French fishermen; and his said Most Christian Majesty engages not to fortify the said islands; to erect no buildings upon them but merely for the conveniency of the fishery; and to keep upon them a guard of fifty men only for the police.

VII. In order to re-establish peace on solid and durable foundations, and to remove for ever all subject of dispute with regard to the limits of the British and French territories on the continent of America; it is agreed, that, for the future, the confines between the dominions of his Britannick Majesty and those of his Most Christian Majesty, in that part of the world, shall be fixed irrevocably by a line drawn along the middle of the River Mississippi, from its source to the river Iberville, and from thence, by a line drawn along the middle of this river, and the lakes Maurepas and Pontchartrain to the sea; and for this purpose, the Most Christian King cedes in full right, and guaranties to his Britannick Majesty the river and port of the Mobile, and every thing which he possesses, or ought to possess, on the left side of the river Mississippi, except the town of New Orleans and the island in which it is situated, which shall remain to France.

37. A Program of "Radical Reconstruction"

WITH THE STATUS of Canada definitively settled by the Treaty of Paris, the time had come for Britain to adopt a policy for her new colony. The problem was a difficult one, for the British had no precedent to show them how to integrate into their empire a firmly settled population that was neither English nor Protestant. Initially, the government decided that this strange new block must be made to conform in language, laws, religion, and political institutions to the established British colonial pattern. This policy is outlined in the Royal Proclamation of October, 1763—which also applied to the newly acquired territories of East Florida, West Florida, and Grenada—and in the royal instructions to General James Murray, first British governor of Canada.

SOURCES: Document A, Royal Proclamation of October 7, 1763, Shortt and Doughty, *Documents Relating to the Constitutional History of Canada, 1759–1791,* I, 163–168; Document B, Instructions to Our Trusty and Wellbeloved James Murray . . . the Seventh Day of December 1763. *Ibid.* 181–205.

A. *Royal Proclamation of October, 1763*

BY THE KING
A PROCLAMATION

WHEREAS We have taken into Our Royal Consideration the extensive and valuable Acquisitions in America, secured to our Crown by the late Definitive Treaty of Peace, concluded at Paris, the 10th Day of February last; and being desirous that all Our loving Subjects, as well of our Kingdom as of our Colonies in America, may avail themselves with all convenient Speed, of the great Benefits and Advantages which must accrue therefrom to their Commerce, Manufactures, and Navigation, We have thought fit, with the Advice of our Privy Council, to issue this our Royal Proclamation. . . .

First—The Government of Quebec bounded on the Labrador Coast by the River St. John, and from thence by a Line drawn from the Head of that River through the Lake St. John, to the South end of the Lake Nipissim; from whence the said Line, crossing the River St Lawrence, and the Lake Champlain, in 45. Degrees of North Latitude, passes along the High Lands which divide the Rivers that empty themselves into the said River St Lawrence from those which fall into the Sea; and also along the North Coast of the Baye des Chaleurs, and the Coast of the Gulph of St Lawrence to Cape Rosieres, and from thence crossing the Mouth of the River St Lawrence by the West End of the Island of Anticosti, terminates at the aforesaid River of St John. . . .

And to the end that the open and free Fishery of our Subjects may be extended to and carried on upon the Coast of Labrador, and the adjacent Islands, We have thought fit, with the advice of our said Privy Council, to put all that Coast, from the River St John's to Hudson's Streights, together with the Islands of Anticosti and Madelaine, and all other smaller Islands lying upon the said Coast, under the care and Inspection of our Governor of Newfoundland.

We have also, with the advice of our Privy Council, thought fit to annex the Islands of S[t] John's [Prince Edward Island] and Cape Breton, or Isle Royale, with the lesser Islands adjacent thereto, to our Government of Nova Scotia. . . .

And whereas it will greatly contribute to the speedy settling our said new Governments, that our loving subjects should be informed of our Paternal care, for the security of the Liberties and Properties of those who are and shall become Inhabitants thereof, We have thought fit to publish and declare, by this Our Proclamation, that We have, in the Letters Patent under our Great Seal of Great Britain, by which the said Governments are constituted, given express Power and Direction to our Governors of our Said Colonies respectively, that so soon as the state and circumstances of the said Colonies will admit thereof, they shall, with the Advice and Consent of the Members of our Council, summon and call General Assemblies[1] within the said Governments respectively, in such Manner and Form as is used and directed in those Colonies and Provinces in America which are under our immediate Government; and We have also given Power to the said Governors, with the consent of our Said Councils, and the Representatives of the People so to be summoned as aforesaid, to make, constitute, and ordain Laws, Statutes, and Ordinances for the Public Peace, Welfare, and good Government of our said Colonies, and of the People and Inhabitants thereof, as near as may be agreeable to the Laws of England, and under such Regulations and Restrictions as are used in other Colonies; and in the mean Time, and until such Assemblies can be called as aforesaid, all Persons Inhabiting in or resorting to our Said Colonies may confide in our Royal Protection for the Enjoyment of the Benefit of the Laws of our Realm of England; for which Purpose We have given Power under our Great Seal to the Governors of our said Colonies respectively to erect and constitute, with the Advice of our said Councils respectively, Courts of Judicature and public Justice within our Said Colonies for hearing and determining all Causes, as well Criminal as Civil, according to Law and Equity, and as near as may be agreeable to the Laws of England, with Liberty to all Persons who may think themselves aggrieved by the Sentences of such Courts, in all Civil

1 "So soon as the state and circumstances of the said Colonies will admit thereof" meant when a sufficient number of English Protestant inhabitants would be settled in Canada. There was no intention at this early date of granting the franchise to the French Canadians.

Cases, to appeal, under the usual Limitations and Restrictions, to Us in our Privy Council.

We have also thought fit, with the advice of our Privy Council as aforesaid, to give unto the Governors and Councils of our said Three new Colonies, upon the Continent full Power and Authority to settle and agree with the Inhabitants of our said new Colonies or with any other Persons who shall resort thereto, for such Lands, Tenements and Hereditaments, as are now or hereafter shall be in our Power to dispose of; and them to grant to any such Person or Persons upon such Terms, and under such moderate Quit-Rents, Services and Acknowledgments, as have been appointed and settled in our other Colonies, and under such other Conditions as shall appear to us to be necessary and expedient for the Advantage of the Grantees, and the Improvement and settlement of our said Colonies. . . .

And whereas it is just and reasonable, and essential to our Interest, and the Security of our Colonies, that the several Nations or Tribes of Indians with whom We are connected, and who live under our Protection, should not be molested or disturbed in the Possession of such Parts of our Dominions and Territories as, not having been ceded to or purchased by Us, are reserved to them, or any of them, as their Hunting Grounds.—We do therefore, with the Advice of our Privy Council, declare it to be our Royal Will and Pleasure, that no Governor or Commander in Chief in any of our Colonies of Quebec, East Florida, or West Florida, do presume, upon any Pretence whatever, to grant Warrants of Survey, or pass any Patents for Lands beyond the Bounds of their respective Governments, as described in their Commissions. . . .

And, We do further declare it to be Our Royal Will and Pleasure, for the present as aforesaid, to reserve under our Sovereignty, Protection, and Dominion, for the use of the said Indians, all the Lands and Territories not included within the Limits of Our said Three new Governments, or within the Limits of the Territory granted to the Hudson's Bay Company, as also all the Lands and Territories lying to the Westward of the Sources of the Rivers which fall into the Sea from the West and North West as aforesaid. . . .

B. Royal Instructions to Governor Murray, December 7, 1763

3. And You are forthwith to call Our said Council together, or such of them as can be conveniently assembled, and to cause Our

said Commission to You to be read at such Meeting; which being done, You shall then take yourself, and also administer to Our Lieutenant Governors respectively, and to the Members of Our said Council, the Oaths mentioned in an Act, passed in the first Year of the Reign of His Majesty King George the First, intituled, "An Act for the further Security of His Majesty's Person and Government, and the Succession of the Crown in the Heirs of the late Princess Sophia, being Protestants, and for extinguishing the Hopes of the pretended Prince of Wales, and his open and secret Abettors;"—as also to make and subscribe, and cause them to make and subscribe the Declaration mentioned in an Act of Parliament made in the Twenty fifth Year of the Reign of King Charles the Second, intituled, "An Act for preventing Dangers which may happen from Popish Recusants." . . .

11. And whereas it is directed, by Our Commission to You under Our great Seal, that so soon as the Situation and Circumstances of Our said Province will admit thereof, You shall, with the Advice of Our Council, summon and call a General Assembly of the Freeholders in Our said Province; You are therefore, as soon as the more pressing Affairs of Government will allow to give all possible attention to the carrying this important Object into Execution: But, as it may be impracticable for the present to form such an Establishment, You are in the mean time to make such Rules and Regulations, by the Advice of Our said Council, as shall appear to be necessary for the Peace, Order and good Government of Our said Province, taking Care that nothing be passed or done, that shall any ways tend to affect the Life, Limb or Liberty of the Subject, or to the imposing any Duties or Taxes. . . .

28. And whereas We have stipulated, by the late Definitive Treaty of Peace concluded at Paris the 10th Day of February 1763, to grant the Liberty of the Catholick Religion to the Inhabitants of Canada, and that We will consequently give the most precise and most effectual Orders, that Our new Roman Catholick Subjects in that Province may profess the Worship of their Religion, according to the Rites of the Romish Church, as far as the Laws of Great Britain permit; It is therefore Our Will and Pleasure, that you do, in all things regarding the said Inhabitants, conform with great Exactness to the Stipulations of the said Treaty in this respect.

29. You are, as soon as possible, to summon the Inhabitants to meet together, at such Time or Times, Place or Places, as you shall find most convenient, in order to take the Oath of Allegiance, and

make and subscribe the Declaration of Abjuration mentioned in the aforesaid Act passed in the first Year of the Reign of King George the First, for the further Security of His Majesty's Person and Government, and the Succession of the Crown in the Heirs of the late Princess Sophia, being Protestants, and for extinguishing the Hopes of the pretended Prince of Wales, and his open and secret Abettors; which Oath shall be administered to them by such Person or Persons as you shall commissionate for such Purpose; and in case any of the said French Inhabitants shall refuse to take the said Oath, and make and subscribe the Declaration of Abjuration, as aforesaid, You are to cause them forthwith to depart out of Our said Government. . . .

32. You are not to admit of any Ecclesiastical Jurisdiction of the See of Rome, or any other foreign Ecclesiastical Jurisdiction whatsoever in the Province under your Government.

33. And to the End that the Church of England may be established both in Principles and Practice, and that the said Inhabitants may by Degrees be induced to embrace the Protestant Religion, and their Children be brought up in the Principles of it; We do hereby declare it to be Our Intention, when the said Province shall have been accurately surveyed, and divided into Townships, Districts, Precincts or Parishes, in such manner as shall be hereinafter directed, all possible Encouragement shall be given to the erecting Protestant Schools in the said Districts Townships and Precincts, by settling, appointing and allotting proper Quantities of Land for that Purpose, and also for a Glebe and Maintenance for a Protestant Minister and Protestant School-Masters; and you are to consider and report to Us, by Our Commissioners for Trade and Plantations, by what other Means the Protestant Religion may be promoted, established and encouraged in Our Province under your Government. . . .

38. The Views of a Francophile Governor

DESPITE HIS instructions to carry out a policy of Anglification, James Murray almost immediately adopted a pro-French attitude. With his council he passed an ordonnance extending the lifespan of French laws of tenure and inheritance; he also helped to obtain the consecration of

Grand Vicar Jean-Olivier Briand as bishop of Quebec in 1766 by urging his appointment in official dispatches to the government and in private correspondence with Church of England officials.

Murray's policy was continued and intensified by his successor Guy Carleton, Lord Dorchester, governor of Canada from 1766 to 1778 and from 1786 to 1791. In a series of memorable dispatches, Carleton vigorously attacked the very foundations of the policy of 1763. He argued that instead of seeking to undermine the French character of Canada, the British government should recognize and accept it in order to win the loyalty and devotion of the new subjects.

Further Reading: A. L. Burt, Guy Carleton, Lord Dorchester, 1724–1808 (Ottawa: Canadian Historical Association Booklet, 1964).

SOURCE: Document A: Guy Carleton to William Petty, Earl of Shelburne, secretary of state for the southern department, November 25, 1767, in Shortt and Doughty, Documents Relating to the Constitutional History of Canada, 1759–1791, I, 281–285. Document B: Carleton to Shelburne, January 20, 1768, in ibid., I, 294–296.

A. Carleton to Shelburne,
November 25, 1767

I take for granted, that the natural Rights of Men, the British Interests on this Continent, and the securing the Kings Dominions over this Province, must ever be the principal Points in View, in forming it's Civil Constitution, and Body of Laws; And that the last, is the Foundation of all, without which, other schemes can be little better than meer Castles in the Air; it will naturally follow, I should first shew, How far this Foundation is, or is not firmly laid— . . .

The King's Forces in this Province, supposing them compleat to the Allowance, and all in perfect Health, Rank and File, would amount to sixteen hundred and twenty seven Men, The King's old subjects in this Province, supposing them all willing, might furnish about five hundred Men, able to carry Arms, exclusive of his Troops; that is supposing all the King's Troops and old Subjects collected in Quebec; with two Months hard Labour, they might put the Works in a tolerable State of Repair, and would amount to about one third of the Forces necessary for it's Defence.

The new Subjects could send into the Field about eighteen

thousand Men, well able to carry Arms; of which Number, above one half have already served, with as much Valor, with more Zeal, and more military Knowledge for America, than the regular Troops of France, that were joined with them.

As the common People are greatly to be influenced by their Seigneurs, I annex a Return of the Noblesse of Canada, shewing with tolerable Exactness, their Age, Rank, and present Place of Abode, together with such Natives of France, as served in the Colony Troops so early in Life, as to give them a Knowledge of the Country, an Acquaintance and Influence over the People, equal to Natives of the same Rank; from whence it appears, that there are in France, and in the French Service, about one hundred Officers, all ready to be sent back, in Case of a War, to a Country they are intimately acquainted with, and with the Assistance of some Troops, to stir up a People accustomed to pay them implicit Obedience. It further shews, there remain in Canada, not many more than seventy of those, who ever had been in the French Service; not one of them in the King's Service, nor one who, from any Motive whatever, is induced to support His Government and Dominion; Gentlemen, who have lost their Employments, at least, by becoming His Subjects, and as they are not Bound by any Offices of Trust or Profit, we should only deceive ourselves by supposing, they would be active in the Defence of a People, that has deprived them of their Honors, Privileges, Profits and Laws, and in their Stead, have introduced much Expence, Chicannery, and Confusion, with a Deluge of new Laws unknown and unpublished. Therefore all Circumstances considered, while Matters continue in their present State, the most we may Hope for from the Gentlemen, who remain in the Province, is a passive Neutrality on all Occasions, with a respectful Submission to Government, and Deference for the King's Commission in whatever Hand it may be lodged; this they almost to a Man have persevered in, since my Arrival, notwithstanding much Pains have been taken, to engage them in Parties, by a few, whose Duty, and whose Office should have taught them better. This Disposition the French Minister seems to have foreseen, as appears by Orders calculated to draw them from Canada into France, well knowing that such as remained, were bound by Duty and Honor to do nothing against their Allegiance to the King, under whose Government they live, whereas those, who go to France, are to all Intents and Purposes

Officers in the French Service, and liable to be sent on any Service. . . .

Having arrayed the Strength of His Majesty's old and new Subjects, and shewn the great Superiority of the Latter, it may not be amiss to observe, that there is not the least Probability, this present Superiority should ever diminish, on the Contrary 'tis more than probable it will increase and strengthen daily: The Europeans, who migrate never will prefer the long unhospitable Winters of Canada, to the more chearful Climates, and more fruitful Soil of His Majesty's Southern Provinces; The few old Subjects at present in this Province, have been mostly left here by Accident, and are either disbanded Officers, Soldiers, or Followers of the Army, who, not knowing how to dispose of themselves elsewhere, settled where they were left at the Reduction; or else they are Adventurers in Trade, or such as could not remain at Home, who set out to mend their Fortunes, at the opening of this new Channel for Commerce, but Experience has taught almost all of them, that this Trade requires a Strict Frugality, they are Strangers to, or to which they will not submit; so that some, from more advantagious Views elsewhere, others from Necessity, have already left this Province, and I greatly fear many more, for the same Reasons, will follow their Example in a few Years; But while this severe Climate, and the Poverty of the Country discourages all but the Natives, it's Healthfulness is such, that these multiply daily, so that, barring Catastrophe shocking to think of, this Country must, to the end of Time, be peopled by the Canadian Race, who already have taken such firm Root, and got to so great a Height, that any new Stock transplanted will be totally hid, and imperceptible amongst them, except in the Towns of Quebec and Montreal.

B. Carleton to Shelburne, January 20, 1768

In my Letter I have given the Military state of this Province, with a scheme for strengthening it by a Citadel; I shall now add, that, was this already constructed, and I could suppose it impossible for any foreign Enemy to shake the King's Dominion over the Province, still I shall think the Interests of Great Britain but half advanced, unless the Canadians are inspired with a cordial Attachment, and zeal for the King's Government; How far they are removed from that desirable Disposition, may easily be discovered, if brought to the Test, and examined by the general Cause of the Attachments of Men, Self-Interest; if it shall not be found more their Interest to remain as at present, than to return under the Dominion of their former Sovereign, they certainly have not all those Motives, which induce Men of Honor to disregard the general Rule; there remain, 'tis true, an Oath of Allegiance, which may keep some Quiet in Case of a French Expedition, and the Punishments due to Traitors, which will be regarded, as long as Government has Force sufficient to inflict them; it therefore seems to me highly expedient, that, at least, those Causes of Complaint, which affect the Bulk of the People, and come home almost to every Man, should be removed; That they should be maintained in the quiet Possession of their Property, according to their own Customs, which Time immemorial, has been regarded by them and their Ancestors, as Law and Equity; and that the Approach to Justice and Government, for the Redress of Wrongs, be practicable and Convenient, in Place of being ruinous by Delay, and an Expence disproportioned to their Poverty; but this is neither in the Power of Justice or Government here to grant him, while the Supreme Court is obliged to Judge according to the Laws of England, and the different Offices can claim, as their Right, Fees calculated for much wealthier Provinces.

But, Beside these Points of Justice, as long as the Canadians are deprived of all Places of Trust and Profit, they never can forget, they no longer are under the Dominion of their natural Sovereign; tho' this immediately concerns but few, yet it affects the Minds of all, from a national Spirit, which ever interests itself at the general Exclusion of their Countrymen: three or four of their principal Gentlemen, with the Rank of Counsellors, was it little more than Honorary, tho' on many Occasions they might prove useful; a few Companies of Canadian Foot judiciously officered, with three or four trifling Employments, in the Civil Department, would make very considerable Alterations on the Minds of the People; It would divide the Canadians at least, and secure a Part, in Case of a French War, that would emulate the zeal of the King's National Troops; It would hold up Hopes to the Gentlemen, that their Children, without being bred up in France, or the French Service, might support their Families in the Service of the King their

Master, and by their Employments preserve them from sinking into the lower Class of People, by the Division and Subdivision of Lands every Generation.

I have found in Canada, what I believe may be found everywhere, the People fond of the Laws and Form of Government they have been educated under, tho' scarcely a Man that Knows one sound Principle of Government, or Law; Three or four of the old Subjects, about a year ago, brought me the rough Draft of a Petition for a general Assembly, and hoped, I had no Objection to their having it signed by all the British, who wished to have one called; I told them, I had many Objections to great numbers signing a Request of any Kind, that it seldom conveyed the sincere Desire of the Subscribers, that it had an Appearance of an Intention to take away the Freedom of granting or refusing the Request; I had no Objection to Assemblies in General, yet such was the peculiar Situation of Canada, tho' I had turned that Matter often in my Thoughts, I could hit off no Plan that was not liable to many Inconveniencies, and some Danger. . . . On the other Hand the better Sort of Canadians fear nothing more than popular Assemblies, which, they conceive, tend only to render the People refractory and insolent; Enquiring what they thought of them, they said, they understood some of our Colonies had fallen under the King's Displeasure, owing to the Misconduct of their Assemblies, and that they should think themselves unhappy, if a like Misfortune befell them. It may not be improper here to observe, that the British Form of Government, transplanted into this Continent, never will produce the same Fruits as at Home, chiefly, because it is impossible for the Dignity of the Throne, or Peerage to be represented in the American Forests; Besides, the Governor having little or nothing to give away, can have but little Influence; in Place of that, as it is his Duty to retain all in proper Subordination, and to restrain those Officers, who live by Fees, from running them up to Extortion; these Gentlemen, put into Offices, that require Integrity, Knowledge and Abilities, because they bid the highest Rent to the Patentee, finding themselves checked in their Views of Profit, are disposed to look on the Person, who disappoints them, as their Enemy, and without going so far as to forfeit their Employments, they in general will be shy of granting that Assistance, the King's Service may require, unless they are all equally disinterested or equally Corrupt. It therefore follows, where the executive Power is lodged with a Person of no Influence, but coldly assisted by the rest in Office, and where the two first Branches of the Legislature have neither Influence, nor Dignity, except it be from the extraordinary Characters of the Men, That a popular Assembly, which preserves it's full Vigor, and in a Country where all Men appear nearly upon a Level, must give a strong Bias to Republican Principles; Whether the independent Spirit of a Democracy is well adapted to a subordinate Government of the British Monarchy, or their uncontrolable Notions ought to be encouraged in a Province, so lately Conquered, and Circumstanced as this is, I with great Humility submit to the Superior Wisdom of His Majesty's Councils: for my own part, I shall think myself Fortunate, if I have succeeded in rendering clear Objects not allways distinctly discernable at so great a Distance.

39. The Quebec Act, 1774: Reconstruction Abandoned

DENOUNCED BY some historians as part of a dark plot to extinguish British liberties in America, praised by others as the consecration of the right of a non-English people to remain itself, the Quebec Act is in reality a subtle and complex piece of legislation that fits neatly into neither of these two categories. The essential British policy, based on the wishes of the Canadians as interpreted by Guy Carleton, is expressed in the act; the spirit in which the new constitution was to be administered is explained in the accompanying instructions to the governor. The British community in Canada was to be conciliated by the introduction of English laws in a broad range of personal cases, and the doors of Anglification were to be kept ajar by limiting the liberties of the Roman Catholic Church, French Canada's most powerful institution. Carleton, however, almost completely ignored these instructions. He used the Quebec Act to repress the aspirations of the British settlers and to establish his own authoritarian rule.

Further Reading: R. Coupland, The Quebec Act, A Study in Statesmanship (Oxford, 1925); C. Martin, Empire and Commonwealth (Oxford, 1929); E. Arthur, "French-Canadian Participation in the Government of Canada, 1775–1785," Canadian Historical Review, XXXII (1951), 303–314.

SOURCES: Document A: An Act for Making More Effectual Provision for the Government of the Province of Quebec in North America, in Shortt and Doughty, *Documents Relating to the Constitutional History of Canada, 1759–1791*, I, 570–575. Document B: Instructions to our Trusty and Welbeloved Guy Carleton Esquire . . . Given at our Court at St. James's the third Day of January 1775. In the Fifteenth year of Our Reign, in Shortt and Doughty, *ibid.*, II, 599, 602–605.

A. The Quebec Act

May it therefore please Your most Excellent Majesty that it may be enacted; and be it enacted by the King's most Excellent Majesty, by and with the Advice and Consent of the Lords Spiritual and Temporal, and Commons, in this present Parliament assembled, and by the Authority of the same, That all the Territories, Islands, and Countries in *North America*, belonging to the Crown of *Great Britain*, bounded on the South by a Line from the Bay of *Chaleurs*, along the High Lands which divide the Rivers that empty themselves into the River *Saint Lawrence* from those which fall into the Sea, to a Point in Forty-five Degrees of Northern Latitude, on the Eastern Bank of the River *Connecticut*, keeping the same Latitude directly West, through the Lake *Champlain*, until, in the same Latitude, it meets the River *Saint Lawrence*; from thence up the Eastern Bank of the said River to the Lake *Ontario*; thence through the Lake *Ontario*, and the River commonly called *Niagara*; and thence along by the Eastern and Southeastern Bank of Lake *Erie*, following the said Bank, until the same shall be intersected by the Northern Boundary, granted by the Charter of the Province of *Pennsylvania*, in case the same shall be so intersected; and from thence along the said Northern and Western Boundaries of the said Province, until the said Western Boundary strike the *Ohio* . . . and along the Bank of the said River, Westward, to the Banks of the *Mississippi*, and Northward to the Southern Boundary of the Territory granted to the Merchants Adventurers of *England*, trading to *Hudson's Bay*; and also all such Territories, Islands, and Countries, which have, since the Tenth of *February*, One thousand seven hundred and sixty-three, been made Part of the Government of *Newfoundland*, be, and they are hereby, during His Majesty's Pleasure, annexed to, and made Part and Parcel of, the Province of Quebec, as created and established by the said Royal Proclamation of the Seventh of October, One thousand seven hundred and sixty-three. . . .

And whereas the Provisions, made by the said Proclamation, in respect to the Civil Government of the said Province of Quebec, and the Powers and Authorities given to the Governor and other Civil Officers of the said Province, by the Grants and Commissions issued in consequence thereof, have been found, upon Experience, to be inapplicable to the State and Circumstances of the said Province, the Inhabitants whereof amounted, at the Conquest, to above sixty-five thousand Persons professing the Religion of the Church of Rome, and enjoying an established Form of Constitution and System of Laws, by which their Persons and Property had been protected, governed, and ordered, for a long Series of Years, from the First Establishment of the said Province of Canada; be it therefore further enacted by the Authority aforesaid, That the said Proclamation, so far as the same relates to the said Province of Quebec . . . and all Commissions to Judges and other Officers thereof, be, and the same are hereby revoked, annulled, and made void, from and after the First Day of May, One thousand seven hundred and seventy-five.

And, for the more perfect Security and Ease of the Minds of the Inhabitants of the said Province, it is hereby declared, That His Majesty's Subjects, professing the Religion of the Church of Rome of and in the said Province of Quebec, may have, hold, and enjoy, the free Exercise of the Religion of the Church of Rome, subject to the King's Supremacy . . . and that the Clergy of the said Church may hold, receive, and enjoy, their accustomed Dues and Rights, with respect to such Persons only as shall profess the said Religion.

Provided nevertheless, That it shall be lawful for His Majesty, His Heirs or Successors, to make such Provision out of the rest of the said accustomed Dues and Rights, for the Encouragement of the Protestant Religion, and for the Maintenance and Support of a Protestant Clergy within the said Province, as he or they shall, from Time to Time, think necessary and expedient.

Provided always, and be it enacted, That no Person, professing the Religion of the Church of Rome, and residing in the said Province, shall be obliged to take the Oath required by the said Statute passed in the First Year of the Reign of Queen Elizabeth, or any other Oaths substituted by any other Act in the Place thereof; but that every such Person who, by the said Statute is required to take the Oath therein mentioned, shall be obliged, and is hereby required, to take and subscribe the following Oath before the Governor, or such other Person in such Court of Record as His Majesty shall appoint, who are hereby authorized to administer the same; *videlicet*,

I A. B. *do sincerely promise and swear, That I will be faithful, and bear true Allegiance to His Majesty King* GEORGE, *and him will defend to the utmost of my Power, against all traiterous Conspiracies, and Attempts whatsoever, which shall be made against His Person, Crown, and Dignity; and I will do my utmost Endeavour to disclose and make known to His Majesty, His Heirs and Successors, all Treasons, and traiterous Conspiracies, and Attempts, which I shall know to be against Him, or any of Them; and all this I do swear without any Equivocation, mental Evasion, or secret Reservation, and renouncing all Pardons and Dispensations from any Power or Person whomsoever to the Contrary.*

So HELP ME GOD. . . .

And be it further enacted by the Authority aforesaid, That all His Majesty's Canadian Subjects, within the Province of Quebec, the religious Orders and Communities only excepted, may also hold and enjoy their Property and Possessions, together with all Customs and Usages relative thereto, and all other their Civil Rights, in as large, ample, and beneficial Manner, as if the said Proclamation, Commissions, Ordinances, and other Acts and Instruments, had not been made, and as may consist with their Allegiance to His Majesty, and Subjection to the Crown and Parliament of Great Britain; and that in all Matters of Controversy, relative to Property and Civil Rights, Resort shall be had to the Laws of Canada, as the Rule for the Decision of the same; and all Causes that shall hereafter be instituted in any of the Courts of Justice, to be appointed within and for the said Province, by His Majesty, His Heirs and Successors, shall, with respect to such Property and Rights, be determined agreeably to the said Laws and Customs of Canada. . . .

Provided always, That nothing in this Act contained shall extend or be construed to extend to any Lands that have been granted by His Majesty, or shall hereafter be granted by His Majesty, His

Heirs and Successors, to be holden in free and common Soc-cage.[1] . . .

And whereas the Certainty and Lenity of the Criminal Law of *England*, and the Benefits and Advantages resulting from the Use of it, have been sensibly felt by the Inhabitants, from an Experi-ence of more than Nine Years, during which it has been uniformly administered; be it therefore further enacted by the Authority aforesaid, That the same shall continue to be administered, and shall be observed as Law in the Province of *Quebec*. . . .

And whereas it may be necessary to ordain many Regulations for the future Welfare and good Government of the Province of *Quebec*, the Occasions of which cannot now be foreseen, nor, without much Delay and Inconvenience, be provided for, without intrusting that Authority, for a certain Time, and under proper Restrictions, to Persons resident there: And whereas it is at present inexpedient to call an Assembly; be it therefore enacted by the Authority aforesaid, That it shall and may be lawful for His Majesty, His Heirs and Successors, by Warrant under His or Their Signet or Sign Manual, and with the Advice of the Privy Council, to constitute and appoint a Council for the Affairs of the Province of *Quebec*, to consist of such Persons resident there, not exceeding Twenty-three, nor less than Seventeen, as His Majesty, His Heirs and Successors, shall be pleased to appoint; and, upon the Death, Removal, or Absence of any of the Members of the said Council, in like Manner to constitute and appoint such and so many other Person or Persons as shall be necessary to supply the Vacancy or Vacancies; which Council, so appointed and nominated, or the major Part thereof, shall have Power and Authority to make Ordinances for the Peace, Welfare, and good Government, of the said Province, with the Consent of His Majesty's Governor, or, in his Absence, of the Lieutenant-governor, or Commander in Chief for the Time being.

Provided always, That nothing in this Act contained shall extend to authorise or impower the said legislative Council to lay any Taxes or Duties within the said Province, such Rates and Taxes only excepted as the Inhabitants of any Town or District within the said Province may be authorised by the said Council to assess, levy, and apply, within the said Town or District, for the Purpose

1 Soccage: free and entire ownership of land as a result of a grant or by payment of a rent.

of making Roads, erecting and repairing publick Buildings, or for any other Purpose respecting the local Convenience and Oeconomy of such Town or District.

Provided also, and be it enacted by the Authority aforesaid, That every Ordinance so to be made, shall, within Six Months, be transmitted by the Governor, or, in his Absence, by the Lieutenant-governor, or Commander in Chief for the Time being, and laid before His Majesty for His Royal Approbation; and if His Majesty shall think fit to disallow thereof, the same shall cease and be void from the Time that His Majesty's Order in Council thereupon shall be promulgated at Quebec.

Provided also, That no Ordinance touching Religion, or by which any Punishment may be inflicted greater than Fine or Imprisonment for Three Months, shall be of any Force or Effect, until the same shall have received His Majesty's Approbation.

Provided also, That no Ordinance shall be passed at any Meeting of the Council where less than a Majority of the whole Council is present. . . .

B. Instructions to Governor Carleton, 1775

12. The Establishment of Courts, and a proper Mode of administering Civil and Criminal Justice throughout the whole Extent of Our Province, according to the Principles declared in the said Act "for making more effectual Provision for the Government thereof," demand the greatest Care and Circumspection; for, as on the one hand it is Our Gracious purpose, conformable to the Spirit and Intention of the said Act of Parliament, that Our Canadian Subjects should have the benefit and use of their own Laws, Usages, and Customs in all Controversies respecting Titles of Land, and the Tenure, descent, Alienation, Incumbrances, and Settlement of Real Estates, and the distribution of the personal property of Persons dying intestate; so on the other hand, it will be the duty of the Legislative Council to consider well in framing such Ordinances, as may be necessary for the Establishment of Courts of Justice, and for the better Administration of Justice, whether the Laws of England may not be, if not altogether, at least in part the Rule for the decision in all Cases of personal Actions grounded upon Debts, Promises, Contracts, and Agreements, whether of a Mercantile or other Nature; and also of Wrongs

proper to be compensated in damages; and more especially where Our natural-born Subjects of Great Britain, Ireland, or Our other Plantations residing at Quebec, or who may resort thither, or have Credits, or Property within the same, may happen to be either Plaintiff or defendant in any civil Suit of such a nature. . . .

20. The establishment of proper regulations in matters of ecclesiastical concern is an Object of very great importance, and it will be your indispensable duty to lose no time in making such arrangements in regard thereto, as may give full satisfaction to Our new Subjects in every point, in which they have a right to any indulgence on that head; always remembering, that it is a toleration of the free exercise of the religion of the Church of Rome only, to which they are entitled, but not to the powers and privileges of it, as an established Church, for that is a preference, which belongs only to the Protestant Church of England.

21. Upon these principles therefore, and to the end, that Our just Supremacy in all matters ecclesiastical, as well as civil, may have its due scope and influence, it is Our Will and Pleasure,—

First, that all Appeals to, or correspondence with any foreign ecclesiastical jurisdiction, of what nature or kind so ever, be absolutely forbidden under very severe Penalties.

Secondly, That no Episcopal or Vicarial Powers be exercised within Our said Province by any Person professing the Religion of the Church of Rome, but such only, as are essentially and indispensably necessary to the free exercise of the Romish Religion; and in those cases not without a Licence and Permission from you under the Seal of Our said Province, for, and during Our Will and Pleasure, and under such other limitations & restrictions, as may correspond with the spirit and provision of the Act of Parliament, "for making more effectual provision for the Government of the Province of Quebec;" And no person whatever is to have holy Orders conferred upon him, or to have the Cure of Souls without a License for that purpose first had or obtained from you.

Thirdly, That no person professing the Religion of the Church of Rome be allowed to fill any ecclesiastical Benefice, or to have and enjoy any of the Rights or Profits belonging thereto, that is not a Canadian by birth, (such only excepted, as are now in possession of any such Benefice,) and that is not appointed thereto by Us, or by, or under Our Authority, and that all Right, or claim of right in any other Person whatever to nominate, present, or appoint to any vacant Benefice, other than such as may lay claim to the patronage of Benefices, as a Civil Right, be absolutely abolished. No Person to hold more than one Benefice, or at least not more than can reasonably be served by one and the same Incumbent.

Fourthly, That no person whatever, professing the Religion of the Church of Rome, be appointed Incumbent of any Parish, in which the Majority of the Inhabitants shall solicit the appointment of a Protestant Minister; in such case the Incumbent shall be a Protestant, and entitled to all Tythes payable within such Parish; But nevertheless the Roman Catholicks may have the use of the Church for the free exercise of their Religion at such time, as may not interfere with the Religious Worship of the Protestants: And in like manner the Protestant Inhabitants in every Parish, where the Majority of Parishioners are Roman Catholicks, shall notwithstanding have the use of the Church for the exercise of their Religion at such times, as may not interfere with the Religious Worship of the Roman Catholicks.

Fifthly, That no Incumbent professing the Religion of the Church of Rome, appointed to any Parish, shall be entitled to receive any Tythes for Lands, or Possessions occupied by a Protestant. . . .

Eighthly, That such Ecclesiasticks, as may think fit to enter into the holy state of Matrimony, shall be released from all Penalties, to which they may have been subjected in such Cases by any Authority of the See of Rome.

Ninthly, That freedom of Burial of the Dead in Churches and Church yards be allowed indiscriminately to every Christian Persuasion.

Tenthly, That the Royal Family be prayed for in all Churches and Places of Holy Worship, in such manner and form, as are used in this Kingdom; and that Our Arms and Insignia be put up not only in all such Churches and Places of holy Worship, but also in all Courts of Justice; and that the Arms of France be taken down in every such Church or Court, where they may at present remain.

Eleventhly, That the Society of Romish Priests, called the Seminaries of Quebec and Montreal, shall continue to possess and occupy their Houses of Residence, and all other Houses and Lands, to which they were lawfully intitled on the 13th of September 1759; and it shall be lawful for those Societies to fill up Vacancies, and admit new Members according to the Rules of their Foundations, and to educate Youth, in order to qualify them for the Service of Parochial Cures; as they shall become vacant. It is nevertheless Our Will and Pleasure, that not only these Seminaries, but all other Religious Communities, so long as the same shall continue, be subject to visitation by You Our Governor, or such other Person or Persons, as you shall appoint for that purpose, and also subject to such Rules and Regulations, as you shall, with the Advice and Consent of Our Council, think fit to establish and appoint.

Twelfthly, It is also Our Will and Pleasure, that all other Religious Seminaries and Communities (that of the Jesuits only excepted) do for the present and until We can be more fully informed of the true State of them, and how far they are, or are not essential to the free exercise of the Religion of the Church of Rome, as allowed within Our said Province, remain upon their present Establishment; but you are not to allow the admission of any new Members into any of the said Societies or Communities, the Religious Communities of Women only excepted, without our express orders for that purpose. That the Society of Jesuits be suppressed and dissolved, and no longer continued, as a Body corporate and politic, and all their Rights, Possessions and Property shall be vested in Us for such purposes, as We may hereafter think fit to direct and appoint; but We think fit to declare Our Royal Intention to be, that the present Members of the said Society, as established at Quebec shall be allowed sufficient stipends and Provisions during their natural Lives. . . .

40. The American Revolution

THE AMERICAN REVOLUTION caused the first important social cleavage in the history of French Canada. In 1775 an army commanded by Richard Montgomery advanced up the Richelieu, captured Montreal, and then joined forces with the army of Benedict Arnold before Quebec. The assault on the capital of Canada took place on December 31 and was repelled by the defenders, commanded by Carleton. During this crucial year the clergy and the seigneurs, who had been elated by the Quebec Act, stood firmly by the British (see the address of Bishop Briand to the people of Canada—Document A), but only a small number of habitants followed their example. The rest remained neutral, and some even went over to the Americans. (Document B).

In 1778 France entered the Revolutionary War and the situation once more became critical for the British in Canada. In October, Charles Hector, comte d'Estaing, the French admiral in American waters, sent an address to the French Canadians (Document C) that was widely circulated in Quebec. A. L. Burt believes that the French would have received massive Canadian support had they followed up this appeal with an invasion of Canada.

Further Reading: G. M. Wrong, Canada and the American Revolution (Toronto, 1935); G. Lanctot, Canada and the American Revolution (Toronto, 1967); H. Verreau, Invasion du Canada, collection de mémoires recueillis et annotés (2 vols., Montreal, 1873).

SOURCES: Document A: Têtu and Gagnon, Mandements, lettres pastorales et circulaires des Evêques de Québec 1659–1887, II: 264–265; translated by the editor. Document B: Guy Carleton to William Legge, Earl of Dartmouth, October 25, 1775, Public Archives of Canada, series Q, vol. 11, pp. 267–270. Document C: O'Callaghan (ed.), Documents Relative to the Colonial History of the State of New York, X, 1165–1167.

A. The Reaction of the Church, 1775

Jean-Olivier Briand, by the goodness of God and the grace of the Holy See, Bishop of Quebec, etc., etc.

To all the people of this colony, greetings and benediction.

A troop of subjects in revolt against their lawful sovereign, who is also our own, have just made an irruption into this province, less with the hope of maintaining themselves in it than with the view of drawing you into their revolt or at least of engaging you not to oppose their pernicious design. The remarkable goodness and gentleness with which we have been governed by His Very Gracious Majesty, King George III, since the fortune of arms have subjected us to his rule, the recent favors which he has bestowed upon us by restoring the usage of our laws, the free exercise of our religion, and in letting us participate in all the privileges and advantages of British subjects would no doubt suffice to excite your gratitude and ardor in support of the interests of the British Crown. But motives still more pressing must speak to your hearts at the present moment. Your oaths, your religion, place upon you an obligatory duty to defend with all your might your country and your king. Therefore shut your ears, dear Canadians, and do not listen to the rebels, who are seeking to make you unhappy and to stifle in your hearts the feelings of obedience to your lawful superiors which religion and upbringing have shaped. Gladly carry out everything that will be commanded of you on behalf of a benevolent governor who only has your interests and happiness in view. There is no question of carrying war into remote provinces; we only ask you to lend a hand to repel the enemy and prevent the invasion with which this province is threatened. The voice of religion and that of your interests are here united and assure us of your zeal in the defense of our frontiers and our properties.

Given at Quebec under our seal, our coat of arms, and the signature of our secretary, May 22, 1775.

B. The Reaction of the Habitants, 1775

Montréal October 25th 1775

My Lord

After my Letter by Lord Pitt, the Disobedience of this People encreased, & bore some proportion to the encrease of the Rebels on the opposite side of the River; these received several Reinforcements, & their Emissaries travelled through the Country with less danger than the King's Servants.

The 24th of September it was so generally believed the Rebels wou'd cross the River & storm the Town, that all those who had Ladders in the Suburbs, were ordered to lodge them within the Walls; this they refused with Insolence, & even Menaces, against whoever shou'd attempt to carry it into Execution; it was very doubtful if a Guard for the Gates cou'd be procured from the Militia the next day; We had about sixty soldiers in the place, the Walls extensive & defenceless.

The next morning it was rumoured the Rebels had crossed the River in the night, & were posted about three Miles below the Town, this was soon confirmed; the Drums beat the alarm, all the old Gentlemen & better sort of Citizens English and Canadian, turned out under Arms, some of the lower Classes followed their Example; they were ordered to joyn the Troops at the Barracks, & from thence to the further end of the Quebec [sic] Suburbs; Captain Crawford with thirty Soldiers marched first; a few, mostly Colonists, then stept forward & turned off the contrary way, the rest, with some Officers who have retired, or are on the Staff, and a few Indians, followed the Troops very gallantly, & hurried them forward without further command & without much Order; They soon came up to the Rebel's Post, & in a little time put them to the Rout. These were about one hundred & fifty in number, two thirds Canadians; they say they expected all in the Suburbs, some in the Town, & many from the neighbouring Parishes wou'd have joyned them, & that they were to march in without opposition; Ethan Allen their Chief, & about thirty five men, were taken Prisoners, five of these wounded.

Major Carden who was our senior Officer in the Action, & very capable of conducting an Affair of this sort, was mortally wounded; Mr. A. Patterson, an english merchant, received a bad wound, but is likely to recover, three or four soldiers & discharged soldiers killed or wounded. This for a time, gave a favorable turn to the Minds of the People; some of the Parishes now began to send in their Quotas from the Militia.

On information that Mr. Walker[1] still continued to preach up Disobedience & Rebellion, a party of Troops with some Canadians were sent to apprehend & bring him Prisoner, he had prepared his House for defence, & fired several shot at those who surrounded it, Ensign Macdonald was wounded in the arm, & a Soldier received a bad Wound in the Thigh, occasioned by their Humanity; the House was then sett on fire, & Mr. Walker, his Wife & Servants surrendered. This occasioned our Numbers to encrease, & willing to profit by these favorable Events, several Officers were employed to make another Effort to bring up some Militia; Mr. Lanaudière [a seigneur] arrived at Berthier with about seventy, mostly unarmed, the People of this Parish took him Prisoner, & those he led immediately dispersed; their first design was to have him carried to the Rebels, but those who had charge of him repented & let him go; he has since joyned Lt. Colonel Maclean, who, about this time, marched with the small remains of the Troops from Quebec, & with what Militia he cou'd assemble below, has taken post at Sorel.

I had purposed on the first alarm to have formed a considerable Corps here, & shou'd have encamped them at Chambly, had not this wretched People been blind to Honor Duty & their own Interest.

1 Thomas Walker was a merchant who came to Canada from Boston soon after the conquest. He opposed the policy of Murray and Carleton and disseminated American propaganda during the revolutionary period.

Rigouville [a seigneur], on the same business, met with still a worse fate at Verchère, the Inhabitants of that Parish sent for some Bostonions & joyning them attacked him in the night, he had but one old man killed out of an hundred & forty, all armed, he was taken Prisoner & carried off, the rest of his party returned in their Boats.

These two events, trifling as they are, have occasioned great Desertion, I had assembled about nine hundred Men since our little Combat, but they disappear thirty or forty of a night, & if this continues a little longer, we shall be in as forlorn a state as before. Chambly surrendered about a week ago, the Garrison are Prisoners, this I fear, will sink their Spirits still more.

About three score Savages from one of our Villages are come in this Evening . . . I expect many more soon, but they are as easily dejected as the Canadian Peasantry, & like them, choose to be of the strongest side, so that when they are most wanted they vanish. . . .

C. Comte d'Estaing's Proclamation to the People of Canada, 1778

To all his Countrymen in North America:

You were born French; you never could cease to be French. A war, which was declared against us only by seizing nearly all our seamen, and the principal advantages of which our common enemies entirely owed to the courage, the talents and the numbers of the brave Americans, who are now fighting against them, has wrested from you that which is most dear to all men; even the name of your country. To compel you, in spite of yourselves, to bear the arms of parricides against it, must complete the measure of misfortune: with this you are now threatened: a new war may justly make you dread being obliged to submit to this most intolerable law of slavery. . . .

As a French gentleman, I need not mention to those among you who were born such, like myself, that there is but one august House in the universe under which the Frenchman can be happy, and serve with pleasure; since its head, and those who are nearly allied to him by blood, have been at all times, through a long line of Monarchs, and are at this day more than ever delighted with bearing that very title which Henry IV regarded as the first of his own. I shall not excite any regrets for those qualifications, those marks of distinction, those decorations, which, in our manner of thinking are precious treasures, but from which, by our common misfortunes, the French Americans, who have known so well how to deserve them, are now precluded. These, I am bold to hope and to promise, their zeal will soon make them recover. They will merit them, when they dare to become the friends of our allies.

I shall not ask the companions in arms of the Marquis de Levi,[2] those who shared his glory, who admired his talents and military tact, who have cherished his cordiality and frankness, the principal characteristics of our *Noblesse*, whether there be other names in other nations, among which they would be better pleased to place their own. Can the Canadians who saw the brave Montcalm fall in their defence, can they become the enemies of his nephews? Can they fight against their former leaders, and arm themselves against their kinsmen, at the bare mention of whose names, the weapons would fall from their hands?

I shall not observe to the Ministers of the altars that their evangelic efforts will require a special protection of Providence to prevent the faith being diminished by example; to prevent worldly interest getting the better, and the political indulgence of Sovereigns, whom force has imposed upon them, becoming less proportionably as those Sovereigns shall have less to fear; that it is necessary for religion, that those who preach it should form a body in the State; and in Canada, that no other body would be more considered, or have more power to do good than that of the Priests taking a part in the government, because their respectable conduct has merited the confidence of the people.

I shall not represent to that people, nor to all my countrymen in general, that a vast monarchy having the same religion, the same manners, the same language, where they find kinsmen, old friends and brethren, must be an inexhaustible source of commerce and wealth, more easily acquired and better secured, by a reunion with powerful neighbors, than with strangers of another hemisphere, among whom everything is different, and who, being jealous and despotic Sovereigns, will, sooner or later, treat them as a conquered people, and doubtless much worse than they treated their late countrymen [the Americans] who made those Sovereigns victori-

2 François-Gaston, chevalier de Lévis, became commander-in-chief of the French forces in North America following the death of Montcalm.

ous. I shall not urge, to a whole people, that to join with the United States is to secure their own happiness; for, a whole people, when they acquire the right of thinking and acting for themselves, must know their own interest; but I will declare, and I now do formally declare in the name of his Majesty, who has authorized and so commanded me, that all his former subjects in North America, who will not acknowledge, any longer, the supremacy of Great Britain may depend upon his protection and support.

Done on board his Majesty's ship the *Languedoc*, in the harbor of Boston, the 28th day of October, 1778.

ESTAING

41. Petition for an Assembly, 1784

THE RIFT OPENED *in Canadian society by the Quebec Act and the American Revolution did not mend following the return of peace in 1783. While the upper classes continued to stand by the constitution of 1774, a large number of French Canadians began to press for a democratization of government. In 1784, this group joined forces with the British mercantile community, which had repeatedly asked for an elective assembly, English commercial law, and habeas corpus, since the mid-1760's. The result was a petition to the king that bore some 2,300 signatures, over half of them French.*

SOURCE: Shortt and Doughty, *Documents Relating to the Constitutional History of Canada, 1759–1791,* II, 742–746, gives the petition and the English signatures only. *Petitions from the Old and New Subjects, Inhabitants of the Province of Quebec, to the right honourable the Lords Spiritual and Temporal* (London, 1791) gives the petition with the French and English signatures.

The humble Petition of Your Majesty's Ancient and New Subjects Inhabitants of the Province of Quebec.

MAY IT PLEASE YOUR MAJESTY.

After the Conquest of the Province of Canada by the Arms of Great Britain, Your Petitioners in compliance with Your Majesty's gracious and royal Proclamation, bearing date the 7th day of October 1763, Settled and became established, in the New acquired Colony of Quebec; in the full reliance on the faith of the Crown of Great Britain, as expressed in that Proclamation, for the enjoyment of those Laws, that Freedom and Security in Canada, which the Principles of the English Constitution afforded, in every part of the British Dominions in America. YOUR PETITIONERS and the Inhabitants of the Province, have chearfully on every occasion, obeyed the Controuling power of the Parliament of Great Britain, and with patience have suffered, during a period of Anarchy and War, rather than wound Your Majesty's feelings, or embarrass the Throne with Remonstrances and Petitions, at a time when the safety of the Nation, made sacred every moment of Public deliberation. The Actions and Conduct of Your Petitioners when truly represented, will best express to Your Majesty, the Sincerity of their Loyalty and Attachment to the Crown and Government of Great Britain.

YOUR PETITIONERS look with Concern on the burthen of Great Britain, and with great Pain and Commiseration they see the distresses of Your Majesty's loyal Subjects, who, driven from their Estates, Wealth, and Possessions are daily taking Shelter in this British Colony; though their unsettled and distressed Situation, may for the present hinder them from bringing forward their Petitions and their Claims; Your Majesty will readily perceive that a Government similar or Superior, to that under which they were born, had lived, and were happy, must be considered by those Your Majesty's unfortunate Subjects as an Affectionate proof of Your Majesty's Paternal Care and Regard for them; and the first Comfort which Your Majesty in relief to their Distresses can now grant: And the more so, as it will be a Blessing not merely granted to them, but extended to their Children and Posterity. YOUR PETITIONERS fully persuaded that the Welfare and Happiness of Your Majesty's Subjects, are objects of Your Majesty's serious, and benign Consideration—beg leave to lay their Petition at the foot of the Throne and ardently to request Your Majesty's Interposition for the Repeal of the Quebec Bill; allowing such Priviledges as are already granted to the Roman Catholick Religion; as being inadequate to the Government of this extensive Province; the Cause of much Confusion in our Laws, and fraught with trouble and uneasiness to Your Majesty's loyal Subjects here. And that Your Majesty will be pleased to Concur in establishing your affectionate Subjects of this Province, in the full Enjoyment, of their civil Rights as British Subjects; and in granting them a Free, Elective House of Assembly. In these hopes they humbly presume to Suggest, that Clauses of the following Import, may be inserted in the Act of Parliament, which shall be made to Confirm a free Constitution to this Country.

1ˢᵗ THAT the House of Representatives or Assembly,—be chosen by the Parishes, Towns and Districts of the Province, to be Composed of Your Majesty's Old and New Subjects, in such manner as to Your Majesty's Wisdom may seem most proper, that the Assembly be triennial, and the Members elected every three Years.

2ᵈ THAT the Council consist of not less than Thirty Members and in case of Division on any measure before them, that no Act shall be passed, unless at least Twelve Members agree to carry the Vote. That the appointment of the Members, may be during their residence in the Province, and for Life; yet subject to temporary leave of Absence, as mentioned in the 11ᵗʰ Article; And that they serve as Councellors, without Fee or Reward.

3ᵈ THAT the Criminal Laws of England be continued, as at present established by the Quebec Act.

4ᵗʰ THAT the ancient Laws and Customs of this Country, respecting landed Estates, Marriage Settlements, Inheritances and Dowers, be continued; yet subject to be altered by the Legislature of Quebec; And that Owners may alienate by Will, as provided by the 10ᵗʰ Section of the Quebec Bill.

5ᵗʰ THAT the Commercial Laws of England, be declared to be the Laws of this Province, in all Matters of Trade and Commerce, subject to be Changed by the Legislature of Quebec, as in the preceeding Article.

6ᵗʰ THAT the Habeas Corpus Act, the 31ˢᵗ Charles 2ᵈ be made part of the Constitution of this Country.

7ᵗʰ THAT Optional Juries be granted, on all Trials in Courts of Original Jurisdiction. That they be regularly Baloted for, and a Pannel formed as in England; either in the Case of an ordinary or a Special Jury, at the option of the Party applying for the same, And that Nine Members out of the Twelve, may in Civil Causes, be sufficient to Return Verdicts, subject to be Modified by the Legislature of Quebec, as in the 4ᵗʰ Article. . . .

14ᵗʰ YOUR PETITIONERS beg leave, humbly to Represent to Your

Majesty; that from their Proximity to the United States, who from Situation and Climate, have many advantages over them, the Internal Regulations for promoting the Trade, Agriculture and Commerce, of this Province; are now become more intricate and difficult; and will require great Care and Attention, on the part of the Legislature here; to watch over the Interests of this Country. They therefore request, that the Assembly may have the Power, of laying the Taxes and Duties, necessary for defraying the Expences of the Civil Government of the Province. And for that purpose, that the Laws now existing, laying Taxes and Duties to be levied in the Province, may be repealed.

SUCH MAY IT PLEASE YOUR MAJESTY are the Intreaties and Prayers of Your loyal Subjects; and in full Confidence they trust, that Your Majesty will relieve them from the Anarchy and Confusion, which at present prevail, in the Laws and Courts of Justice of the Province, by which, their Real Property is rendered insecure, Trade is clogged, and that good Faith, which ought, and would subsist among the People, and which is the Life and Support of Commerce, is totally destroyed. And be Graciously pleased to Secure to them, a Constitution and Government, on such fixed, and liberal Principles, as may promote the desire Your Affectionate Subjects of this Province have, of rendering this Mutilated Colony, a bright Gem in the Imperial Crown of Great Britain. And that may call on the present Generation, for their unceasing Acknowledgements and Gratitude. And upon the future, to feel as the present, that the Security and Happiness of the People and Province of Quebec; depend on an Union with, and Submission to, the Crown and Government of Great Britain.

Quebec 24th November 1784

42. The Constitutional Act of 1791

THE ELECTIVE ASSEMBLY for which the British mercantile community, the newly arrived United Empire Loyalists, and the French Canadian liberals had pressed was finally conceded in 1791 under the Constitutional Act. The accompanying division of the colony into the provinces of Upper Canada and Lower Canada, however, dismayed the British merchants of Montreal and Quebec. They had hoped to control the legislature with the support of the Loyalists but instead found themselves reduced to a small minority in a province that was overwhelmingly French. Conversely, the French Canadians now occupied a commanding position in a territory which they soon began to regard as their own national state.

SOURCE: Shortt and Doughty, *Documents Relating to the Constitutional History of Canada, 1759–1791*, II, 1031–1041.

An Act to repeal certain Parts of an Act, passed in the Fourteenth Year of His Majesty's Reign, intituled, *An Act for making more effectual Provision for the Government of the Province of Quebec, in North America*; and to make further Provision for the Government of the said Province.

Whereas an Act was passed in the Fourteenth Year of the Reign of His present Majesty, intituled, *An Act for making more effectual Provision for the Government of the Province of Quebec in North America*: And whereas the said Act is in many Respects inapplicable to the present Condition and Circumstances of the said Province: And whereas it is expedient and necessary that further Provision should now be made for the good Government and Prosperity thereof: May it therefore please Your most Excellent Majesty that it may be enacted; and be it enacted by the King's most Excellent Majesty, by and with the Advice and Consent of the Lords Spiritual and Temporal, and Commons, in this present Parliament assembled, and by the Authority of the same, That so much of the said Act as in any Manner relates to the Appointment of a Council for the Affairs of the said Province of Quebec, or to the Power given by the said Act to the said Council, or to the major Part of them, to make Ordinances for the Peace, Welfare, and good Government of the said Province, with the Consent of His Majesty's Governor, Lieutenant Governor or Commander in Chief for the Time being, shall be, and the same is hereby repealed.

II. And whereas His Majesty has been pleased to signify, by His Message to both Houses of Parliament, His Royal Intention to divide His Province of Quebec into Two separate Provinces, to be called The Province of Upper Canada, and The Province of Lower

Canada; be it enacted by the Authority aforesaid, That there shall be within each of the said Provinces respectively a Legislative Council, and an Assembly, to be severally composed and constituted in the Manner herein-after described; and that in each of the said Provinces respectively His Majesty, His Heirs or Successors, shall have Power, during the Continuance of this Act, by and with the Advice and Consent of the Legislative Council and Assembly of such Provinces respectively, to make Laws for the Peace, Welfare, and good Government thereof, such Laws not being repugnant to this Act. . . .

III. And be it further enacted by the Authority aforesaid, that for the Purpose of constituting such Legislative Council as aforesaid in each of the said Provinces respectively, it shall and may be lawful for His Majesty, His Heirs or Successors, by an Instrument under His or their Sign Manual, to authorize and direct the Governor or Lieutenant Governor . . . to summon to the said Legislative Council, to be established in each of the said Provinces respectively, a sufficient Number of discreet and proper Persons, being not fewer than Seven to the Legislative Council for the Province of *Upper Canada,* and not fewer than Fifteen to the Legislative Council for the Province of *Lower Canada.* . . .

IV. Provided always, and be it enacted by the Authority aforesaid, That no Person shall be summoned to the said Legislative Council, in either of the said Provinces, who shall not be of the full Age of Twenty-one Years, and a natural-born Subject of His Majesty, or a Subject of His Majesty naturalized by Act of the *British* Parliament, or a Subject of His Majesty, having become such by the Conquest and Cession of the Province of *Canada.*

V. And be it further enacted by the Authority aforesaid, That every Member of each of the said Legislative Councils shall hold his Seat therein for the Term of his Life. . . .

XX. And be it further enacted by the Authority aforesaid, That the Members for the several Districts, or Counties, or Circles of the said Provinces respectively, shall be chosen by the Majority of Votes of such Persons as shall severally be possessed, for their own use and Benefit, of Lands or Tenements within such District, or County, or Circle, as the Case shall be, such Lands being by them held in Freehold, or in Fief, or in Roture, or by Certificate derived under the Authority of the Governor and Council of the Province of *Quebec,* and being of the yearly Value of Forty Shillings

Sterling, or upwards, over and above all Rents and Charges payable out of or in respect of the same; and that the Members for the several Towns or Townships within the said Provinces respectively shall be chosen by the Majority of Votes of such Persons as either shall severally be possessed, for their own Use and Benefit, of a Dwelling House and Lot of Ground in such Town or Township, such Dwelling House and Lot of Ground being by them held in like Manner as aforesaid, and being of the yearly Value of Five Pounds Sterling, or upwards, or, as having been resident within the said Town or Township for the Space of Twelve Calendar Months next before the Date of the Writ of Summons for the Election, shall bona fide have paid One Year's Rent for the Dwelling House in which they shall have so resided, at the Rate of Ten Pounds Sterling per Annum, or upwards. . . .

XXVII. Provided always, and be it enacted by the Authority aforesaid, that the said Legislative Council and Assembly, in each of the said Provinces, shall be called together Once at least in every Twelve Calendar Months, and that every Assembly shall continue for Four Years from the Day of the Return of the Writs for chusing the same, and no longer, subject nevertheless to be sooner prorogued or dissolved by the Governor or Lieutenant Governor of the Province, or Person administering His Majesty's Government therein.

XXVIII. And be it further enacted by the Authority aforesaid, That all Questions which shall arise in the said Legislative Councils or Assemblies respectively shall be decided by the Majority of Voices of such Members as shall be present; and that in all Cases where the Voices shall be equal, the Speaker of such Council or Assembly, as the Case shall be, shall have a casting Voice. . . .

XXX. And be it further enacted by the Authority aforesaid, That whenever any Bill which has been passed by the Legislative Council, and by the House of Assembly, in either of the said Provinces respectively, shall be presented, for His Majesty's Assent, to the Governor or Lieutenant Governor of such Province, or to the Person administering His Majesty's Government therein . . . and he is hereby authorized and required to declare, according to his Discretion, but subject nevertheless to the Provisions contained in this Act, and to such Instructions as may from Time to Time be given in that Behalf by His Majesty, His Heirs or Successors, that he assents to such Bill in His Majesty's Name, or that he withholds

His Majesty's Assent from such Bill, or that he reserves such Bill for the Signification of His Majesty's Pleasure thereon.

XXXI. Provided always, and be it further enacted by the Authority aforesaid, That whenever any Bill, which shall have been so presented for His Majesty's Assent to such Governor, Lieutenant Governor, or Person administering the Government, shall . . . have been assented to in His Majesty's Name, such Governor, Lieutenant Governor, or Person as aforesaid, shall, and he is hereby required, by the first convenient Opportunity, to transmit to One of His Majesty's principal Secretaries of State an authentick Copy of such Bill so assented to; and that it shall and may be lawful, at any Time within Two Years after such Bill shall have been so received by such Secretary of State, for His Majesty, His Heirs or Successors, by His or their Order in Council, to declare His or their Disallowance of such Bill. . . .

43. The French Canadian *Habitants* at the Beginning of the Nineteenth Century

IN 1806, an Englishman named John Lambert landed in Quebec. His mission, officially sponsored by the Board of Trade, was to encourage the cultivation of hemp in Lower Canada in order to render Great Britain independent of the supply of northern Europe. The project soon fell through, but Lambert stayed on for a year in Lower Canada and then made a six-month tour of the United States. His book of travels in North America was published in 1810 and quickly went through three editions. It contains a description that is highly informative about, if not always sympathetic toward, the manners and character of the French Canadian habitants in the early years of the nineteenth century.

SOURCE: John Lambert, *Travels through Lower Canada, and the United States of North America, in the years 1806, 1807, and 1808* (3 vols., London, 1810), I, 153–165.

The French Canadians, are an inoffensive, quiet people, possessed of little industry, and less ambition. Yet from the love of gain, mere vanity, or that restlessness which indolence frequently occasions, they will undergo the greatest hardships. There cannot be a stronger proof of this, than in those who labour in the spring to collect the sap of the maple tree: their exertions for five or six weeks while the snow is on the ground, are excessive. None also undergo severer trials than those who are employed in the fur trade. They penetrate the immense forests of the north-west for thousands of miles, exposed to all the severities of the climate, and often to famine and disease. That vanity should be a predominant characteristic of the Canadians, is no more than might be expected from the children of France, whose national character is vanity.

The Habitans content themselves with following the footsteps of their forefathers. They are satisfied with a little, because a little satisfies their wants. They are quiet and obedient subjects, because they feel the value and benefit of the government under which they live. They trouble themselves not with useless arguments concerning its good or bad qualities, because they feel themselves protected, and not oppressed by its laws. They are religious from education and habit, more than from principle. They observe its ceremonies and formalities, not because they are necessary to their salvation, but because it gratifies their vanity and superstition. They live in happy mediocrity, without a wish or endeavour to better their condition, though many of them are amply possessed of the means. Yet they love money, and are seldom on the wrong side of a bargain. From poverty and oppression they have been raised, since the conquest, to independent affluence. They now know, and feel the value of money and freedom, and are not willing to part with either. Their parsimonious frugality is visible in their habitations, their dress, and their meals; and had they been as industrious and enterprizing, as they have been frugal and saving, they would have been the richest peasantry in the world.

Their houses are composed of logs slightly smoothed with the axe, laid upon each other, and dove-tailed at the corners. Sometimes a frame work is first constructed, and the logs laid upon each other, between two grooves. The interstices are filled with clay or mud, and the sides of the building washed outside and in, with lime dissolved in water. This, they say, has the property of preserving the wood better than paint, from the effects of the weather, and vermin; at all events it has the property of being cheaper, which is a consideration of more importance to them, than weather or vermin.

The roofs is constructed with boards, and generally covered with shingles. Sometimes they are white-washed, but oftener allowed to remain in their natural state. In a few months the weather changes the colour of the wood, and gives the shingles the appearance of slate, which, with the white sides have a pleasing effect. The whole, however, falls very short of the neat wooden farm-houses in the United States, which are generally clapboarded over the rough logs, and neatly painted. They present a more complete and finished appearance, than the rough outsides of the Canadian farm-houses.

The Canadian habitations consist of only one story or ground floor, which is generally divided into four rooms. Over them, is a garret or loft formed by the sloping roof. Some of the small houses have only one or two apartments, according to the affluence, or poverty of their owners. The better sort of farmers have always four rooms. . . .

The chimney is built in the centre of the house; and the room which contains the fire-place, is the kitchen. The rest are bed-rooms, for it matters not how many apartments a house consists of, they are seldom without one or two beds in each, according to the size of the family. This indispensable piece of furniture, which is always placed in one corner of the room, is a sort of four-post bedstead without the pillars, and raised three or four feet from the ground. At the head there is generally a canopy or tester fixed against the wall, under which the bed stands. Upon the bedstead is placed a feather or straw bed, with the usual clothes, and covered with a patchwork counterpane, or green stuff quilt. In winter, the men frequently lay themselves along the hearth, or by the stove, wrapped up in a buffalo robe. In the middle of the night, they will get up, stir the fire, smoke their pipe, and lie down again till morning. . . .

The furniture of the Habitans, is plain and simple, and most commonly of their own workmanship. A few wooden chairs with twig or rush bottoms, and two or three deal tables, are placed in each room, and are seldom very ornamental; they, however, suffice, with a proper number of wooden bowls, trenchers, and spoons, for the use of the family at meals. A press, and two or three large chests, contain their wearing-apparel, and other property. A buffet in one corner, contains their small display of cups, saucers, glasses, and tea-pots, while a few broken sets may perhaps grace the mantle-piece. A large clock is often found in their best apartment, and the sides of the room are ornamented with little pictures, or waxen images of saints and crucifixes; of the holy virgin and her son. An iron stove is generally placed in the largest apartment, with a pipe passing through the others into the chimney. The kitchen displays very little more than kettles of soup—tureens of milk—a table, a dresser, and a few chairs. The fire-place is wide, and large logs of wood are placed on old fashioned iron dogs. A wooden crane supports the large kettle of soup, which is for ever on the fire.

Their chief article of food, is pork, as fat as they can procure it. They all keep a great number of swine, which they fatten to their liking. Peas-soup, with a small quantity of pork boiled in it, constitutes their breakfast, dinner, and supper, day after day, with very little alteration, except what is occasioned by a few sausages, and puddings made of the entrails, when a hog is killed; or during Lent, when fish and vegetables only, will suffice. They are extremely fond of thick sour milk, and will often treat themselves with a dish of it, after their pork. Milk, soup, and other spoon-meat, are eaten out of a general dish, each taking a spoonful after the other. Knives and forks are seldom in request.

The old people will sometimes treat themselves with tea or coffee, in which case, they generally have to boil their water in the frying-pan; for it rarely happens that they have a tea-kettle in the house. . . .

Milk and water is the usual drink of the females and younger part of the family. Rum is, however, the cordial balm which relieves the men from all their cares and anxieties. They are passionately fond of this pernicious liquor, and often have a debauch when they go to market with their commodities. . . .

Very few of the country people who frequent the markets in the towns, return home sober, and in winter time, when there is not room for more than one cariole on the road, without plunging the horse four or five feet deep in snow, these people, having lost their usual politeness by intoxication, do not feel inclined to make way for the gentry in carioles, and will often run their sleighs aboard, and upset them.

The Canadian country-people bake their own bread, which is made of wheat-flour and rye-meal; but for the want of yeast, it has a sour taste, and is coarse and heavy. Their ovens are built of wicker-work, plaistered inside and out with a thick coating of clay or mortar. Some are built of bricks or stones, but the former are more general. They are situate at a short distance from the house, to prevent accidents from fire, and are raised about four feet from the ground, covered with a roof of boards, supported by four posts, to keep off the rain.

The dress of the Habitant is simple, and homely; it consists of a long-skirted cloth coat or frock, of a dark grey colour, with a hood attached to it, which in winter time, or wet weather, he puts over his head. His coat is tied round the waist by a worsted sash of various colours, ornamented with beads. His waistcoat and trowsers are of the same cloth. A pair of moccasins, or swamp-boots, complete the lower part of his dress. His hair is tied in a thick long queue behind, with an eelskin; and on each side of his face a few strait locks hang down like, what are vulgarly called, "rats' tails." Upon his head is a bonnet rouge, or in other words, a red night-cap. The tout ensemble of his figure is completed by a short pipe, which he has in his mouth from morning till night. A Dutchman is not a greater smoker than a French Canadian.

The visage of the Habitant is long and thin, his complexion sunburnt and swarthy; and not unfrequently of a darker hue than that of the Indian. His eyes, though rather small, are dark and lively. His nose prominent, and inclined to the acquiline or Roman form. His cheeks lank and meagre. His lips small and thin. His chin sharp and projecting.

Such is the almost invariable portrait of a Canadian Habitant, or countryman, and more or less of the lower order of French people in the towns. It is, in fact, a portrait of five-sixths of the male inhabitants of Lower Canada. It is very seldom that any alteration takes place in the dress of the men; unless in summer, the long coat is exchanged for a jacket, and the bonnet rouge for a straw hat; but it oftener happens that the dress which I have described is worn the whole year round.

The dress of the women is old-fashioned; for the articles which compose it never find their way into Canada, until they have become stale in England. I am now speaking of those who deck themselves out in printed cotton gowns, muslin aprons, shawls, and handkerchiefs; but there are numbers who wear only cloth of their own manufacture, the same as worn by the men. A petticoat and short jacket, is the most prevailing dress; though some frequently decorate themselves in all the trappings of modern finery, but which, in point of fashion, are generally a few years behind those of Europe. The elderly women still adhere to long waists, full caps, and large clubs of hair behind. Some of the younger branches of the countrywomen are becoming more modern, having imbibed a spirit for dress from the French girls who live in the towns, as servants.

The Habitans have almost every resource within their own families. They cultivate flax, which they manufacture into linen; and their sheep supply them with the wool, of which their garments are formed. They tan the hides of their cattle, and make them into moccasins and boots. From woollen yarn they knit their own stockings and bonnets rouge; and from straw they make their summer hats and bonnets. Besides articles of wearing apparel, they make their own bread, butter, and cheese; their soap, candles, and sugar; all which are supplied from the productions of their farm. They build their own houses, barns, stables, and ovens. Make their own carts, wheels, ploughs, harrows, and canoes. In short, their ingenuity, prompted as much by parsimony as the isolated situation in which they live, has provided them with every article of utility, and every necessary of life. A Canadian will seldom or never purchase that which he can make himself; and I am of opinion, that it is this saving spirit of frugality alone, which has induced them to follow the footsteps of their fathers, and which has prevented them from profiting by the modern improvements in husbandry, and the new implements of agriculture introduced by the English settlers.

44. The Coming of a New Era, 1810

ONLY FOUR YEARS after Lambert had concluded that the French Canadians were inoffensive and quiet, Governor James Craig declared dramatically that they viewed the English with sentiments of envy, mistrust, jealousy, and hatred. Since Craig wrote these lines shortly after engaging in a bitter conflict with the legislative assembly, which was dominated by the politically conscious French Canadian middle classes, he was no doubt inclined to exaggerate the strength of anti-English sentiment across the province. His dispatch, however, unmistakably tells of the growth of nationalist sentiment among the élite and of the influence this group was beginning to exert on the masses through the elective system established in 1791.

SOURCE: James Craig to Robert Jenkinson, Earl of Liverpool, secretary of state for the colonies, May 1, 1810, in A. G. Doughty and D. A. MacArthur (eds.), *Documents Relating to the Constitutional History of Canada, 1791–1818* (Ottawa, 1914), pp. 387–397.

In the consideration which may be given to the various objects, which I may feel myself called on to submit to your Lordship, I must request that the particular situation in which this Province stands, as being a conquered Country, may never be put out of view, and I claim that it may always be recollected that I speak of a Colony, the population of which, is usually estimated at 300,000 souls, and which, calculating upon the best data in our possession, I myself believe to exceed 250,000. Of these 250,000 souls about 20,000 or 25,000 may be English or Americans, the remainder are French. I use the term designedly My Lord, because I mean to say, that they are in Language, in religion, in manner and in attachment completely French—bound to us by no one tie, but that of a Common Government, and on the contrary viewing us with sentiments of mistrust & jealousy, with envy, and I believe I should not go too far, were I to say with hatred.

So compleat do I consider this alienation to be, that on the most careful review of all that I know in the Province, there are very few whom I could venture to point out as [not] being tainted with it; the line of distinction between us is completely drawn. Friendship [and] Cordiality are not to be found—even common intercourse scarcely exists—the lower class of people to strengthen a term of contempt add Anglois—and the better sort with whom there formerly did exist some interchange of the common civilities of Society have of late entirely withdrawn themselves—the alledged reason is that their circumstances have gradually declined in proportion as ours have increased in affluence; this may have had some effect, but the observation has been made also, that this abstraction has taken place exactly in proportion as the power of the French in England has become more firmly established. . . .

Their attachment to France is equally undoubted, and it is now even supposed to be not a little directed to the Person of Bonaparte, who since the concordat, is considered among them as the Restorer of the Roman Catholic Religion.

Of the Legislative Council it is not necessary to say much, it is certainly composed of every thing that is respectable in the Province, and I believe the Members to be on all occasions animated by the best intentions towards His Majesty's Service, & the public good; It is an Object of great jealousy to the Lower House, who seem anxious to seize every opportunity of showing the little respect in which they hold it, It is thought that an increase of numbers would add to their weight, at present they seldom exceed five or six in the House.

To a People circumstanced as I have described these to be, ignorant and credulous in the extreme, having no one common tie of affection, or union, viewing us with Jealousy, mistrust, and hatred, having separate & distinct Interests, It has been thought proper to give a share in the Government of the Country, by a House of Representatives, in which they must ever have the Majority; It is very far from my intention to question the liberal views on which the measure was originally founded, but it is my business to point out the consequences that have ensued from it.

Your Lordship is aware that tho' the Constitutional Act has established a qualification for the Electors, there is none required in the Representation, I mean with respect to Property. The Numbers of English in the House has never exceeded 14 or 15, in the two last Parliaments there have been 12, in the present there are ten, some of these have of late come from a pretty low step in the scale of society, but in general they are composed of two, or three Avocats, about the same number of Gentlemen possessing Landed property, and the remainder of Merchants of Character & estimation; Upon the first establishment of the House, the few Canadian Gentlemen that existed in the Country stepped forward, and some were elected, but they soon found that nothing was to be gained by it, on the contrary, that their absence from home and their attendance at Quebec, during three months of the year, was given at an expence that very few of them could afford, and they gradually withdrew: now that some of them have attempted to resume the stations they abandoned, they have found it impossible; but at all times, their numbers were inconsiderable: the House has ever been as it is now, in great proportion as to the Canadian part, filled up with Avocats, and Notaries, shop-keepers, and with the Common Habitants, as they are called, that is, the most ignorant of Labouring farmers, some of these, can neither read nor write. In the last parliament there were two who actually signed the Roll by marks, and their [sic] were five more, whose signatures were scarcely legible, and were such as to shew that to be the extent of their ability in writing. . . .

In such a House of Assembly as I have described, Your Lordship will easily perceive that it is impossible that Government can possess any influence, they are certainly the most independant Assembly that exists, in any known Government in the world, for a Governor cannot obtain among them even that sort of influence that might arise from personal intercourse, I can have none with Blacksmiths, Millers, & Shopkeepers, even the Avocats & Notaries, who compose so considerable a portion of the House, are generally speaking, such as I can nowhere meet, except during the actual sitting of Parliament, when I have a day of the week expressly appropriated to the receiving a large portion of them at dinner.

Of the Party who had the House, I have already had occasion to speak in a former dispatch, and have been induced to enter into the Characters of a few of them; They consist mostly of a set of unprincipled Avocats, and Notaries, totally uninformed as to the Principles of the British Constitution or parliamentary proceedings, which they profess to take for their Model, with no property of any sort, having everything to gain, and nothing to lose by any change they can bring about, only any state of Confusion into which they may throw the Province:—That these people have gradually advanced in audacity, in proportion as they have considered the power of France as more firmly established by the Successes of Bonaparte in Europe is obvious to every one, and that they are using every endeavour to pave the way for a change of Dominion, and a Return under that Government, is the general opinion of all ranks with whom it is possible to converse on the Subject. . . .

In considering the probability of these people having in view their return to their own Government, it may be urged that they have been hitherto quiet & faithful subjects, during the long lapse of 50 years, in which it would rather be to be supposed that their old attachment should have gradually decreased, so that there should be the less likelihood of their assuming now a disposition, of which they have hitherto shown no indication; to all this however it may be replied, that no circumstance whatever has occurred to awaken their attachment to their Mother Country, nor have any pains ever been taken to produce such a change, their habits, language and religion, have remained as distinct from ours as they were before the Conquest. Indeed it seems to be a favourite object with them to be considered as [a] separate Nation; La Nation Canadienne is their constant expression, and with regard to their having been hitherto quiet & faithful subjects, it need only be observed that no opportunity has presented them an encouragement to shew themselves otherwise . . . but during all this period to which I have hitherto alluded they had no foreign assistance to look to, nor any head to direct them, to France they now direct their view for the former, and I am pointing out those who I fear are preparing to offer themselves for the latter, and certainly under the most formidable shape under which a head could be found. . . .

The first and most obvious remedy that presents itself, is to deprive them of the constitution, as they term it, that is of that representative part of the Government which was unquestionably prematurely given them—neither from habits, information or assimilation, with the Government of England, were they prepared for it, nor was this circumstance of their unprepared state unforeseen by many of the best informed of the Canadians themselves, who opposed its being granted to them. It was in fact brought about by the English part of the Inhabitants, who in their Enthusiasm for the Constitution which they so justly Esteemed as it exists in their own Country, could not conceive that any inconvenience, or any thing but happiness, and prosperity, could result from its establishment elsewhere. The since Catholic Bishop Denaud a very worthy Man, observed at the time to an English Gentleman who was very warm on the subject, (tho' now quite the reverse) "You do not know my Countrymen, they are not at all prepared for the Constitution you wish to give them, once let the rein loose, and be assured they will never know when to stop." . . .

Next to this great measure, that which is most generally looked up to, is the Reunion of the Two Provinces, so as to Balance the Canadian Party in the House. Of the success of this measure I confess I have doubts. It would produce a heterogeneous mixture of opposite principles and different interests, from which no good could be expected, and if it did not avert, I should apprehend it might accelerate the evil. I am more inclined to keep the Province of Upper Canada as a foreign, and distinct population, which may be produced as a resource against that of this Country in case of necessity, It must always be interested in opposing revolution of every sort here, the great distance and general poverty of the people, appear to me further obstacles to such a measure scarcely to be overcome. . . .

Short of the decisive step of taking away the House altogether, one or other of these two measures either of reuniting the Provinces, or of forming a new division of the Counties seems to offer the only option, from which a hope can be entertained of rendering that House less capable of doing mischief; when I say this, I mean as offering the only expectation of ever effecting a Balance, to the Canadian Party, but under any shape in which it may be thought proper to continue the House, the enactment of a qualification with respect to the Representatives seems to be indispensably necessary, It really My Lord appears to me an absurdity, that the Interests of certainly not an unimportant Colony, involving in them those also of no inconsiderable portion of the Commercial concerns of the British Empire, should be in the hands of six petty shopkeepers, a Blacksmith, a Miller, and 15 ignorant peasants who form part of our present House, a Doctor or Apothecary, twelve Canadian Avocats, and Notaries, and four, so far respectable people that at least they do not keep shops, together with ten English members compleat the List; there is not one person coming under the description of a Canadian Gentleman among them.

The qualification that I think best adapted to the circumstances of the Country, would be one hundred pounds Currency, clear annual revenue arising from Land actually the property of the person presenting himself, for twelve Calendar Months previous to the day of election, or two thousand pounds Currency in personal property clear of all debts or demands.